A PARADE OF GRIEF

Also by Robert Fraga

The Greening of Oz (2019), Wasteland Press.

The Road through San Judas (2020), PM Press.

Calculus for a New Century (1999),
Mathematical Assn of America

A PARADE OF GRIEF

Gun Violence in America

Robert Fraga

Anamcara Press LLC
Lawrence, Kansas

Published in 2023 by Anamcara Press LLC
Author © 2023 by Robert Fraga
Cover and Book design by Maureen Carroll
Palitino Linotype, Minion Pro, Corbel, DINosour
Printed in the United States of America.

Book description: Armed authorities pitted against unarmed Black men. Increased suicides. Tattered lives. Our means of preventing gun violence is fatally flawed. Robert Fraga covers the history, statistics and more, answering the question: *what can be done?*

All rights reserved. No part of this publication may be reproduced, distributed, or transmitted in any form or by any means, including photocopying, recording, or other electronic or mechanical methods, without the prior written permission of the publisher, except in the case of brief quotations embodied in critical reviews and certain other noncommercial uses permitted by copyright law. For permission requests, write to the publisher, addressed "Attention: Permissions Coordinator," at the address below.

ANAMCARA PRESS LLC
P.O. Box 442072, Lawrence, KS 66044
https://anamcara-press.com

Ordering Information:
Quantity sales. Special discounts are available on quantity purchases by corporations, associations, and others. For details, contact the publisher at the address above. Orders by U.S. trade bookstores and wholesalers. Please contact Ingram Distribution.

ISBN-13: A Parade of Grief, 978-1-941237-97-7 (Paperback)
ISBN-13: A Parade of Grief, 978-1-941237-98-4 (EBook)
ISBN-13: A Parade of Grief, 978-1-941237-99-1 (Hardcover)
TRU002020 TRUE CRIME / Murder / Mass Murder
POL022000 POLITICAL SCIENCE / Constitutions
SOC051000 SOCIAL SCIENCE / Violence in Society
SOC004000 SOCIAL SCIENCE / Criminology

Library of Congress Control Number: 2023935603

CONTENTS

Foreword vii
PROLOGUE ix
CHAPTER ONE: Stats 1
CHAPTER TWO: In the Heartland 31
CHAPTER THREE: Assassinations 47
CHAPTER FOUR: The Towers 61
CHAPTER FIVE: A Litany of Massacres 75
CHAPTER SIX: Thoughts and Prayers 121
CHAPTER SEVEN: The Amendment 135
CHAPTER EIGHT: What Can Be Done? 150
Acknowledgments 201
References 203
About The Author 207

Foreword

As explained in the first chapter, the genesis of this book lies in the senseless attack on Alex Melchert. I am grateful for the cooperation of the entire Melchert family in the writing of this book and hereby dedicate it to Alex, in particular, and to all victims of gun violence in this country.

I need to acknowledge the assistance and insight which Valerie Johnson, Shawn Johnson's mother, offered in compiling material for the first chapter of this book.

Let me express my gratitude to two clinical psychiatrists, Paul Linde and Michael Seely, who offered their professional help with the actions of some of the characters who appear in these pages. Paul's experience in this country and in Africa were especially illuminating.

I thank Edward Brunt for his careful and insightful reading of the chapter on Kansas. A 30-year veteran of the Lawrence police force, he offered helpful criticism of that chapter.

I am indebted to Dan Close of the *Wichita Eagle* for helpful advice about making contact with potentially recalcitrant interviewees. Without my journalistic sources, principally *The New York Times*, the *Washington Post*, and the British daily *The Guardian*, this book would never have seen the light of day.

PROLOGUE

A Christmas Card

The Melcherts' card arrived with a batch of others. It began the way many others did. "It was wonderful to receive your Christmas card," they wrote. Then news of the family. Christmas is the one time of the year when we communicate. First a perfunctory run-down of what the older children were doing; then that their younger son Alex had begun his freshman year at the College of Wooster. At that point the card changed tone: "Unfortunately Alex was shot six times coming back from a weekend in Columbus. Sunday morn at 11 a.m. a nutcase blasted him at a rest stop. No reason, no explaining."

That card—that sentence—persuaded me to write this book.

This is what happened on the morning of Sunday, October 2, 2016. Alex Melchert had been returning with a classmate after visiting a mutual friend. He hadn't showered that day and wanted to freshen up before getting back to college. Halting at a rest stop on Interstate 71, he went to the men's room to splash water on his face. There were no paper towels in the men's room, so he returned to his car to retrieve a towel from the back seat. Someone shouted, and Alex turned. It was then that he heard three shots.

"I couldn't hear anything more with the ringing in my ears," he later said.

The gunman had pumped six bullets into the young man's

body, five in his abdomen, one in his upper arm. A witness told police that he was hearing pops, and he saw that there was a gun in the shooter's hand. "It was very small," he said. "It looked like a starter pistol." In fact, it was a 9mm revolver.

What Alex could remember was lying on the ground in a pool of blood, draining from his arm "which had kinda exploded."

Over the course of the next few days, the young collegian underwent a battery of operations at a hospital in Columbus, Ohio. One third of the patients in the hospital, the Melcherts later learned, had suffered gun wounds. Alex underwent four operations all told, the first to stop the bleeding, two to repair the wounds in his diaphragm and abdomen, the fourth to rebuild his injured right arm. Alex played the cello, and he hoped to resume playing in the fullness of time.

One of the bullets to strike Alex had nicked his liver which became infected. Most of the bullets were removed, but one slug remained lodged in his back. A rib had prevented that bullet from severing his aortic artery.

His parents, his older brother, and his sister all rushed to Columbus to be with Alex during the first few agonizing days of his recovery. For the first two days, he could not breathe without a breathing tube. It was removed the Tuesday after the shooting. At first, he could not speak. He communicated by writing. That took an effort because Alex was right-handed, but he could only use his left hand. What did he write? "He told us to be happy, to stay calm," his sister Adriane said. 'Don't be worried." All that Alex could manage then was to cope with the pain riveting his body, a pain which he later described as "insane." There was no question of reflecting on what had happened to him or to think of anything but that pain. The pain killers, which in the hospital he had taken intravenously, alleviated intolerable suffering for months afterward.

Reaction to the attack on Alex at Wooster was immediate. The day following the shooting, there was a vigil on campus organized by the college's Dean of Students. Students wrote letters and get-well cards. The Columbus Dispatch reported that a cantor in Israel had offered a service in his honor.

***

Melchert's assailant was a twenty-five-year-old man named Shawn Johnson. The man had a troubled past. He lived with his mother in Columbus. Two days before he shot Melchert, the two had quarreled. Johnson's mother locked him out of the apartment they shared. Later that day, Johnson broke in and punched his mother in the head. She then alerted police who issued a warrant for his arrest on Saturday, October 1. That was the day before Johnson shot Alex Melchert.

After the shooting, Johnson fled in a Camry that belonged to his mother. The police were in hot pursuit. Johnson led them on a high-speed chase north along I-71. The cops laid down road spikes which blew the car's tires and brought it to a halt, but not before the Camry had darted from one lane to another at speeds the police estimated to be in excess of 90 mph. In trying to pass a tractor-trailer on the right, Johnson slammed into the side of the truck, swerved in front of the vehicle, then smashed into cable barriers along the highway median. The State Highway Patrol had an armored vehicle which had come from Columbus. Their caution was standard procedure in such a situation: The Camry had tinted windows, and it was impossible to see what was going on inside. The cops kept yelling at Johnson to come out, but there was no response. Finally police used a battering ram to smash the passenger window of the car. They found Johnson's body inside. He had died from a self-inflicted gun wound.

When Alex Melchert heard that Johnson was dead, he wept. This was the one and only time he cried during the whole ordeal. "I'm sorry he's dead," he said. "He didn't need to shoot himself."

Why had Shawn Johnson shot Alex Melchert, someone he didn't know from Adam?

"I was worried that my son would commit suicide," his mother, Valerie Johnson, told *USA Today* in a phone interview. "But I had no idea that he would ever shoot somebody like that."

"He was never violent," she continued.

Five years before the shooting, Johnson was driving home

with a friend when the friend's car was struck by a drunken driver. Johnson was knocked unconscious. Upon regaining consciousness, his personality changed. He began to hear voices in his head. "The voices of demons," he said. Sometimes he answered back. "Who you talking to?" Valerie once asked him. "The Devil," he responded. He would wake up in the middle of the night, screaming that demons were attacking him. Shawn came to believe that he was the Angel Gabriel.

Hearing voices like that had occurred in Valerie Johnson's family before: Her great grandmother and two uncles had experienced the same phenomenon. Hearing voices is not as uncommon as one might think. Estimates run as high as twenty-eight percent of the general population who hear voices unheard by others. Psychiatrists regard the phenomenon as an auditory hallucination, a symptom of schizophrenia caused by chemical and genetic factors.

I interviewed Paul Linde, a clinical professor of psychiatry at the University of San Francisco School of Medicine, who was reluctant to discuss Shawn's case in detail since he was unfamiliar with the particulars. He did, however, offer some general observations. Linde has had extensive experience dealing with psychiatric emergencies. He told me that traumatic head injury can make people more prone to violence, and untreated psychosis can lead to violent behavior. Shawn may have been suffering from posttraumatic stress disorder. But it is more likely that he was experiencing a psychotic disorder brought on by a traumatic brain injury. It was not known whether any brain imaging was done after Shawn's accident. Linde points out that damage to some parts of the brain are more closely linked to psychosis than others. Religious delusions could make someone like Shawn feel that he was doing God's work when voices in his head commanded him to kill. They told him that he himself had less than one year to live.

Linde spent a year working in an asylum in the east African nation of Zimbabwe. He wrote his experiences in a book entitled *Of Spirits and Madness: An American Psychiatrist in Africa*. Some of the patients he encountered exhibited symptoms like Shawn Johnson's. One such man whom Linde calls Tichaona heard voices which he attributed to ancestral bewitchment. The psychiatrist reported that in Zimbabwe, patients who suffered from auditory hallucinations heard the voices of their ancestor spirits rather than the voice of Jesus Christ. As Shawn's mother was to tell me, a couple of Linde's patients said that they were hearing the voices of their great grandmothers. Tichaona was one of these. His great grandmother may have suffered from schizophrenia.

"Could it be," Linde asked, "that Tichaona inherited his great grandmother's spiritual abilities along with her mental illness?" Could she be the 'ancestral spirit' who was communicating with Tichaona?

In Tichaona's culture, symptoms of madness can indicate the appearance of a healer—a n'anga in his Shona tongue. Remember that Shawn Johnson, who was raised in a Christian tradition, said that he was the Angel Gabriel.

Phenomena, reminiscent of Johnson's, arise in classical Greek mythology: The priestess at the Oracle of Delphi—known as Pythia—was consulted for her prophecies when she acted as a conduit for the god Apollo. (The original mythic name for Delphi was Pytho, from the Greek verb puthein, meaning to rot—a reference to the odor of the decomposing body of the monster Python, killed by Apollo.) It is possible that the Pythia prophesized while under the influence of ethylene gas which rose through fissures in the floor where she was sitting. We have examples of supernatural communication closer to our own times. Among Christians, particularly French Catholics, Joan of Arc is said to have heard the voices of saints commanding her to do certain things, and specifically to support the French Dauphin in his struggle with the English. Conveniently for Jeanne d'Arc, all these saints spoke French.

The creativity that Shawn evinced when he was younger—he had started drawing when he was six years old and even did some online commissions for small sums of money—began to dry up after his car accident. He was studying graphic design at the time he shot Alex.

It was evident to his mother who was a registered nurse—she told me that she had been a nurse "for a long time"—that

Shawn needed professional help. Her insistence that he seek help is what precipitated their row on the Friday before the shooting. "Get help," she told him, or she would leave. Shawn then started screaming. He threatened to kill someone. He had a concealed carry permit which he had obtained legally despite his mental problems. Shawn had purchased the gun—a Taurus PT111 Millenium G2 Compact—at a Gander Mountain store in Columbus a few months before that particular branch of the outdoor retailer closed. It had cost him almost $300. According to the manufacturer, this weapon was the "ideal concealed carry handgun."

"I wanted him to be arrested, not as a criminal but as a person who had psychological issues," his mother told *USA Today*. She had been in therapy since the fall of 2016 and had had to cut back on her work load.

"He didn't want to face the fact that he had issues," Valerie Johnson said. "I told him that he needed medication, but he wouldn't listen." He wouldn't listen whenever someone told him that he needed help. One of Shawn's sisters was supportive and sympathetic, the other sister told him what his mother had said... that he needed help. When Shawn heard that, he would stop listening. His mother enlisted the assistance of Shawn's father, a retired sergeant in the armed services. She asked him to speak to Shawn, which he did. Valerie never found out what they discussed.

At Valerie's insistence, Shawn saw psychiatrists at Netcare, a local substance abuse and mental health clinic. Somehow, he persuaded the doctors that he was mentally stable. According to Dr. Terry Kukor of Netcare, many patients "seek to minimize the problems that they're having" because of the social stigma which comes with mental illness. Valerie Johnson felt that men, in particular—men like Shawn who needed help—were the most likely to deny that they needed it.

What is often available to care providers is little more than a snapshot of a patient's mental health. That's why family involvement is critical to an assessment of patients' risk to others and to themselves. "Information provided by people close to a patient is important," said Dr. Kukor, "if they think that their loved one might not be sharing the full story."

That was precisely the issue that frustrated Valerie so much, the way things failed to work out in Shawn's case despite her insistence that there was something going on inside Shawn's head, something that was seriously amiss. The message she wanted to get out was this: "When a family member says that someone like Shawn needs help, the authorities need to take this opinion seriously."

On Saturday, October 1, Shawn and his mother spoke on the phone. Shawn said that he couldn't come home. "You have to respect that I'm ready to die," he told his mother. God, he said, had let him know that he shouldn't celebrate his birthday because the time for him to die was at hand. When Valerie Johnson continued to insist that he needed help, he told her to go to hell. The next day he nearly killed Alex Melchert.

***

THE COLLEGE OF WOOSTER FRESHMAN STAYED in a Columbus hospital for more than three weeks before being discharged and flown back to Wisconsin in a family friend's private jet. He had suffered the loss of his spleen and his lungs collapsed. Still, he recuperated faster than might have been expected. "A few nurses said that, for injuries like I had, people are in the hospital for about three times as long," Alex told *USA Today* at the end of October. Valerie Johnson had heard that Alex had died, but I told her that that was not the case; he was recuperating at his parents' home in Wisconsin.

Back home, he began the arduous task of physical and occupational therapy. He was still on pain killers: 400mg doses of gabapentin and 45 mgs of oxycodone, every four to six hours a day. These were supplemented by morphine. Rehabilitation continued apace, mostly in his own home. The goal was to increase the range of motion of his mangled right arm. He missed a full year of school at the College of Wooster, during which time he enrolled in an environmental studies course at the University of Wisconsin-Green Bay. The course met four times a week, and Alex believed that the credits he earned in the course would transfer to Wooster.

Alex confessed that he was now interested in questions of gun control although he had experience while in high school firing both a pistol and a shotgun. He told his parents that he wanted to keep the five bullets which had been extracted from his body. They were part of him. The sixth bullet was still lodged in his back a year after the shooting.

After several efforts, Shawn's mother, Valerie, succeeded in telephoning Alex's mother, Rebecca Melchert. The conversation went on for an hour. According to Rebecca, Valerie had been most gracious. She was most concerned that the Melcherts not blame her or her family for what Shawn had done. Rebecca assured her that no one blamed her. Although Alex was still in constant pain and would be for the foreseeable future, he was still alive and even managed to play the cello at his aunt's wedding the previous summer. Valerie's pain was also constant—she had lost her son. Bonded by grief, Rebecca and Valerie agreed to stay in touch.

Shawn was African-American, and I asked Alex if this had affected his attitude toward Black people. No, Alex said that he had more of an adverse reaction to seeing in the street a guy in a hoodie with his hands in his pockets.

This story has a relatively happy ending. Alex was able to return to the College of Wooster. I last talked to him during his junior year, when he was following classes online because the coronavirus pandemic had closed the college. Although an MRI showed that he had lost use of half of one lung, he told me that he was up to 185 pounds and felt strong. He was majoring in psychology. One can only speculate how his brush with death at the hands of a mentally disturbed young man influenced his choice of majors.

One thing more: His older brother recently bought a pistol.

CHAPTER ONE:
Stats

St. Charles, Missouri was the scene of the crime. At the end of 2018, a man called Richard Darren Emery shot and killed two children, both pre-teens. He killed their grandmother who was trying to protect them and their mother who had been Emery's girlfriend. A shootout with the cops ensued. Emery was wounded and bleeding profusely. He abandoned his pickup truck and tried to carjack another vehicle, first stabbing the driver before fleeing into the woods. The police finally nabbed him in the men's room of a convenience store. The clerk at the store had alerted the police. Emery appeared so traumatized at his arraignment that all he could do by way of a response to the charges he faced was to nod his head yes or no. He did ask later how the driver he had stabbed was faring, and he apologized for shooting at the police who had tried to apprehend him. He did not utter so much as a syllable of remorse for the four souls he had snuffed out earlier that day.

An extraordinary story? Yes. An isolated instance of butchery? Not so extraordinary, unfortunately. Not so isolated either. The country is awash in guns. People use them to kill other people. A study of gun ownership was conducted by a consortium of universities including Harvard and the University of Washington. The study, published in 2017 in the American Journal of Public Health, found that three million Americans pack loaded handguns every day. Researchers estimated that thirteen to fourteen million Americans hold concealed-carry permits. There were 265 million guns, most of them handguns, in circulation in the US. There are still more people than guns in the US but not by as much as one might expect. A minority of Americans—one estimate puts the number at one in three—own guns. Still, people with multiple weaponry make up for those who are armless. Case in point: Police who raided the hotel room where Stephen Paddock, the gunman who killed fifty-eight people and wounded hundreds more in the Las Vegas massacre on October 1, 2017, found a total of twenty-three guns there.

The rash of gun ownership—and a flouting of the rules which govern their possession—has reached into the halls of Congress. A Texas congressman evaded a metal detector in the Capitol. In so doing, he was reported to have sneered, "You can't stop me." Another congressman told police who tried to scan him after he set off the machine, "Nah, I'm not going to do that." And a third member of Congress, Lauren Boebert of Colorado, refused to let the police search her handbag after she bragged that she was going to carry a loaded Glock handgun to Congress. "We need strong Christians to go on the offensive against socialists who want to rip our country apart," chirped Marjorie Taylor Greene, a newly elected congresswoman from Georgia, who posted an image of herself on Facebook cradling an assault rifle in her arm beside three Democratic congresswomen known for their progressive views. One of those women, Alexandria Ocasio-Cortez, said on CNN that she didn't feel safe around other members of Congress.

The profile of a typical handgun carrier in this country is that of a conservative, middle-aged white male, raised among guns and living in a Southern suburban community. Twenty percent of gun owners are veterans. Less than thirty percent have children.

What do gun owners do with their weapons? Some of them shoot themselves or, like Stephen Paddock, they shoot other people before shooting themselves. What prompted Paddock to commit mass murder is a mystery and will probably remain so. Police found no suicide message in the hotel room which he had occupied. The room normally rented for $590 a night, but the hotel let Paddock—a regular high-roller at the hotel's casino—have it for free. In response to why he might have committed such a heinous crime, the FBI agent in charge of the agency's Las Vegas office said simply, "He didn't want people to know."

***

HERE IS A SAMPLING OF GUN-VIOLENCE ANECDOTES, the first three of which have been taken from a web site called *Parents Against Gun Violence*:

- I was too drunk to drive, so I got an Uber. In the back seat, I moved my legally-concealed handgun from one pocket to another and it went off. I shot my driver in the back but he was really nice about it.
- My dad caught me doing some stuff on my computer so he took it away. I was really mad, so I shot him and I also shot his roommate's girlfriend because she happened to be there at the time.
- My wife moved out so I shot our two daughters dead and then I shot my wife in the legs and told her I wanted her to live so she can suffer with the grief. I had permits for my guns.
- In January 2022, an English astrophysicist named Matthew Wilson lay in bed. He was visiting his girlfriend in the Atlanta region when he was struck and killed by a stray bullet. His killing made headlines in the U.K., a country with one of the world's lowest gun homicide rates.
- Another stray bullet ended the life of a 12-year-old child who had just written the Governor of Tennessee to oppose reducing the state's restrictions on guns. He argued that "the new law will be bad and people will be murdered."

A staff writer for the *Washington Post,* John Woodrow Cox, wrote a book entitled *Children Under Fire*. It tells the way the country's epidemic of gun violence affects the young. One chapter in the book about 11-year-old Tyler Paxton, was excerpted as an article in the *Post*. The Paxton boy, the son of a church-going evangelical couple, retrieved a .357 magnum revolver from a cabinet in his parents' bedroom. Of all the guns in the cabinet, it was the only one that was loaded. Tyler pressed the muzzle of the revolver against his temple, pulled the trigger and shot himself in the head. There was no apparent reason for him to commit suicide. He had not been depressed, he had many friends, and he seemed perfectly well-adjusted to his life. Why then had he pointed the barrel of his father's pistol at his temple and taken his own life? Was it curiosity? A child's unthinking experiment? The answer went to the grave with Tyler.

The numbers speak for themselves: From 2000 to 2010, 332,014 people died from gunshot wounds in the US. Of those victims, 2694 were children. Eighty-two of them were under the age of five. At the end of that decade, in 2010, 31,328 people (including suicides) died by gunfire. That was one fatality every 17 minutes. On what might be considered an "average day," 93 Americans died from gun shots.

At the end of January 2018, when this chapter was written, the US had experienced eleven shootings on school property. They occurred all over the country although slightly over half occurred in the South. Four of these—in Kentucky, North Carolina, Arizona and Michigan—involved fatalities. The country was rife with stories of gun violence.

One story to make all the major newspapers occurred in Washington just outside the Nationals Park where, on July 17, 2021, the Washington Nationals were playing the San Diego Padres. In the middle of the sixth inning, the Padres leading 8-4, the game was stopped when inside the stadium, shots could be heard. There had been an exchange of gunfire between people in two cars in an incident that left three people injured. Panic broke out among the fans who sought cover behind seats as announcers advised people to stay inside the park.

"It was just a chaotic scene," the umpire crew chief told the Associated Press. "We heard what sounded like rapid gunfire; we didn't know where it was coming from."

One fan, Jacob DeAngeles, who had been sitting with his girlfriend and a friend, heard someone cry out, "Active shooter!"

"You don't think you will be in that experience, but you hear

'Active shooter' and just run." He and his friends jumped the turnstiles and made it onto the street.

In one of his articles, columnist Leonard Pitts of the *Miami Herald* focused on the reaction of an 8-year-old child to the shooting. It was the second shooting in which she had been tangentially involved.

"I was kind of prepared 'cause I always am expecting something to happen," she told a reporter from a local TV station. Shaking her head, she added, "What are you going to do?"

Pitts' comment was simply: "This is what she has come to understand. This is what normal looks like to her."

From January 2018 to February of the following year, D.C. authorities recovered 40,302 bullet casings from the nation's capital. So how does the US stack up against other countries in instances of gun violence?

We have this statistic for 2012: Sixty percent of the murders in the US were due to firearms. For the same year, that figure for Canada was 31% and 10% for the U.K. For that year, there were thirty deaths by firearms in the U.K. as opposed to nearly nine thousand in the US. The figure for Canada for 2016 was 611. Paradoxically gun ownership in this country has actually fallen off. In 1980, fifty percent of men owned a gun. Forty years later, that percentage had dropped to thirty-five. To counteract this trend, some gun manufacturers have lobbied police forces to shift from their traditional arms—like Smith & Wesson .38 revolvers—to weapons like Glock pistols.

Despite the fall-off in private gun ownership, the firearm-related deaths per 100,000 people show how pervasive violence in the US has become. There were, in 2014, more than ten fatalities by firearms in the US (per 100,000 inhabitants) as compared to far less than one in the U.K. (per !00,000 inhabitants). In Canada there were slightly less than two firearm-related deaths (per 100,000 inhabitants) for a comparable period. In fact, the death rate in the US for years around 2010 was exceeded only by ten countries—Brazil, Guatemala, Columbia, Honduras, El Salvador, Jamaica, Uruguay, Venezuela, Panama, and Swaziland—all, with few exceptions—in Central and South America and the Caribbean.

One apparent contributing factor that puts the US in a category of its own among developed countries is the relative ease of acquiring firearms in the country, even military-type weapons. In 2016, the FBI requested the Bureau of Alcohol, Tobacco, Firearms and Explosives to confiscate more than four thousand guns from buyers who were not qualified to possess them, either because they had criminal records or mental health issues.

Gun violence in the country generated a movement called Black Lives Matter. In our opinion, this was the most socially explosive development of the past twenty years in the saga of police use of guns to control a minority in America. In 2017, police shot and killed nearly one thousand people, according to a *Washington Post* story. This figure has remained more or less steady for three years. The number of unarmed Blacks shot by police actually declined in 2017, when 19 men were killed. There had been 36 such fatalities in 2015. "The national spotlight on this issue has made officers more cautious in unarmed situations," according to Chuck Wexler, the executive director of a Washington-based think tank called the Police Research Forum. "We are giving officers more options," he said.

Still, Black males are shot at a rate which is disproportionately high. Although they are only six percent of the country's population, American Black males were the victims of twenty-two percent of fatal police shootings in 2017. Police violence against Blacks—particularly young Black males—generated a movement that came to rival the civil rights movement of the 1960s. We can touch on only a few instances. These were depressingly common, and the three detailed below are just the most sordid. Only one narrowly defines the category of police shootings. Yet they share similarities—armed authorities pitted against unarmed African-American males.

Black Lives Matter

The Black Lives Matter (BLM) movement grew out of the acquittal of the man who was charged with shooting and killing a teenager named Trayvon Martin. That incident occurred on 26 February 2012, near a gated community in Florida called Sanford. The 17-year-old Martin did not live in Sanford. His father had arranged for him to stay with his girlfriend there after the teenager had been suspended from his high school in Miami. This occurred when a drug residue was found in his book bag. Sanford is about a four-hour drive from Miami. On the night he was shot, the young Martin had gone to a convenience store to buy a snack. On his way home, he encountered a neighborhood watchman who thought the boy's behavior was suspicious. "The guy looks like he's up to no good, or he's on drugs or something," the watchman said at the time. "It's raining and he's just walking around." The watchman, whose name was George Zimmerman, made a 911 call and talked to a police dispatcher who asked him if he was following Martin. Zimmerman admitted that he was. "We don't need you to do that," the dispatcher told him, but Zimmerman followed Martin, anyway.

What happened next is moot. An altercation between the two men broke out. Zimmerman said Trayvon Martin threatened him. They scuffled. Part of the exchange between Zimmerman and Trayvon Martin was captured on his girlfriend's cell phone. At the time of the encounter, Martin was talking to his girlfriend who heard Zimmerman ask Martin what he was doing. Martin responded by asking Zimmerman why he was following him. At this point she lost her connection. The two men scuffled and Zimmerman shot the teenager with a 9mm semiautomatic handgun, hitting Martin in the chest. By the time the police arrived, Martin was dying and Zimmerman was lying, face down in the grass. His nose was bloodied. One police officer thought that Zimmerman's nose was broken. His face appeared to be swollen, and there was blood on the back of his head. Police offered to take him to hospital, but Zimmerman declined their offer. After questioning him, the police let Zimmerman go.

Analysis of scrapings taken from underneath Martin's fingernails contained none of Zimmerman's DNA. You might have expected to find some if a prolonged tussle between the two men had taken place.

Attorney Ben Crump became involved with the Martin family before Zimmerman's trial. The Florida lawyer was to become a nationally recognized spokesman speaking out against the racism implicit in the killings of Black men by the police. He is best known for what he had to say eight years later at the time George Floyd, a 42-year-old African American from Minneapolis, died in May 2020 while in police custody. (A cop named Derek Chauvin had pinned Floyd to the pavement; he dug his knee into the Black man's neck for nearly nine minutes and suffocated him.) Crump later said:

> We all watched the horrific death of George Floyd on video as witnesses begged the police officer to take him into the police car and get off his neck. This abusive, excessive, and inhumane use of force cost the life of a man who was being detained by the police for questioning about a non-violent charge.

Charging Chauvin with third degree murder—upgraded later to second-degree murder—elicited this judgment from Crump: "a significant step forward on the road to justice." A jury found Chauvin guilty as charged.

(What was so special about the Floyd killing? Rashad Robinson, president of a civil rights organization called Color of Change, offered this explanation: "The police officer is looking into the camera as he's pushing the life out of [Floyd].") The incident in Minneapolis sparked nationwide protests. Some of these deteriorated in a welter of opportunistic looting and vandalism.

Years before this all happened, Ben Crump had become involved in the Trayvon Martin killing. During a court hearing, the lawyer prodded Trayvon's father Tracy to offer details on the 2003 killing of Trayvon:

"You said that your teenage son was unarmed?" Crump asked.

"Yes, sir. All he had was a bag of Skittles and a can of iced tea."

Again Crump: "And you said the neighborhood watch volunteer shot him."

"Yes, and he shot Trayvon in the heart."

Despite Crump's assurances to the contrary, Tracy was convinced that nothing would happen to Zimmerman whose defense rested on something called a Stand Your Ground law. This turned out to be prophetic: Florida's Stand Your Ground law permits someone to protect himself, even by deadly force, if he fears "imminent death or great bodily harm." Such a person is immune from criminal prosecution.

A jury of six women and six men acquitted Zimmerman of second-degree murder in the shooting death of Trayvon Martin. Years later, the US Justice Department declined to pursue a civil rights violation case against Zimmerman. Attorney General Eric Holder said at the time that "though a comprehensive investigation found that the high standard for a federal hate crime prosecution cannot be met under the circumstances here, [Trayvon Martin's] premature death necessitates that we . . . be unafraid of confronting the issues and tensions his passing brought to the surface."

Alicia Garza, a Bay Area activist who rose to prominence in the wake of the Trayvon Martin slaying, said, "Seven years ago, we were treated like we were too radical, too out of the bounds of what is possible. And now, countless lives later, it's finally seen as relevant." The country, she went on to say, had reached its breaking point.

Zimmerman's shooting of Trayvon Martin and his subsequent acquittal of murder ushered in a tumultuous period in his life. He and his wife divorced in the fall of 2013. In early September 2013, the woman soon to be his ex-wife told a police dispatcher, "He is in his car and he continually has his hand on his gun and he keeps saying, 'Step closer.' He is just threatening all of us." A couple of months later, he was charged with aggravated assault after pointing a shotgun at his then-girlfriend who claimed that he had first broken a table with it. The girlfriend later recanted, and the charges against Zimmerman were dropped.

The man went on a litigation binge, suing NBC in 2013. Zimmerman charged that the chain had edited a story to make it appear that he had voluntarily told a 911 operator that Trayvon Martin was Black. (The Florida judge handling the case threw the lawsuit out.) In 2019, Zimmerman sued Martin's family, their lawyer, Benjamin Crump, and Crump's publisher. The suit claimed that Zimmerman was a "victim of a conspiracy along with malicious prosecution and defamation." Crump's office issued a rejoinder, stating that Crump had "every confidence that this unfounded and reckless lawsuit will be revealed for what it is—another failed attempt to defend the indefensible and a shameless attempt to profit off the lives and grief of others." If that were not enough, Zimmerman went on the following year to sue candidates Elizabeth Warren and Pete Buttigieg for a whopping $265 million for their tweets which he alleged were malicious although they did not mention him by name.

Litigation did not take up all of Zimmerman's time. He managed to dabble in the arts, producing works with political content. In 2014 he showed a work entitled "Angie," a portrait of prosecutor Angela Corey, with the chyron "I have this much respect for the American judicial system." In 2015, he produced a piece featuring Confederate flags for the benefit of a "Muslim-free gun shop." In September of that year, he re-tweeted a picture of Trayvon Martin with the comment, "I sure hate offending people that have plotted and tried to kill me and my family."

In January, 2016, Zimmerman criticized Barak Obama for crying while discussing mass shootings. He called the president "a disgrace to the country" and "a piece of garbage."

After Zimmerman was acquitted, Alicia Garza posted a message on Facebook:

"I continue to be surprised at how little Black lives matter," she wrote. It was this message that would generate a defining slogan—Black Lives Matter—for a nationwide civil rights movement. "Stop giving up on Black life."

Opal Tometi, a Nigerian-American activist who was born in Phoenix, AZ, but who later moved to New York, had just viewed a film about the police slaying of the young Black man, Oscar Grant, in Oakland when she learned that George Zimmerman had been acquitted of the murder of Treyvon Martin. "I remember sitting on the street corner and getting a slew of text messages and tweets from folks who were frantic," she said. At a conference in Washington, D.C., Tometi said:

> I remember in that moment [when Zimmerman was acquitted] just sitting with the fact that everybody knew what took place. And despite all the knowledge, despite the testimonies, despite all that, Treyvon Martin was put on trial for his own death . . . I was struck by the fact that my younger brother—who was fourteen at the time—could have been Treyvon.

Motivated by Alicia Garza's post on Facebook, Tometi joined in the movement: "We need to have other people interact with this message and also share the work that they're doing to ensure Black lives matter, and how can we, as a collective… make sure that we are coordinated and uplifting a message that will ensure that all of our Black lives would matter?"

The two women, together with Patrisse Khan-Cullors, a performance artist and queer activist from Los Angeles, went on to found the Black Lives Matter movement. It was Khan-Cullors who provided the movement's hashtag which she began posting on social media.

"Before BLM there was a dormancy in our Black freedom movement," Khan-Cullors said in an interview with the British newspaper, *The Guardian*. "Obviously many of us were doing work, but we been able to reignite a whole new generation, not just inside the US but across the globe, centering Black people and centering the fight against white supremacy."

Khan-Cullors wrote a book entitled *When They Call You a Terrorist: A Black Lives Matter Memoir* of which she told *The Guardian* that "What was most important for me is that I could share what I experienced as a young person, in particular what impact incarceration of family members and policing had on my life and my family's life."

Both her father and her older brother had scrapes with law enforcement. Her brother suffered from a schizoaffective disorder for which the family lacked access to treatment. This led to the boy's repeated arrests. He was, in Khan-Cullors' words, "a big, loving, unwell, good-hearted brother" who "never, never hurt another human being." He was arrested in the middle of a psychiatric episode. Her brother's arrest and the time he subsequently spent in jail precipitated Khan-Cullors' activism.

Of her father, she wrote: "his real addiction [was] to the fast-paced energy of it all; how else was a man like him ever going to have some money in his pocket, decent clothes, be viewed as someone who mattered?"

Zimmerman tried three times to auction off the gun he used to kill Trayvon Martin. These attempts all provoked a storm of protests. His first two attempts attracted a number of fake bids. It was reported that the high bid the third time around was $138,900. It was submitted by a prospective buyer who identified himself as John Smith.

Police Violence

POLICE VIOLENCE AGAINST YOUNG AFRICAN Americans, in just this century, has opened the floodgates to a literary torrent. We cite only a few examples of this subject. In the summer of 2014, a white officer killed a Black teenager named Michael Brown. The incident generated street riots in the small Missouri town where it happened. Days before he was to enroll in a technical college in St. Louis, MO, Brown and a friend named Dorian Johnson went to a convenience store in Ferguson, MO, a suburb of St. Louis. There young Brown pilfered some cigarillos. The clerk at the store challenged Brown who grabbed the clerk by the collar of his shirt and shoved him. Johnson later said that he "was being a real good friend and staying with [Brown] even though I know he committed a crime." When the two Black youths left, the clerk alerted the police.

An officer—a white man named Darren Wilson—arrived shortly before noon. A native of Texas, Wilson, his mother and sister moved to the St. Louis area where Darren found work in construction. When the housing market collapsed in 2008, he opted for a career in the police force, focusing on the region north of St. Louis, a poor and rough area called North County, as a way to speed up his career advancement in the police forces. Wilson was fortunate to have for his field-training officer a man called Mike McCarthy. McCarthy, a ten-year veteran of the force who had grown up in North County, cultivated good relations with the Black population. "You have no idea what's going on behind that façade until you stop and try to know," he said. Many of his colleagues were unwilling to make that effort. "Too many cops weren't interested in understanding the root causes of crime," he said. McCarthy, who talked to Jake Halpern, the author of a profile of Wilson for *The New Yorker*, showed the reporter a police log dealing with an African-American accused of shooting a cop. The suspect was released "due to his lack of mental capacity." Someone had written in the log "Kill the Fucker." Another entry detailed the apprehension of two Black males on suspicion of robbery. Written beside this entry was the remark, "Men, you better leave your wallets at home. Niggers are going to come in the police station next and rob us."

McCarthy could empathize with the Blacks in North County. He was gay and understood what it meant to be a victim of marginalization. "In the US, where everybody is supposed to be equal, I'm not," he told Halpern. "That's a major thing." Wilson admired the way McCarthy could relate to people in the underprivileged areas where he served. "Mike, I don't know what I'm doing," he confessed. "This is a culture shock. Would you help me? Because you obviously have that connection, and you can relate to them. You may be White, but they still respect you. So why can they respect you and not me?" For his part, McCarthy was impressed by Wilson. "Darren was probably the best officer that I've ever trained," he said. "Just by his willingness to learn."

Wilson's first assignment as a cop was in a town called Jennings. That was before he was assigned to Ferguson. The department in Jennings had a reputation for racism. (The log entries cited above come from a Jennings police log book.) The town has changed since Wilson worked there. It has elected a Black mayor who could remember African-Americans telling her that they avoided the town like the coronavirus. "I ain't going there," they would say.

Wilson would deny that he was racist. "What happened to my great-grandfather is not happening to me." Regardless what his experiences in Jennings were, Wilson was not deterred from working at other locations in North County. "When I left Jennings, I didn't want to work in a White area," he told *The New Yorker*. "I liked the Black community . . . I had fun there. There's people who will just crack you up."

In Ferguson, a town which was two-thirds Black, cops routinely arrested people for failing to comply with police directives. The Justice Compartment found that trivial charges like "manner of walking in a roadway" were leveled almost exclusively against Blacks. In any event, the overwhelming majority of those arrested for their "failure to comply"—94%—were African-American. Wilson was involved in one such instance. He had detained a man outside a minimart who Wilson maintained was known to be selling drugs. When ordered to put his hands on the police car, the suspect refused, and Wilson arrested him for "failure to comply." Wilson would later admit that the "failure to comply" ordinance was "an easy way to arrest someone."

On August 9, 2014, Wilson spotted two men on a street called Canfield Drive. One of them matched the description of the youth who had taken the cigarillos from the convenience store. Wilson ordered the men to move from the roadway to the sidewalk. The exchange between the cop and the youths is in dispute. Wilson claims that Brown had said "Fuck what you have to say." Dorian Johnson denies this and contends that Wilson's order had itself been laced with profanity: "Get the fuck on the sidewalk," he claimed Wilson had said.

Wilson blocked the roadway with his S.U.V. This, according to the president of the Missouri Fraternal Order of Police, is a common maneuver which offers protection to officers if a gun battle ensues. But there is another way to look at what Wilson did. Jonathan Fenderson, who teaches African-American Studies at St. Louis' Washington University, observed that "Wilson's decision to blockade the street sent a message: You will defer to the power that I exhibit, or I am going to force you back into place."

Michael Brown was six foot five. He weighed just under 300 pounds. His father worried that his size would make him a target of police harassment. His advice to his son, if he were stopped by the police, was simple. It boiled down to one word: Obey. "After you thought that you were being disrespected, get a name and a badge number," the senior Brown said, "so your parent can reach out to the police department and file a complaint." On August 9, Michael ignored his father's advice.

Wilson and Brown get into an argument during which Wilson claimed that Brown had reached through the driver's window to try to wrest Wilson's revolver away from him. Wilson fired twice from inside his vehicle. One bullet, later found to have lodged in the driver's door, seemed to miss Brown entirely. The other struck Brown's hand. The cop claimed that Brown had taunted him: "You are too much of a pussy to shoot me."

Michael Brown tried to escape by running east on Canfield Drive. After a brief chase, Brown turned to confront Officer Wilson. Exactly what happened next is murky. Rumors of all sorts, most of them false, flew in the aftermath of the incident. The most poignant of these was that Brown had cried out, "Hands up, don't shoot!" True or not, this was to become a kind of slogan for protestors, later in Ferguson and elsewhere in the country. Wilson pumped six bullets into Brown's body, hitting him in the arm, chest, and forehead. Wilson later testified before a grand jury that Brown looked "like he was almost bulking up to run through the shots, like it was making him mad that I'm shooting at him." A commentator on MSNBC, Melissa Harris-Perry, later said that Wilson's language conformed to "the myth of the Black brute incapable of pain himself bent on inflicting pain on others."

Brown's body lay on the baking asphalt of Canfield Drive for four and a half hours after he was shot. This, remember, was in the heat of an August day. (Police later admitted that this had been a mistake.) During that time, crowds formed. The housing estate adjacent to the spot where Brown lay dead, was almost exclusively occupied by African-Americans.

Within the hour, Michael Brown's immediate family began to congregate at the scene of his shooting. They arrived individually: His mother, his stepfather, his father. A local reporter interviewed Brown's mother, Lezley McSpadden, who cried out, "You didn't have to shoot him eight [sic] times. You just shot all through my baby's body."

The reporter later said, "This was a scene that I had never seen before, a heartbreak that I had never felt before from the people I was interviewing . . . Something wasn't right. This wasn't the typical police shooting scene."

Leaving Brown's body to lie in the street for so long after he was shot stoked a predictable outcry. Said a pastor of a church in St. Louis: "For the police to shoot somebody, and leave him lying in the street in the heart of a community, in front of his family and friends and neighbors . . . to me that was tantamount to slavery."

After the police had removed Brown's body, church groups began to arrive. They surrounded McSpadden and her husband, praying, singing, and hugging one another. When these groups dispersed, a more violent mood overtook the crowd. People began to yell. One of the protestors set fire to a dumpster. A shouting match erupted between demonstrators and police. Armed youths began grabbing merchandise from a filling station called QuikTrip which they may have confused with the convenience store where Brown had been videoed assaulting the man who had called the cops. Rioters ripped an ATM machine off the wall and set the filling station afire. It soon burned to the ground. The image of the store ablaze is what caught the public's eye, that more than the actual killing of Michael Brown.

Later that night Wilson and his wife watched the demonstrations in the streets of Ferguson. They viewed the scenes of civil unrest with disbelief. "Oh, my God, what's going on?" Darren Wilson's wife cried out incredulously. Darren got on the phone to Mike McCarthy, who had recently been involved in a shooting incident himself. What did he feel about what had transpired in Ferguson? "It just tore me up," he said, "because here you had a young kid who was doing nothing more than his job—and was doing a job that I encouraged him and taught him how to do." McCarthy could empathize with the rage which underpinned first the protests and, later, the riots that broke out in Ferguson, but he firmly believed that the shooting had nothing to do with race.

People still wanted answers to their questions: Why had Brown been shot? Why had his body lain on the street so long?

A childhood friend of Michael Brown spoke to a reporter from the *Washington Post* a couple of days after the shooting. He told the reporter:

"People are tired of being misused and mistreated, and this is an outlet for them to express their outrage and anger. Everyone is looking for an outlet to express their emotions. This is a reason . . . all the looting and what's going on, but people want to be heard, and they don't know how to do it. So that's why they lash out."

A press conference was held at the Jennings Mason Temple, a church in St. Louis. Brown's family, wearing T-shirts that read "Rest in Peace" attended and spoke of their grief and thirst for justice.

Ben Crump came up from Florida to speak at the church. Crump, the author of the book Open Season, describing the police violence directed against young Black men, told the congregation: "He was executed in broad daylight when it was clear he had no weapon."

Then, once again, in a booming voice that reverberated off the stained-glass windows of the church, he shouted: "Their baby was executed in broad daylight!"

He went on: "To some it has become a cliché. To us these are our children. Our children. Don't they deserve the dignity and respect of law enforcement?

When it came time for her to speak, Lezley McSpadden tearfully said, "That was my firstborn son...ask anyone and they'd tell you how much I loved my son...I just wish I could have been there to help him."

That very day Mike Brown was to have begun classes at a vocational school in St. Louis. He had just passed the summer course he needed to obtain his high school diploma.

Street demonstrations continued for weeks afterward. Night after night, crowds gathered outside the Ferguson police station, chanting: "Indict, convict, send that killer to jail. The whole damn system is guilty as hell." Their thirst for justice was not to be slaked.

On November 24, 2014, a grand jury failed to bring criminal charges against Darren Wilson. Lezley McSpadden stood outside that station, giving voice to her outrage at the grand jury's decision: "They wrong!" she yelled at the phalanx of officers arrayed before her. "Y'all know y'all wrong!"

A tsunami of protests erupted in the wake of the grand jury's decision. These turned violent as mobs, rampaging through the streets of Ferguson, broke store windows and torched buildings. Police in riot gear used smoke and tear gas to control the rioters who were looting and burning stores. The St. Louis suburb was undergoing what looked like a mini-blitz. The governor of Missouri called up the National Guard to protect the town's police station.

Ben Crump said that the Brown family had never trusted the prosecutor, Bob McCulloch, to try the case against Wilson. "They are going to try to see if they can do something to get positive change out of this because they understand this system needs to be changed." Criticism of McCulloch was trenchant. He had exhibited what the *Washington Post* claimed was "cartoonish defiance" and he had knowingly allowed one witness to give false testimony on behalf of Wilson. The Brown family issued a statement expressing their disappointment at the verdict but urged restraint in the protests. The statement said, in part, "While we understand that many others share our pain, we ask that you channel your frustration in ways that will make a positive change."

Seven months after the slaying of Michael Brown, the Justice Department issued first a finding that Wilson had not willfully violated Michael Brown's civil rights, then a report on police practices and court proceedings in Ferguson. That report asserted that law enforcement impacted African-Americans disproportionately. It is true that a majority of the population in Ferguson is African-American. But they accounted for more than a mere majority of the arrests made in the city in 2012-2014: A whopping ninety-three percent. The report buttressed its findings with examples of the police's racial prejudices.

Not included in the Department of Justice report was an incident involving the reporter from the *Washington Post* whose interview with a childhood friend of Michael Brown was cited above. On the night of the killing, the biracial reporter, whose name was Wesley Lowery, had walked three blocks to a McDonald's restaurant to recharge his iPhone. Cops, kitted out in riot gear, entered the restaurant and suggested that Lowery and another reporter leave because a volatile situation could become dangerous once the sun had set. Both reporters declined to budge. The police suggestion became an order. Neither reporter responded fast enough to satisfy the cops. Sixty seconds after telling the reporters to clear out, one of the officers said, "Okay, let's take him." Lowery felt them grab him from behind. Despite his protest that he was complying with their orders, a cop said, "You're resisting, stop resisting."

Lowery later wrote of this experience and other racially-saturated conflicts across the country in a book entitled *They Can't Kill Us All*. In his book, he complained of the "sting of the plastic zip tie" as the police secured his wrists. This was the first time that Lowery had ever been arrested, and he hadn't expected it to go this way. Once outside MacDonald's, Lowery and his fellow reporter waited in the middle of the street for a vehicle to take them to jail. Both men remembered that they were journalists, and they spent their time bombarding the police with questions about their arrest.

"This is a mistake," Lowery exclaimed. "This is going to be on the front page of the *Washington Post* tomorrow."

"Yeah, well, you're going to be sleeping in our jail cell tonight," was the response of one self-assured cop. That, it turned out, was wrong.

Half an hour after being booked at the Ferguson police station, Lowery and his colleague were released. Pressure from the *Post* and a variety of media did the trick.

The prosecutor at the Wilson grand jury hearing lost his bid for reelection four years after Brown was killed. An Black councilman, running on a campaign to "fundamentally change the culture" in Ferguson law enforcement, defeated him in the Democratic primary.

The killing of Michael Brown acted like a spray of kerosene on the smoldering fire of Black Lives Matter. What began as a protest burst overnight into a full-fledged civil rights movement.

Ben Crump seemed to be omnipresent when it came to cases involving the gunning down of young African-American men. "If you turn on your TV and see Benjamin Crump," began a profile of the lawyer to appear in the June 22, 2020 issue of *The New Yorker*, "it usually means that something terrible has happened." How does that happen? "There aren't many options for Black people when they get killed by the police," he explained. "What are you gonna do? Turn to the police? They're the ones who killed you." The lawyer has fought more than 200 police-violence cases. He's garnered cash settlements in all of them. When he wins a case, he takes a third of the award. (If he loses, he takes nothing.) Crump was not universally admired, even within the Black Lives Matter movement. One adherent of BLM tweeted: "If I am ever killed by [the] police or by a White person, please make sure my family does not hire Ben Crump! He is just as horrible as those ambulance chasing attorneys."

Ahmaud Arbery

In the spring of 2020, a young Black man named Ahmaud Arbery was shot and killed by Greg and Travis McMichael, a father-son duo, as he jogged through their neighborhood in Brunswick, Georgia. The parallels between his slaying and the shooting of Trayvon Martin were striking and unnerving. They both involved a stand-your-ground defense appeal; they both involved a failure of the local police to immediately arrest the men responsible for the shooting deaths. The catalyst which resulted in arrests in the Arbery shooting was a 36-second video shot at the time Ahmaud confronted the men who ended his life.

Benjamin Crump was retained by the Arberys as part of a legal team representing the family. When he viewed the video,

Crump pronounced it to be the lynchpin in the eventual arrests that were made. "If Ahmaud's murder hadn't been caught on video, I fear that his killers would've gotten away with taking his young life," he tweeted.

The man who shot that video, William "Roddie" Bryan, Jr. was himself charged with "felony murder and criminal attempt to commit false imprisonment." Officials appeared to believe that there was evidence Bryan was acting in collusion with the McMichaels although Bryan at first denied this.

The Arbery family was pleased that the police had apprehended the man. Attorneys for the family claimed that Bryan had helped trap Ahmaud although Bryan's lawyer said that his client was "not now and never has been more than a witness to the shooting."

At a preliminary hearing, a Georgia investigator testified that Bryan had heard Travis McMichaels call Arbery a "fucking nigger" after shooting the young Black. For his part, Greg McMichael said that his son "had no choice" but to shoot Arbery. The police who arrived at the scene of the shooting appeared deferential toward the McMichaels. "Why would [Travis] be in cuffs?" one of them said. When Travis said, "I just shot a man, last thing I ever wanted to do in my life," one officer commiserated: "Trust me; I can truly understand that." A police video suggests that the cops offered no assistance to Arbery, who was still breathing when they arrived.

Two whole months elapsed between the slaying of Ahmaud Arbery and the arrest of the McMichaels and Roddie Bryan. Why the delay? Greg McMichael was a retired investigator who had worked three decades in the Glynn County District Attorney's office. There was a cascade of recusals, officials excusing themselves because they had known one or both of the defendants. Nonetheless, it's unclear if that accounted for the delay which only the public release of the Bryan video footage brought to an abrupt and sensational end. Ironically enough, it was Greg McMichael who was responsible for giving the video to a local TV station. (If there was no collusion/cooperation between the McMichaels and Bryan, how could that have happened?) Greg McMichael managed that through the intervention of a Brunswick lawyer who said at the time, "I didn't want the neighborhood to become a Ferguson."

Some context for the shooting may be useful. The neighborhood where Arbery was jogging was tense. Residents were fearful of break-ins. One hotspot which figures in the Arbery slaying was a house under construction where a surveillance camera caught a man—later identified as Ahmaud—on the property. The house belonged to Larry English, a contractor who was doing the construction himself. One incident which sticks out occurred on February 11, almost two weeks before Ahmaud was shot. Travis McMichael, who had heard reports that someone was trespassing on English's property, was driving past the site when he spotted a man there. He reversed his pick-up truck. "I was leaving the neighborhood and I caught a guy running into a house being built," he said, and he called 911. English's motion sensor camera had pinged, showing that someone was at the house. English texted a neighbor who went to the site where he found Travis. Shortly thereafter, Greg walked up from his house to join in the search for the intruder. The Arbery family lawyers admitted that Ahmaud was the man who had visited the house under construction, but they said that he had just "stopped by a property under construction where he engaged in no illegal activity."

February 23, the day of the shooting, began the same way. Someone called 911 to report an intruder at the English construction site. Greg McMichael was in his front yard at the time. "Travis," he called out to his son who lived with Greg, "this guy is running down the street. Let's go." Armed with a shotgun and a .357 magnum handgun, father and son jumped in their pickup and tore down Satilla Drive where they parked at an intersection and waited. When Arbery appeared, a scuffle broke out, and Travis shot and killed the young Black man.

The aftermath of the shooting opened a can of worms for both the police and for the family of the man who was gunned down. The Atlanta Journal-Constitution revealed that Ahmaud had been placed on probation for carrying a gun at a high school basketball game in 2013. *The Guardian* obtained a copy of a police video which dealt with an incident dating back to 2017. The incident took place in a park which the police contended was known for drug activity. In the video, Ahmaud Arbery is shown sitting in his car. A police officer orders him out of the car. Arbery protests although he complies with police orders. The cop testifies later that he became alarmed that Arbery "was becoming enraged and [might] turn physically violent." He calls for backup, and another cop drives up and actually attempts to taser Arbery. (The taser malfunctions.) When told that the police are looking for criminal activity, Arbery protests, "I'm in a fucking park…I'm up early in the morning trying to chill. I'm just aggravated because I work hard, six days a week." During the altercation, the police discover that Arbery's driver license has expired. He is permitted to leave the park but his car stays behind. Afterward, Arbery family lawyers remarked that the video clearly showed "a situation where Ahmaud was harassed by Glynn County police officers."

In another incident later that year—one also captured on a police video camera (the incidents involving Ahmaud's run-ins with the police and his murder on February 23 are the most videoed incidents in this book), the young Arbery and three of his friends had been arrested for attempted theft at a Brunswick-area Walmart. What they were trying to make off with according to a Walmart security guard, an off-duty Glynn County policeman, was a 65" TV.

"Tell me about the TV," says the Glynn County policeman.

"What TV? We don't have any TV."

In one of several scandal-induced black eyes for the authorities, the police chief and three of his high-ranking officers were indicted for perjury less than one month after the Arbery shooting: It was alleged that they had ignored evidence that one of their own "was consorting" with a local drug dealer. The year before, the police department had disbanded a specialist narcotics unit after evidence was uncovered that one of its investigators had had sex with two confidential informants.

The death of Ahmaud, like those of Trayvon Martin and Michael Brown became a case which ignited public outrage which spilled into the streets.

Not surprisingly, Leonard Pitts commented on the killing. He had this to say about it:

> Racism is not hurt feelings. It is systematized oppression that bars you from opportunity and steers you toward calamity every waking day from cradle to grave, that allows you to be murdered on camera, in cold blood in broad daylight—and your assailants to be home in time for dinner.

Jury selection resulted in a lopsided panel of 11 Whites and one Black member. The presiding judge, Timothy Walmsley, admitted that there appeared to be "intentional discrimination in the panel," but that there was nothing he could do to alter the imbalance since the defense had made race-neutral arguments in dismissing potential jurors. The county in which the trial was taking place was more than one quarter Black. The Arbery family was outraged. "How did we get to this result?" a spokeswoman for the family asked. "My mind kept going from White juror to White juror who met the precise parameters that they were describing for omitting Black jurors."

Did the racial imbalance of the jury affect its verdict? The eleven Whites and one Black found the defendants guilty of murder. "I never thought this day would come," said Arbery's mother when the verdict was read.

President Biden said that the outcome of the Arbery trial is "a devastating reminder of how far we have to go in the fight for racial justice in this country." The younger McMichael, the man who actually shot Arbery, was found guilty of malice murder, which in Georgia law involves the deliberate intent to kill someone. The district attorney who tried the case—a woman brought all the way down from suburban Atlanta—rejected his contention that he had acted in self-defense because Arbery was trying to seize his shotgun and he feared for his life. "You can't start it and claim self-defense," the DA retorted. "And they started it."

Travis McMichael's father Gregory was acquitted of malice murder but found guilty of felony murder, the charge when death occurs during the commission of another felony. Their neighbor, William "Roddie" Bryan, was convicted of three counts of felony murder. All three defendants were sentenced to life in prison, the McMichaels with no possibility of parole. Because he had cooperated with investigators, Bryan would be able to seek parole after 30 years. With good behavior, Roddie Bryan might be a free man in 2051.

Judge Walmsley said that Arbery went for a jog and wound up running away from his killers for five minutes. To dramatize the terror of that chase, Walmsley had the court observe a minute of total silence. Arbery's mother said that:

> They chose to target my son because they didn't want him in their community. They chose to treat him differently than other people who frequently visited their community. And when they couldn't sufficiently scare or intimidate him, they killed him.

Arbery's father told the court that "not only did they lynch my son in broad daylight, they killed him while he was doing what he loved doing more than anything: running."

During the trial, several civil rights leaders, including the Rev. Al Sharpton and the Rev. Jesse Jackson, appeared in the public gallery of the courtroom. This prompted one of the defense attorneys, Kevin Gough, to complain that there were only so many pastors the Arbery family could have. "If their pastor's Rev. Al Sharpton, that's fine [although he had called Sharpton's presence `intimidating']. But that's it. We don't want any more Black pastors in here."

The Arbery family was having none of this: "We are going to bring one hundred Black pastors to pray with the family," said Ben Crump representing Arbery's father. "And we welcome all those who want to show their support and add their prayers to ours."

More bad news for the defendants: After their State trial, the McMichaels and Bryan were hauled into a Federal court where they were convicted of a hate crime. Their convictions will certainly face a chunk of prison time, even if their state convictions are overturned or their sentences reduced. Copious evidence of the men's racial prejudices was critical to obtaining their convictions. Said Derrick Johnson, president of the NAACP:

> Two years ago none of us knew of Ahmaud Arbery, but two years [later], his story shook the conscience of our nation and world. Ahmaud Arbery was lynched in broad daylight, and today's verdict brings us one step closer to justice.

Here is another case with racial overtones. It ran at the same time as the trial of the three men accused, and eventually convicted, of killing Ahmaud Arbery. This trial took place in Kenosha, Wisconsin. The defendant was an 18-year-old man named Kyle Rittenhouse who had showed up at a demonstration in Kenosha to protest the police shooting of a Black man, Jacob Blake. Rittenhouse opened fire with his AR-15, killing two men and injuring a third. All the victims, like Rittenhouse, were White. As in the Arbery case, Rittenhouse's lawyers claimed that their client had acted in self-defense. In Wisconsin, someone who fears that he/she is at risk of death or serious bodily harm can respond with deadly force. According to *The New York Times*, Kyle Rittenhouse was pursued by a man who Rittenhouse feared would seize his gun. Rittenhouse shot and killed him. This signaled to the crowd that Rittenhouse was dangerous and hostile. The second of Rittenhouse's victims attacked him with a skateboard. Rittenhouse shot and killed him, too. A third man pulled out a handgun, and Rittenhouse shot him in the arm.

Unlike the Arbery case, the jury accepted the defense's arguments and found Rittenhouse not guilty of all charges. "When people look at this…they're not recognizing just how high the prosecutors' burden is here," *The New York Times* quoted Cecelia Klingele, a University of Wisconsin professor of law. "It was a real uphill battle to get out from under self-defense." The jury did not consider whether Rittenhouse was wrong to bring a gun to a volatile situation. A former Wisconsin Supreme Court justice, Janine Geske, argued that the jury in Rittenhouse's trial could have reached a guilty verdict. It could, for example, have concluded that his fear of death or great bodily harm was not justified.

The verdict provoked a predictable storm of controversy. Right-wing politicians were ecstatic. Several Congressmen suggested that they might offer Rittenhouse an internship in their offices. Marjorie Taylor Greene (R-Georgia) sponsored a bill to award the young man a congressional medal of honor for protecting the town on Kenosha. Those on the left saw matters differently. In an op-ed piece for *The New York Times* entitled "Rittenhouse and the Right's Vigilante Heroes," Charles Blow wrote: "The great threat, and real possibility, is that there are other Rittenhouses out there—young men who watched this verdict and saw how the right has embraced and celebrated a murderer, and now want to follow his lead." Commentator David French agreed. "The Trumpist right is wrongly creating a folk hero out of Rittenhouse," he wrote. "When you turn a foolish young man into a hero, you'll see more foolish young men try to emulate his example."

***

How did the authorities act in the cases we have cited and others? There were lapses, egregious at times, in all of them. An example was the length of time—two months—it took to arrest the McMichaels and Bryan for the murder of Ahmaud Arbery.

The police killings of young Black males in the 2020s opened the sluice gates on a survey of police violence directed against the African-American community in the country.

"In 2019, data of all police killings in the country compiled by Mapping Police Violence, [showed] Black Americans were nearly three times more likely to die from police than white Americans." This is the conclusion of Willem Roper, writing in Statista in June 2020. Police killed 1098 people in 2019. Twenty-four percent of these were Blacks. There were only 27 days when police didn't kill someone. Ninety-nine percent of police killings in the period 2013-2019 did not result in officers being charged with a crime.

The Washington Post reported that, since 2015, the police have shot and killed 5,100 people as of this writing. To put the matter in perspective, the paper pointed out that the "overwhelming majority of people killed were armed. Nonetheless, "whether armed or not, Black people are still shot and killed at disproportionate rates."

The Rev. Graylan Hagler of Plymouth United Church of Christ, D.C. is quoted in the article to say that "White Americans generally thought police to be friendly protectors and... generally looked at stories of police misconduct cynically, and all of a sudden they have to come face-to-face with the myth that they have been living with."

On the other hand, says Los Angeles police chief Michael Moore (and here we paraphrase): To ask an officer to not defend himself is not difficult; it's impossible.

To comment extensively on the police slaying of George Floyd in Minneapolis would take us too far afield, but the incident unleashed nationwide demonstrations, the most passionate since the assassination of Martin Luther King, Jr., and it cannot pass without some mention. Writing in *The Atlantic*, Wesley Lowery quoted an activist in the Minneapolis/St. Paul area as saying:

> I would never condone violence, ever. But sometimes, when people feel like their voices are being ignored over and over and over, violence is the only answer. They have to burn own their own community down to get people to listen to them. We're at a breaking point.

Another activist, this one with a national reputation, Al Sharpton, made the observation that "the Obama-era reforms, ultimately, did not reduce the number of police killings." The ex-president once confided to Sharpton that he considered himself to be into community service, not community activism, however, Sharpton believed that we might be witnessing "the birth of Obama the activist." Obama himself stoked the fire of such a belief when he said, "We have seen in the last several weeks, the last few months, the kinds of epic changes and events in our country that are as profound as anything that I've seen in my lifetime."

Apart from my sons and cousins, I am the only living American in a Canadian family. Relatives have asked me to comment on police shootings in the country. What to say? I referred a brother-in-law to an article which appeared in *The Guardian*. Written by a former FBI agent, Mike German, it argued that for decades the Federal Bureau of Investigation has warned of links between law enforcement and far-right militias. A redacted version of a 2006 assessment of the situation, entitled *White Supremacist Infiltration of Law Enforcement*, warns of "strategic infiltration by organized groups and self-initiated infiltration by law enforcement personnel sympathetic to white supremacist causes." White supremacists and far-right militias have killed more people in the last ten years than any foreign terrorist organization. When a Congressman asked the FBI counter-terrorism chief, Michael McGarrity, about his concern about supremacist infiltration of the police since the publication of the Bureau's 2006 assessment, McGarrity said that he had not read the report. He was "suspect" of white supremacist cops," he said, "but their beliefs were protected by the first amendment." The 2006 assessment took this into account, but it stated:

> Although the First Amendment's freedom of association provision protects an individual's right to join white supremacist groups for the purpose of lawful activity, the government can limit the employment opportunities of group members who hold sensitive public sector jobs, including jobs within law enforcement, when their memberships would interfere with their duties.

It does not take much digging to find evidence of explicit racism within law enforcement. More than one dozen states provide such evidence. Police openly fraternize with extremists and wear the logos of extremist groups on their uniforms. Prosecutors—and here we quote from German's article—"Keep a register of law enforcement officers whose previous misconduct could reasonably undermine the reliability of their testimony and need to be disclosed to defense attorneys."

Not to exaggerate the problem, German cites the "consummate professionals" with whom he worked, although the small contingent of white supremacists in law enforcement are a "matter of urgent concern." He quotes a Georgetown law professor who posits that the criminal justice system "can never achieve its purported goal of fairness while white supremacists continue to hide within police departments."

In 2020, Zack Beauchamp did a survey of police attitudes

towards Blacks for the online journal Vox. What he found was illuminating if not surprising. "It's better to understand the majority of officers as ordinary Americans who are thrown into a system that conditions them to be violent and to treat Black people, in particular, as the enemy," he writes. Beauchamp found what he called "clear evidence" of structural racism in American policing. One cop, who was subsequently dismissed from his force, was heard to say that he couldn't wait for a new civil war in which Whites would "wipe [Blacks] off the fucking map." A human resources manager in San Francisco quit after putting in a 2-year stint on anti-bias training in that city's police force. He wrote in an exit email that "the degree of anti-Black sentiment throughout SFPD is extreme." He went on to write that "while there are some at SFPD who possess somewhat of a balanced view of racism and anti-Blackness, there are an equal number (if not more) who possess and exude deeply rooted anti-Black sentiments."

In his survey, Beauchamp interviewed a US Army vet, Arthur Rizer, who had served in the police force. Rizer told Beauchamp of a young man who joined the police "because he wanted to make a difference." The young man told Rizer after serving six months that "They're animals, all of them."

"The cops, the people I patrol, everybody. They're just fucking animals."

Some time after this conversation, the young man quit—pushed out, in Rizer's words, "by a system that takes people in and breaks them, on both sides of the law."

CHAPTER TWO:
In the Heartland

The preceding cited chapter and verse on how the country is awash in weaponry. We live in a culture of gun violence. That was (and remains) the opinion of NRA president, Oliver North, who said: "The problem that we've got is that we're trying like the dickens to treat the symptom without treating the disease. And the disease, in this case, is youngsters who are steeped in a culture of violence."

No region, no state, no city is spared. I give you proof from my own state, Kansas, and my own city, Lawrence, seat of the University of Kansas. In an eight-hour standoff between police and the man who had phoned them, the caller fired off several shots, then threatened both his neighbors and the police who responded to his call. The cops brought in an armored vehicle to evacuate people in the vicinity. When the shooter emerged from his house, gun in hand, officers used what the local newspaper called "less lethal weapons" to subdue him. He was taken to the hospitalfor treatment of non-life-threatening injuries and mental health evaluation. The police did not release the identity of the man they apprehended because of the mental health issues involved in the incident, nor did they offer any other details about the arrest.

Lawrence could not be described as a crime-infested city although it has a history of sporadic violence. It is a small Midwestern city which sits placidly in the farmland of northeast Kansas, forty miles southwest of Kansas City. Like other university towns in the country, it experienced civil unrest during the Vietnam War.

Much of the gun violence in America occurs in the Northeast, the South, and major cities in the Midwest, but it is not limited to those places. It pops up in what might seem, at first blush, the most unlikely of venues. It should come as no surprise really that gun violence did erupt in Kansas. This, after all, was Bleeding Kansas, the territory which earned its sobriquet when pro-slavery and anti-slavery forces battled each other in the years which led up to the Civil War. This was the state where John Brown perpetrated a massacre of five pro-slavery men hustled out of their homes to be hacked to death by Brown and his sons. Kansas was born in violence, and violent episodes punctuated its history even after its admission to the Union in 1861 as a free state.

Post Civil War Kansas was home to Dodge City, the cow town so beset by violence that it invited Wyatt Earp to come as its Chief Deputy Marshall in the 1870s. The city council instituted what it called the "Deadline" along the railroad yards along Front Street. The yards separated the north end of town, where guns were prohibited. Cowboys packing heat there were arrested immediately and unceremoniously packed off to jail. In the free-wheeling south end, pretty much any behavior went unchecked. In June of 1879, a local paper ran this article:

> The boys and girls across the deadline had a high old time last Friday. They sang and danced, and fought and bit, and cut and had a good time generally, making music for the entire settlement. Our reporter summed up five knockdowns, three broken heads, two cuts and several incidental bruises. Unfortunately none of these injuries will prove fatal.

In the same year, a photograph showed a street sign in Dodge warning that "The carrying of fire arms is strictly prohibited."

You Are All Watching It Live

LAWRENCE WAS FOUNDED BY NEW ENGLAND abolitionists as a Free State stronghold. It is now a suburb of 100,000 souls less than one hour's drive southwest of Kansas City. The city chooses to believe— naively it turns out—that civic unrest occurs principally when the University of Kansas basketball team wins an important game. The city is not immune to the problems that afflict other communities in the country. In April 2019, a middle school student was arrested and charged with making a threat to shoot people on the last day of school. The incident made the front page of the local newspaper, but it was not an isolated case of threatened violence.

Sometimes violence erupted on the streets of the city. On the night of October 1, 2017, a shooting occurred in downtown Lawrence. Three of the five victims died. An Uber driver later told the local newspaper, the Lawrence Journal World, that "something felt wrong" that evening, even before the shooting. Earlier in the night, there had been a big concert at a downtown music club called the Granada, but the club's owner expressed doubt that the shooting had anything to do with his club which had closed more than half an hour before the incident.

A video taken shortly after the shooting recorded the chaos that ensued. An officer who attempted to reach one of the shooting victims later testified that "People were surrounding him. There was a mass of people who both appeared to be trying to help him, trying to revive him, a lot of people were just standing around videotaping, using their cellphones to record him and his surroundings."

Police were seen administering CPR before the victims were whisked away in an ambulance. None of the dead were from Lawrence: Two came from Topeka, the State Capitol which is 20 miles west of Lawrence; the third fatality, a young woman Leah Brown, was from suburban Kansas City. She had come to Lawrence which was considered "safe." She died from a stray bullet shot into a throng of people who were innocently milling about.

One man taking video filmed for more than ten minutes. He aimed at one of the victims lying on the sidewalk. Onlookers urged him to stop, but he persisted, saying: "This shit is crazy. You all are watching it live."

"We ain't going to watch him die," objected one man in the crowd which numbered, according to one estimate, in the hundreds.

A smaller crowd of about twenty people gathered in the parking lot of the hospital to which the victims were taken. A hospital attendant came out and hugged several of them. A young man kept crying out, "I'm sorry! I'm sorry!"

One of the men killed had just become a father. The mother of his child later said on Facebook that "[He] gave me the greatest gift I could ever ask for, our daughter. Her first word was Dada. My promise to him is to make him proud and always remind our daughter how much he loved her."

Police ultimately arrested three men for the crime. They all lived in Topeka. One of their friends had attended the concert in Lawrence earlier that night. After the concert, the friend was beaten up. Driving back to Topeka, he roused his friends, the 20-year-old men who became the defendants in the shooting incident. The men then returned to Lawrence hankering for revenge. They parked close to the Granada and walked back in the direction of the music hall. About a block away from the club, they encountered a group of men whom they knew from Topeka. An argument broke out. The men began brawling. Then gunfire erupted. Witnesses testified that they heard about twenty gunshots. A surveillance camera caught muzzle flashes. By the time police arrived at the scene, a crowd had formed around the dead and the wounded who lay, sprawling on the pavement. The officers found some onlookers uncooperative. It was difficult to approach the victims because the crowd would not let the police pass. Said one officer, "The crowd was so hostile and so crowding in, I was concerned about all of our safety."

Another cop said, "It was so loud, the volume of voices I couldn't hear my radio. Nobody was listening to any orders."

The same officer later said, "It took me probably fifteen minutes to tell people to back away from a deceased body that was lying on the street."

Here is one reason why people were so hostile: Most of them were Black. The police officers were White. It's easy to imagine that the crowd's hostility was fallout from the Trayvon Martin and Michael Brown shootings.

Apart from Leah Brown, the victims were all African American men from Topeka. They and the defendants knew one another. Some were even friends on Facebook, had been for months, even years. All three defendants had gotten into trouble with the law, mostly because of drug possession and the illegal possession of firearms. Two of the men had spent time in jail just weeks before the Lawrence shooting. One of the men was convicted of violating his probation on several occasions.

During a preliminary hearing, one of the defendants kept leaning back in his chair and shaking his head. Another defendant yelled at the prosecutors and victims' family, "Fuck you, I didn't shoot nobody!"

Originally the three defendants were scheduled to be tried together, but difficulties arose with this scenario during jury selection. One of the defendants' lawyers made a number of errors and engaged in what the presiding judge called "hostile and aggressive questioning" of potential jurors. One of those potential jurors approached the bailiff asking to be excused. She couldn't be fair, she said, in light of the antipathy she felt toward the lawyer. The two other defense attorneys also complained of the collateral damage the third lawyer might do to their clients' cases. Shortly thereafter the judge called the third lawyer "incompetent to try this case" and discharged her. She then declared a mistrial and dismissed the jury pool. Separate trials for each of the three defendants were scheduled for the spring of 2019. In March of that year, one of the men pleaded guilty to a misdemeanor battery. He was sentenced to less time than he had already served in jail. "[My client] is pleased with the outcome," said the defendant's lawyer.

"By entering his plea, [the defendant] acknowledges his role in starting the fight [which led to the shooting]," said the District Attorney for Douglas County, in which Lawrence is located. "Resolving this case allows the State to concentrate on the two remaining and more serious cases."

One of those cases involved Anthony L. Roberts, 22, who asked the judge to find that he had acted in self-defense when he shot three people to death and injured a fourth. The judge rejected Roberts' request, saying that there was no evidence to support it.

A second defendant pleaded guilty of attempted voluntary manslaughter in early April 2019. The judge in the case said that the defendant would be required to register as a violent offender for fifteen years. That development made it possible for the district attorney's office to "prioritize" the case against the remaining defendant, charged with all three homicides.

Jurors deliberated for a total of four and a half hours before finding Roberts guilty on all counts. The presiding judge was in the process of scheduling a sentencing date when Roberts burst out, "You might as well sentence me now! It's a life sentence!"

Roberts was bundled out of the courtroom before the hearing was resumed.

The aunt of one of the victims said, "Thank you, Jesus. He answered all of our prayers. We've been waiting for this for two years."

Less upbeat was the reaction of Leah Brown's mother: "I think that there's no justice for Leah. She's not here and won't walk on this earth with us ever again."

On August 1, 2019, Judge Sally Pokorny sentenced Roberts to serve two life sentences for the murder of two of his victims. In addition, he was to serve 13 years 9 months for the killing of his third victim, 5 years 1 month for the attempted murder of his fourth victim. The sentences were to run consecutively.

"This is not closure," said Pokorny. "This is something that will always affect everyone. None of these families will be able to walk down [the street where the shootings occurred] and not wonder if they can feel safe."

A man speaking on behalf of Leah Brown told the court, "Leah and her best friend were in an appropriate place at an appropriate time until suddenly one of them was dying in her best friend's arms."

Religious leaders in the community were not slow to comment on the shooting. A protestant minister, Eleanor McCormick, wrote a letter to God which she read aloud from the pulpit:

> *Dear God (well actually Hi, God)*
>
> *On the corner of 11th and Massachusetts, a few steps from our sanctuary door, I read a text message saying: five shot, three dead: Colwin Lynn Henderson III, 20, Tre'Mel Dupree Dean 24, and Leah Elizabeth Brown, 22. In less than 24 hours, there were 58 more dead in Las Vegas. God, I was just so sad as I write these words. I turned to the Book of Lamentations because I didn't know where else to go or what to do. I read the five poems there, mostly out loud. These five poems are an anguished response to the destruction of Jerusalem... I read these communal and individual laments in which the speakers attempt to persuade you, God, to intervene in the face of unbelievable crisis. It's anguished writing, with its unsparing focus on destruction and pain and suffering. It is an honest expression of the harsh realities of a very violent world.*

The woman killed in this incident, Leah Brown, became an organ donor, honored by the Donate Life Rose Parade float which took part in the New Year's Day parade in Pasadena, CA in 2019.

***

To the east of Lawrence, in the suburban belt which wraps around the western edge of Kansas City lies the town of Olathe. For thirty years, Austin's Bar & Grill had been an Olathe landmark, a "neighborhood fixture" in the words of one of the sports bar's co-owners. On the night of February 22, 2017, two cricket-playing friends were enjoying a drink at Austin's. The men were immigrants from India who had come to the States to pursue graduate work. After arriving they had found work as engineers at a factory that made GPS devices.

A 51-year-old man police later identified as Adam Purinton approached the two Indians and demanded to know what country they came from. The Indians tried to ignore him, but Purinton became increasingly agitated and abusive. Another Austin patron, Ian Grillot, asked him to leave. Purinton did leave. He stumbled around the parking lot before getting into his pickup truck and driving away. That, it seemed, was the end of the incident. But Purinton came back. This time he came with a gun. "Get out of my country!" he screamed at the Indians whom he mistook for Iranians. Ian Grillot, a white American, tried again to intervene. Purinton shot him in the hand and chest. He turned his gun on the Indians, killing one of them outright and injuring the other. He then made good his escape, driving southeast of Kansas City to Clinton, Missouri, where he entered an Applebee's Restaurant. He was seeking a place to hide, he told a bartender. Purinton believed that he had just killed two Iranians. "So I'm a bartender at Applebee's," said the man Purinton had confided to. "And this guy told me he had done something really bad and he was on the run from the police."

About eighteen months before the shooting in Austin's Bar & Grill, Purinton had lost his father to pancreatic cancer. The two were close, and Purinton, who had always been a heavy drinker, went downhill from there. He became, in the opinion of a neighbor, "a drunken mess."

Federal authorities described the shooting as a hate crime. Support for Purinton's victims poured in. Two days after the crime, the First Baptist Church of Olathe held a prayer vigil attended by hundreds of mourners. More than one million dollars was raised on GoFundMe, an online fundraising platform, for the victims of the attack. This included $400,000 to cover Ian Grillot's medical expenses.

In India, condemnation of the crime came swift and fierce. *The Hindustan Times* noted the difference in the way crime was reported in the US: Why did the shooting in Olathe receive less attention than crimes involving White victims? The paper did observe, however, that Ian Grillot, the man who had interceded on behalf of the Indian engineers, was a hero in India, "possibly a household name." And why, asked *The Times*, hadn't President Trump spoken out about the attack? (A Pakistani-American comic tweeted, "The President could say, 'Don't shoot innocent brown people; it's wrong.'")

What happened in Olathe did nothing to reassure South Asian immigrants to stay in the States. An organization that tracks acts of violence against Americans of South Asian descent reported 140 acts of violence and harassment in the twelve months beginning in November 2016. This compared with 76 between January 2011 and April 2014. The vast majority of those incidents involved anti-Muslim bigotry.

What accounted for this increase? Some observers attributed it in part to anti-immigrant rhetoric by Donald Trump. Calling Mexican immigrants rapists and murderers certainly set the tone for the actions of some of his more bigoted disciples.

The mother of the murder victim in Olathe said that she would not allow her younger son to return to the US. "I don't want to lose another son," she sobbed.

The president of an association for parents of Indians living abroad said, "Many of our young prefer to go to America for higher education . . . Now the situation has changed after Trump has become president of the United States. Racism is high, and this incident is a clear example."

An official of the ruling party in India added his voice to the chorus of complaints: "People in America are apprehensive about their security."

It's not hard to find examples of anti-immigrant bigotry in America. A Harvard Law School student told *The New York Times* that a man swore at him while he was on his cell phone, called him a Muslim (which he wasn't), and followed him around the store where he had gone to shop. The man demanded to know what country the student was from.

A wedding was called off when the bride, who lived in India, told her fiancé in the States that she could not live in America. The Indian-born writer Sandip Roy said, "There were slurs and snide comments about smelling like curry, but it never crossed my mind that America needed to be made great again, because I had already been seduced by its own conviction in its greatness." Roy moved back to India six years ago.

The funeral for the engineer killed in the Olathe bar was held in his hometown of Hyderabad, India. Politicians showed up carrying "Down with Trump" signs. Relatives of the victim carried his rose-covered bier to the cremation site 23 miles away where two hundred mourners attended the ceremony. The government of India indicated that it would raise the issue of safety for its citizens with the Trump administration.

The widow of the slain engineer had misgivings about returning to America from her native India, and there were problems with her legal status in the country which was dependent on her marriage, but she obtained a temporary work visa and decided to come back. In her words: "I returned for all the love that flowed around me after this terrible tragedy. For all the people, near and far, who went out of their way to show me America cannot and must not be judged by the actions of one man. I returned because America is my home now."

When Purinton pleaded guilty to the crimes he had committed—murder and attempted murder—in Austin's Bar & Grill, she issued a statement declaring, "Let us continue to work for peace, understanding, and love—all the things Srini [her husband] stood for and will be his legacy." A judge in Missouri sentenced Adam Purinton to life in prison with no possibility of parole for fifty years.

"Our goal is to make sure that he never walks in the community again," said the district attorney in the case. "I believe that this sentence will achieve that result." Purinton also faced federal hate-crime charges which could have earned him the death penalty, but he avoided this by pleading guilty.

***

These two incidents were drawn from the same part of the state, the northeast corner of Kanas within the metro region of Kansas City, but the problem of gun violence affected all parts of the state. A random culling of stories from around Kansas produced the following two examples:

> A friend brought to my attention the story of the shooting by a police officer of Joey Weber, an autistic man, in the western part of the state. It occurred in the fall of 2016. As a county attorney told the local newspaper, the cop—whose name was Brandon Hauptman—tried to stop Weber who was driving a vehicle with an expired car tag. The man attempted to elude the officer by driving into an alley. Hauptman then called for reinforcements. Three police vehicles pursued Weber until he finally brought his car to a stop. Hauptman ordered Weber "at gunpoint" to lie on the ground. Weber ran away but fell to

the sidewalk, with Hauptman on top of him. Weber tried to wrestle the cop's gun away from him. Hauptman then pushed his gun into Weber's chest, fired, and killed him.

The County Attorney said later that no crime had been committed because "Hauptman was acting in self-defense."

> Kansas' first experience of a mass shooting took place in the spring of 2016. Hesston is a Mennonite community about fifty miles from Wichita. It is also the home of Excel, a lawn equipment factory, which employed around one thousand people, most of whom commuted to Hesston. They could not afford housing prices closer to work, so they drove in from nearby Newton.

On February 25, 2016, a 38-year-old Excel worker named Cedric Ford, came into the factory with a handgun and an AK-47. His ex-girlfriend had given him these weapons although, as a convicted felon with a record in the state of Florida, Ford should not legally have possessed any firearms. Driving up from Newton where he lived in a mobile home, he blasted the windshields of a couple of cars which he encountered on route. At the Excel factory, Ford alternated between his AK-47 and a semi-automatic Glock 22 handgun. In the course of a few minutes, he shot several coworkers.

Ford had told the manager of his trailer park that he had moved north "to turn his life around," although the Floridian had spent some time in a Kansas jail. Impressions of the man varied: One of his coworkers at Excel said that Ford "was just a normal guy," who was enchanted by his first visit to a local zoo. He confided to his Facebook page that "I never seen wildlife in my life besides a pit bull and Rottweiler puppies." On the other hand, his girlfriend had requested a restraining order from the police. In her complaint, she said that Ford had placed me in a chokehold from behind . . . I couldn't breathe."

The time line for the afternoon of the shooting went like this:

- 2:15 Ford reported for the second shift at Excel;
- 3:30 The sheriff serves him with a restraining order;

- 4:30 Ford fails to return to work after a break.

   Ironically that Thursday had started out as a "slow" day at the local police department. So slow that Police Chief Doug Schroeder decided to take an exam on workplace violence for a course he was following. Meanwhile workers at Excel began pouring out of the factory. One of them contacted the police: "We need police at Excel Industries. A guy just popped out with an AK-47 and started shooting. I was in my car. I took off." Ford was inside the factory randomly shooting people. One coworker later said that Ford had pointed a gun at him and pulled the trigger, but the magazine was empty. Another Excel employee said that Ford "looked happy; it was almost like a smile on his face." An autopsy later indicated that there was methamphetamine and alcohol in Ford's blood, a combination that can produce psychosis, even delusions.

   Schroeder, who by now had finished his exam, struggled into a ballistic vest and drove south to the Excel factory, one mile away. When he got there, he found workers milling about outside. He entered the factory on cat's paws and followed a path of bloody footprints between the machinery. Excel felt like a ghost town. Untended machines buzzed away on both sides of him. At the front of the factory, Schroeder caught sight of Ford and let off a shot from his AR-15. Ford fired back, but he missed. Schroeder let off four more shots, three of which struck the gun man. Ford fell to the ground, mortally wounded.

   He had killed three people and wounded 14 others. An autopsy determined that he had been high on methamphetamines and alcohol at the time of the shooting. His motive for the rampage? Ninety minutes earlier he had been served with a restraining order. That, in the opinion of a local sheriff, was what set Ford off.

   Doug Schroeder earned an A in his class and went on to graduate with a 4.0 average in professional studies. He taught criminal justice at the college level and considered going on to get a Ph.D. Schroeder won a Medal of Valor for what he did that day in February, 2016. His wife keeps it in a plastic case in the basement of their house. She plans to have it framed someday.

Hesston was traumatized by the shooting. "If it could happen here," one resident said, "it could happen anywhere." Senator Pat Roberts said that he was praying "for the victims of this senseless act of violence" and President Barack Obama noted that "the real tragedy is the degree to which this has become routine."

Fight Guns With Guns

KANSAS TURNED A BLIND EYE (legislatively) to the gun violence in the state. . For the most part, Kansas believed that you fight guns with more guns. In 2013, then-Governor Sam Brownback signed a bill which expanded the right of citizens to carry a concealed weapon. Previously gun owners needed a permit. The 2013 bill did away with this requirement. It also did not require gun owners to get any training in the use of firearms.

Flanked by representatives of the NRA and the Kansas State Rifle Association, Brownback affixed his signature to the bill. He mentioned at the time that his son had benefitted from an "excellent course" in the handling of firearms. If that was the case, a reporter asked the governor, why was he signing a bill which did away with this requirement?

"You don't have to get the permission slip from the government," Brownback replied. "It is a constitutional right and we're removing a barrier to that right."

A state representative said at the time, "We haven't had any Wild West shoot-out; we haven't had any of the blood running in the streets that folks feared."

The president of the Kansas State Rifle Association asserted that the bill capped a decade-long campaign. As for the training requirement in the earlier bill, that had simply been the result of "political horse trading." Wyatt Earp must have been spinning in his grave.

Attempts to modify the 2013 bill in the State Legislature ran up against stonewalling, if not outright opposition. A bill to prohibit guns on campus never made it out of a Senate committee.

"I'm incredibly angry," said the co-president of the Kansas Coalition for A Gun-Free Campus. "The university community and the hospital community and all the students overwhelmingly support extending this exemption, and it's incredibly clear who the senators on this committee work for, which is the gun lobby and not the people."

Gun rights advocates were ecstatic. "A win for the Second Amendment," crowed the Republican Party Chairman.

One day later a House committee heard testimony on a bill identical to the one that had stalled in the Senate committee. There was an overflow crowd which spilled outside the hearing room. A loudspeaker conveyed what was happening in the hearing room to those who couldn't make it inside. Some people were following the proceedings on live stream posted by other people who had made it inside the hearing room. The vast majority of citizens testifying supported the bill.

"All of us have the right to decide if, when and how we want weapons to enter our homes," said a woman representing non-profit nursing homes. "Residents of nursing homes must not and should not be treated any differently."

One university survey found that seventy percent of faculty and staff at Kansas Regents universities were opposed to handguns in campus buildings. One woman from a suburb of Kansas City testified that neither she nor many of her friends would permit their children to attend a college where concealed weapons were tolerated.

"I am disappointed," she said, "that my son won't be able to attend the University of Kansas . . . due to the risks that guns on campus would create."

Only three people spoke against the bill. One of them was from the NRA.

One committee member asked Rabbi Moti Rieber, a supporter of the bill, if he considered the Second Amendment (in the Bill of Rights) a privilege or a right.

"I think that Justice (Antonin) Scalia said that it was within the rights of the states to limit public carrying of weapons,"

Rieber replied. "And he specifically mentioned schools and public buildings."

One of the few opponents of the bill cited the same decision of Scalia. Representative Boog Highberger (D-Lawrence) challenged that citation by asking, "Isn't it true that Justice Scalia pretty clearly acknowledged that states have the right to ban concealed weapons in public places?"

"I don't agree with that particular portion of the ruling," replied the man offering testimony.

That response provoked a wave of derisive laughter in the hearing room.

A heap of written testimony had been submitted to the committee, and its chairman John Barker, a Republican from Abilene assured committee members that they would have ample time to digest it before any vote was taken.

Two weeks after its public hearing, John Barker's committee failed to advance a narrower bill which would have exempted the University of Kansas hospital complex in the Kansas City metro region from having to allow conceal-carry. The vote in committee was a tie 11-11, and Barker's vote would have been needed to advance the bill. Barker declined to cast that vote. "It was disappointing, and I don't want to downplay the significance of not moving that bill out of committee," said a moderate Republican who had supported the bill.

Dennis "Boog" Highberger, another supporter of the bill, was also disappointed. "I thought that there was a slight majority to pass the bill out, so I'm not quite sure what happened," he said.

Highberger is physically disabled. He famously campaigned in a recumbent bike (sort of elongated tricycle). But spina bifida did not stop him from obtaining a law degree from the University of Kansas and going on to serve first as the mayor of Lawrence, then as a liberal stalwart in the Kansas legislature.

Hospital officials had lobbied for the bill that Highberger had supported, arguing that concealed weapons would put patients and staff at risk. But gun rights advocates contended that security was inadequate in the sprawling hospital complex.

    Again it was hard to fight that legislative mantra: It takes more guns to fight guns.

CHAPTER THREE:
Assassinations

Assassinations have played a role in American politics since the middle of the nineteenth century when—in what probably is the most famous of these killings—President Abraham Lincoln was shot point blank. He was seated in a box at Ford's Theatre in Washington, D.C. watching a comedy called "The American Cousin."

The Lincoln assassination was actually part of a bigger plot targeting several government officials. Chief among the conspirators was an actor named John Wilkes Booth, who lived in the North throughout the Civil War despite his Confederate sympathies. Booth's intended targets included General Ulysses S. Grant, commander of the Union armies; Secretary of State, William H. Seward; and Vice-President Andrew Johnson.

Abraham Lincoln had planned to invite General Grant to come to the play at Ford's Theatre, but Grant had already decided to spend time that day, 14 April 1864, in New Jersey with his children whom he had not seen for a while. This was true but it was still a pretext for Mrs. Grant to avoid Mary Todd Lincoln. Mrs. Grant found the President's wife to be imperious. Lincoln invited, instead, Clara Harris, the daughter of a New York Senator, and her fiancé, a major in the Union Army.

At one point in the evening, President Lincoln took his wife's hand, and Mary Todd Lincoln whispered teasingly, "What would Miss Harris think of my hanging on to you so?"

John Wilkes Booth gained entry to the presidential box when Lincoln's bodyguard was absent. He fired a bullet from his Philadelphia Deringer into Abraham Lincoln's head, timing the shot to be drowned out by the guffaws which erupted after the line in the play, "Well, I guess I know enough to turn you inside out, old gal; you sockdologizing old man-trap!"

Clara Harris' fiancé was slow to intervene. When he jumped up, Booth slashed his left forearm with a knife. Then the assassin leaped from the presidential box, falling twelve feet to the stage below and breaking a bone in his left leg. He yelled something which sounded like Sic Semper Tyrannis, the Virginia state motto, before fleeing across the stage through a side door into an alley where a horse stood waiting for him.

Booth's co-conspirators were less successful. The man designated to kill Andrew Johnson lost his nerve, got drunk at the bar in Johnson's hotel, and staggered off into the night without accosting his intended victim. The conspirator assigned to kill Secretary of State Seward, Lewis Powell, managed to get inside Seward's house, but one of Seward's sons intercepted him. Powell knocked him unconscious and barged into Seward's bedroom where he attacked the bedridden Seward with a knife. The Secretary's butler screamed, "Murder! Murder!" and ran outside to secure help. Powell managed to get away. Seward eventually recovered from Powell's attack although he was left with facial scars.

President Lincoln succumbed to his head wound the day following the shooting at Ford's Theatre. Booth made good his escape from Washington but was cornered in the barn of a farmer in Virginia. There he was shot in the head by a Union soldier, much the way he had shot Lincoln. He died a couple of hours later.

Booth's co-conspirators were arrested and four of them, including Lewis Powell, were convicted by a military tribunal and hanged.

In the next forty years, two other US presidents were shot and killed by assassins:

The first of these was James A. Garfield. His assassin, Charles J. Guiteau, had actually drafted a speech on behalf of Garfield during the election of 1880. It was a rewrite of a piece which Guiteau had written on behalf of Ulysses S. Grant. Guiteau convinced himself that his speech had propelled Garfield to a razor-thin win in the election, and he demanded a diplomatic post in return for his services. Specifically he coveted a consulship in Vienna or Paris. He made such a nuisance of himself, pestering Republican officials in Washington, that Secretary of State James G. Blaine told him to go away and never again to broach the topic of a consulship. Guiteau wrote Garfield demanding that he fire Blaine. The White House ignored this letter as it did all the rest of his correspondence.

On July 2, 1881, Garfield went to a railway station in Washington. The station, the Baltimore and Potomac Railroad Station, has long since been demolished. It stood where the West Building of the National Gallery of Art now stands. Garfield's intent was to go first to Williams College, which was his alma mater, to deliver a speech before leaving for his summer vacation. His Secretary of War, Robert Todd Lincoln, son of Abraham Lincoln, was there to see him off. So was Charles Guiteau. Alerted to the President's departure by local newspapers, Guiteau lay in waiting for him. He carried with him a British Bulldog revolver which he had bought expressly for the purpose of killing Garfield.

Guiteau shot Garfield in the back as he walked across the waiting room of the station. Garfield collapsed, and Guiteau attempted to leave the station but was apprehended by a policeman who had heard gunfire. He took Guiteau to a police station where all he would say was that "I am a Stalwart of the Stalwarts! I did it and I want to be arrested!" (The Stalwarts were a faction of the Republican Party which owed its loyalty to General, then President Ulysses S. Grant.)

Clearly delusional, Guiteau appeared to believe that his killing of Garfield would usher in the Millennium. When police apprehended Guiteau, they found in his pocket a letter stating that "the president's tragic death was a sad necessity but it will unite the Republican party and save the Republic. Life is a fleeting dream, and it matters little when one goes."

Robert Todd Lincoln was grief-stricken. "How many hours of sorrow I have passed in this town," he later cried. Carried first to an upstairs room at the railroad station, Garfield asked more than once to be taken back to the White House. An ambulance was called to transport the stricken president away.

"Yes, I shot the president but his physicians killed him," claimed the assassin with some justification. American doctors in the 1880s did not in general subscribe to Joseph Lister's theory of germs. Garfield's attending physicians repeatedly poked their unsterilized fingers into Garfield's wound in searching—unsuccessfully—for the assailant's bullet which had lodged in his back, near his pancreas. Long afterwards medical experts expressed the view that Garfield might have survived if his physicians had been less ignorant. One of these physicians actually punctured his liver while searching for the elusive bullet. Well-intentioned doctors despaired of saving the president's life. In the heat and humidity of a Washington summer, their patient's condition fluctuated. In desperation, they summoned Alexander Graham Bell who had designed something which he called the "inductive balance." Bell claimed that this device could detect hidden metal. That it could, but when used on President Garfield, what it detected was his mattress composed of steel wires.

To lower the temperature of the sickroom and keep the patient comfortable, Navy engineers improvised a sort of air conditioner which employed fans and a box of ice. In early September, staff removed Garfield to the Jersey Shore to escape the intemperate climate of the capital. There, on September 19, 1881, Garfield expired of septic poisoning.

At his trial, Guiteau behaved like a deranged person: He sang "John Brown's Body" in court and recited epic poetry. The jury at his trial were unpersuaded by Guiteau's claim that it was not he who had killed Garfield but the doctors who attended him. He was found guilty of murder and hanged on June 30, 1882. Even on the gallows, Guiteau continued to delight the press with his circus-like antics, dancing up to the noose which ended his life and shaking hands with the executioner who permitted him to recite a poem he had just written, "I am going to the Lordy; I am so glad." When he finished speaking, the executioner slipped a hood over Guiteau's head, and Guiteau dropped the piece of paper on which he had written his poem. This was the sign that he was ready to die. The trapdoor under his feet swung open, and Guiteau fell through. He died on the gallows, his neck broken.

The condemned man's poem figured in Stephen Sondheim's musical Assassins where it was called "The Ballad of Guiteau."

***

During the twenty years that separated presidential assassinations—Garfield's in 1880 and William McKinley's in 1901—a significant change occurred in the country's method of criminal execution. It was one which reflected the tenor of the times: The electric chair came to replace the gallows as the preferred instrument of capital punishment. In his book on the subject, *The Electric Chair: An Unnatural American History*, Craig Brandon wrote: "The electric chair's midwife was greed, the kind of pure, unadulterated greed for which the Gilded Age was famous."

The story centered on the rivalry between Thomas Edison and George Westinghouse, the champions of direct current (DC) and alternating current (AC) respectively. Which was safer? Lucrative contracts were at stake in this contest.

In November 1887, Edison issued a statement which included the remark that he would "join heartily in an effort to abolish capital punishment." But a month later he seemed to change his mind and wrote, "the most suitable [type of electrocution device] is that class of dynamo-electric machinery which employs intermittent currents. The most effective of these are known as `alternating machines' manufactured principally in this country by Geo. Westinghouse."

A Buffalo dentist, Alfred P. Southwick, is credited with inventing the electric chair. His inspiration came when he witnessed the electrocution death of a drunkard who haplessly touched a live generator terminal. Upon reflection, Southwick concluded that the electric chair would be a more humane way to end a criminal's life than either the gallows or the firing squad. He persuaded the New York legislature of this and in 1889, a law authorizing electrocution went into effect. Until then, electrocution had been used as a way to euthanize stray dogs.

After New York State adopted the electric chair as its means of execution, it sent a convicted murderer, William Kemmler, to death by electrocution in August 1890. After the warden at Auburn Prison had attached electrodes to Kemmler's head, he gestured to have a switch flipped and electric current to pass through the criminal's body. Kemmler's shoulders rose slowly. Witnesses smelled burnt clothes and charred flesh. After seventeen seconds had elapsed, two doctors declared him dead, but one of the witnesses yelled, "Great God, he is alive!" True enough, he was still breathing and his heart was beating. A second jolt of higher voltage electricity passed through Kemmler's body. Smoke was seen pouring out of Kemmler's head. Four minutes later he was dead. It took a matter of hours for his body to cool down.

Southwick was exultant. "We live in a higher civilization this day on," he crowed. Westinghouse was less sanguine. "They could have done a better job with an ax," he told reporters. Edison was ready with some thoughtful advice. "The better way is to place the hands in jars of water and let the current be turned on there."

Like Kemmler, the man who assassinated President William McKinley was put to death in the electric chair. Leon Czolgosz was an anarchist who had lost his job in the financial panic of 1893. He decided that it was his duty, as an anarchist, to kill the President. He acted on this conviction during McKinley's visit to the Pan-American Exposition in Buffalo, New York in September 1901. As part of his visit to the exposition, the President greeted well-wishers at the Temple of Music. His personal secretary had tried twice to delete this part of President McKinley's program, but the president overruled him. "No one would wish to hurt me," he said.

Czolgosz joined the line of people wishing to shake hands with McKinley. He held a .32 Iver Johnson revolver in his right hand, concealed in a handkerchief. It looked as if his hand had been injured. When he came up to McKinley, the President saw Czolgosz's right hand wrapped by what looked like a bandage. McKinley extended his left hand to the man who was about to kill him. Czolgosz fired two bullets into William

McKinley's abdomen and the President lurched forward. An onlooker, a detective, and an artilleryman quickly subdued the assailant who cried out, "I done my duty" as his victim staggered backwards into the arms of his secretary. McKinley was whisked away in an electric ambulance to the on-site hospital which was little more than a first-aid station. Nonetheless the interns on duty there decided to operate to remove the bullets in the president's body. One of these bullets had deflected off a button on McKinley's waistcoat; the other, lodged in his back, remained there. The same electric ambulance which had transported him to the hospital now took McKinley to the house in Buffalo where he was staying. The doctors attending the President expressed confidence that their patient would recover, and for the next several days, it appeared that the president would pull through. His Vice President, Theodore Roosevelt, felt so comfortable with McKinley's improved condition that he set off on a camping trip to the Adirondack Mountains, saying that "You may say that I am absolutely sure the president will recover." McKinley did not pull through, however. Gangrene set in on his stomach walls, and he died on September 14, his arm around his sobbing wife.

Justice was swiftly meted out to the 28-year-old anarchist. Electrocuted only six weeks later, on October 29, 1901, Czolgosz said moments before his death that "I killed the president for the good of the laboring people, the good people."

***

Sixty-odd years were to pass before the country endured another presidential assassination. It was like a period of respite although attempts on politicians' lives were made in the early years of the twentieth century. These included attempts on the lives of both Roosevelts—Theodore and Franklin Delano.

Theodore was saved from what might have been a life-threatening wound in his chest by a steel eyeglass case and a 50-page speech crammed into his coat pocket. Undeterred by the attempt on his life, the president went on to address a political rally in Milwaukee. "Friends, I shall ask you to be as quiet as possible," he began. "I don't know whether you fully understand that I have just been shot." He then showed his stunned audience the blood stains on his shirt. "It takes more than that to kill a bull moose," he said before launching into an 84-minute speech. Remember that Teddy had been McKinley's VP. He became president when McKinley was assassinated.

FDR was targeted by Giuseppe Zangara, an unemployed bricklayer, who shot at the president-elect on February 15, 1933, just after he had addressed a crowd of supporters in Miami. Roosevelt had spoken from the back of a green Buick convertible. He had been crippled since 1921 when he was stricken by polio. His disability was a constant challenge for his political career. He used a cane and a wheel chair which he himself had designed, and he needed assistance to walk.

Zangara was short, only five feet tall. So he stood on a rickety chair to get a better view of the people he was about to shoot. "Too many people are starving!" he cried out as he fired. The shooter missed Franklin Roosevelt, his intended victim, but he hit several people including the mayor of Chicago, Anton Cermak, who had come down to Miami to talk to Roosevelt. Roosevelt's driver tried to whisk the president-elect away, but Roosevelt made him turn back to get Cermak. "Tony, keep quiet, don't move," FDR admonished the stricken mayor. Zangara was first given four 20-year sentences, one for each of the people he had shot. Zangara wasn't satisfied with that. "Oh, judge, don't be stingy," he cried out. "Give me a hundred years." Nineteen days after he was shot, Cermak died of peritonitis, and the judge upgraded Zangara's sentence: Cermak's assassination earned the man who had shot him a seat on Old Sparky, Florida's electric chair. Just before his execution, Zangara told the attending priest to "get the hell out of here, you son of a bitch. I go sit down all by myself."

The decade of the sixties came, and with those years, an outpouring of blood which spilled over the political landscape of the country.

First came the assassination of John F. Kennedy, the thirty-fifth president of the country. He came from a wealthy

Irish-American family with roots in New England. His wife, Jaqueline Bouvier, and he were a beautiful couple. Their public image was that of Prince and Princess Charming. JFK—as he was commonly known—was in the third year of his presidency when the couple flew to Texas in an attempt to heal the divisions of that state's Democratic Party. The trip was not without risk. Extremists were active in Texas. In October 1963, one month before the Kennedy junket, U.N. Ambassador Adlai Stevenson had been roughed up in Dallas, a city which was on the president's itinerary.

When Kennedy arrived at Love Field in Dallas on November 22, 1963, his wife received a bouquet of red roses. She wondered about this because at their previous stops in Texas, Jacqueline had received bouquets of yellow roses, inspired no doubt by the folksong, "The Yellow Rose of Texas."

A motorcade carrying JFK and the First Lady, as well as Governor Connally of Texas and his wife, began the ten-mile trip from the airport through the city's downtown to the Trade Mart where the President was to speak to a luncheon crowd. As it came into Dallas' Dealey Plaza, shots rang out, coming apparently from an adjacent building. This was the Texas School Book Depository where a former Marine and Communist, Lee Harvey Oswald, had been hired only the previous October. JFK was struck in the neck and head. Governor Connally was also injured, apparently by one of the bullets which had struck Kennedy. The presidential limousine roared off toward Parkland Memorial Hospital where, despite all that surgeons there could do, Kennedy died at 1 p.m.

A deputy sheriff, Roger Craig, arriving seconds after the shooting, discovered three spent cartridges beside a sixth-floor window in the Depository. Police came across a rifle, determined to be Oswald's, concealed in a stash of cardboard boxes. It was believed that Oswald had smuggled the weapon into the Depository in a brown-paper bag which he told a co-worker contained curtain rods. The police could find no fingerprints on the gun, later identified as an Italian copy of the German Mauser. They did, however, find Oswald's palm print on the stock of the rifle.

Despite his mousey appearance, Lee Harvey Oswald had a swashbuckling past. He traveled to the Soviet Union in the fall of 1959 and lived in Minsk for two and a half years. It was there that he met and married Marina Nikolayevna Prosakova. Oswald petitioned the US Embassy, indicating his wish to return to the US which he and Marina did in May 1962. He held a series of jobs in the Dallas area before being hired at the Texas School Book Depository in mid-October 1963, just over a month before the Kennedy assassination. Weeks before the Kennedy assassination, Oswald had taken the bus to Mexico City where he contacted officials at the Cuban and Soviet embassies. Ostensibly it was his goal to secure a visa to go to Cuba and then on to Russia. Clarence Kelley, J. Edgar Hoover's successor at the FBI, said after reading the Bureau's "raw files" on the assassination, that he was convinced Oswald had offered to kill Kennedy during his talks with the Russians and Cubans.

In March of 1963, the ex-marine, who had achieved sharp-shooter status while in the service, saw an advertisement in *American Rifleman*, a publication of the National Rifle Association (NRA). The rifle advertised "was only slightly used, test fired and head spaced." Oswald clipped a coupon from the ad and, using the alias A. Hidell, purchased the rifle for $21.45. Shortly before ordering that weapon through the mail, Oswald ordered a Smith & Wesson pistol from a company in Los Angeles.

What did he want with these weapons? Marina photographed her husband behind their house in Dallas dressed in what he called his "fascist hunting clothes"—a black short-sleeved shirt and black pants—and holding the rife and the revolver. Oswald told his wife that he had used the rifle in an attempt to assassinate retired General Edwin Walker, a rabid anti-Communist who had militated against admitting James Meredith to the University of Mississippi in the fall of 1962. In a broadcast at that time he had said:

> Now is the time to be heard! Thousands strong from every State in the Union! Rally to the cause of freedom! The Battle Cry of the Republic! [Governor] Barnett yes! Castro no! Bring your flag, your tent and your skillet. It's now or never! The

time is when the President of the United States commits or uses any troops, Federal or State, in Mississippi! The last time in such a situation I was on the wrong side. That was in Little Rock, Arkansas in 1957-1958. This time—out of uniform—I am on the right side! I will be there!

Oswald had fired at Walker, but his bullet struck a window frame, missing the retired general.

How Oswald escaped from the Book Depository on the day Kennedy was assassinated was a matter of conjecture. This was the case for many of the details, and even core issues, of the assassination. Just days after the killing in Dallas, Lyndon Baines Johnson, who succeeded Kennedy as the 36th President of the U.S, created a commission under the chairmanship of Earl Warren, Chief Justice of the Supreme Court. This became known as the Warren Commission. It was charged with investigating the assassination and what happened immediately afterwards. The Commission issued its report, which was several inches thick, the following year. Its analysis and conclusions were never universally accepted, but it is the account of Kennedy's assassination which we follow here, with an indication of the controversy which its findings generated. Conspiracy theorists had a field day with the killing of JFK. Case in point: How did Oswald get away from the scene of the crime? Did he have an accomplice?

According to the Warren Commission's report, Oswald hopped a bus to take him to his neighborhood. Traffic made the going slow, and Oswald left the bus to hail a taxi which took him closer to his rooming house. (An alternative story had Oswald picked up by car in Dealey Plaza. He stayed there only briefly at the residence, then left in a hurry.) In April 1963, Lee and Marina had split, with Marina staying in the Dallas suburb of Irving with a friend while Oswald continued to live in the city. He visited Marina on weekends, so the couple was not estranged.

In the early afternoon of November 22, a patrolman named J.D. Tippit, stopped a man matching the description of the suspected assassin, a description which he had received on police radio. The man Tippit apprehended shot him several times, killing him instantly. The assailant then fled, eventually coming to rest in a movie house which he entered without purchasing a ticket. The cashier notified the police who accosted the man in the theatre. The man was Lee Harvey Oswald. He was heard to utter the phrase, "Well, it's all over now." After a brief struggle, the police subdued Oswald and drove him to police headquarters.

Two days after he was apprehended, Oswald was shot by a night club owner named Jack Ruby while he was being transferred from city to county jail. Millions of Americans witnessed the shooting on live TV. There is an iconic photograph which shows Oswald, his mouth agape, as the bullet from Ruby's revolver pierces his abdomen while a deputy in a light-colored suit watches in wide-eyed disbelief. It was unclear why Ruby shot Oswald. He claimed later that he had wanted to spare Jacqueline Kennedy the pain and anguish of a return to Dallas for a trial. Did he kill Oswald to prevent him from implicating others in the president's assassination? Possibly Ruby thought, by killing Oswald, he would become a national hero. In any event, Ruby's bullet, fired from a 38 caliber Colt Cobra revolver, into Oswald's belly sent the presumed assassin of the President to Parkland Hospital, the same hospital where JFK had expired two days earlier, and where he, too, died on November 24, 1963.

Ruby was convicted of murder although the Texas Court of Criminal Appeals reversed that decision on the grounds that Ruby could not have gotten a fair trial in Dallas. A new trial was scheduled in 1967, but late in 1966, Ruby was admitted to Parkland Hospital (where else?) with pneumonia. There Jack Ruby was diagnosed with lung cancer. He died in January, 1967 from a blood clot in his lung.

***

The Roman Republic had its Gracchi brothers; the US had the Kennedys, John and Bobby. Bobby Kennedy was JFK's Attorney General. That appointment raised—not for the first time but most contentiously—the issue of nepotism in US politics. It led ultimately to the Anti-nepotism Law of 1967.

When John was assassinated, Bob Kennedy stayed on briefly as Lyndon Johnson's AG. But the two men did not get along, and Bobby resigned to run for a Senate seat from the state of New York. He won his race and served as Senator from 1965 until his death three years later. Supporters urged Kennedy to run for the Presidency, and he did so in 1968. At the time, he issued a statement explaining why he had taken this step:

> I do not run for the Presidency merely to oppose any man but to propose new policies. I run because I am convinced that this country is on a perilous course and because I have such strong feelings about what must be done, and I feel that I'm obliged to do all I can.

Lyndon B. Johnson opted not to seek reelection in 1968, leaving Robert Kennedy a strong contender for the Democratic nomination. His position was enhanced in June of that year when he won the California primary.

As Kennedy was leaving a victory celebration at the Ambassador Hotel in Los Angeles on June 5, 1968, he was shot and killed by a Palestinian Christian immigrant name Sirhan Bishara Sirhan. Sirhan had been angered by Kennedy's support for Israel and specifically of his support for the shipment of fifty bombers to that state, planes which he felt would be used against his fellow Palestinians. In the month prior to the killing, Sirhan had written in his diary that "my determination to eliminate RFK is becoming more and more of an unshakable obsession."

"RFK must die (he wrote). RFK must be killed. Robert F. Kennedy must be assassinated before 5 June 1968."

It is thought that the date which Sirhan cited was significant because that was when the Six Day War between Israel and its Arab neighbors had begun the previous year.

Sirhan was tried and convicted the following year and sentenced to death, but his sentence was commuted to life imprisonment in 1972 when the California Supreme Court invalidated all death sentences. Sirhan was incarcerated in a prison in San Diego County. As of the time this book went to press, he had been denied parole fifteen times.

Conspiracy theories grew around the JFK assassination like

mushrooms on a damp log. One would not expect this to be the case in the relatively cut-and-dried murder of his brother Bobby. But one would be wrong. In a book published at the end of 2018, author Lisa Pease postulates that Sirhan was a CIA patsy, hypnotized to enact the assassination of Kennedy. The actual killers were CIA operatives standing behind Kennedy in the pantry of the Ambassador Hotel. Sirhan's gun, so the theory goes, contained blanks. It further presumes that the mastermind behind this plot.

CHAPTER FOUR:
The Towers

THE 1960S WITNESSED THE SENSATIONAL assassinations of the Kennedy brothers and Martin Luther King. In fact, the decade saw an eruption of gun violence, something which the country had seen relatively little of before. August 1, 1966 was the date of the first gun massacre in modern American history, one which took place at the University of Texas in Austin. It occurred at the University's iconic 27-story tower. The shooting was one of the most widely known and sensational, at least up to that point. The criminologist James Alan Fox said of the incident that it "defined our modern concept of mass murder."

The August 1966 massacre was not unprecedented: In 1927, a Michigan man burdened by debt killed his wife, set his farm on fire, and killed something like forty-five people by setting off a bomb in a school building. The murderer was himself killed in the blast.

The perpetrator of the 1966 massacre was an ex-Marine named Charles Whitman. A photograph of him, taken in 1963, shows a burly man with a blonde crew cut. Whitman had been a bright student, an Eagle Scout at age 12. He enlisted in the Marine Corps to escape his abusive father who had once thrown his son into the family swimming pool for coming home drunk. In the Corps, Whitman excelled at marksmanship, especially when it came to shooting rapidly at moving targets. Approved for a Marine scholarship, Whitman enrolled at the University of Texas (UT) at Austin in the fall of 1961. There he joined the university's mechanical engineering program. He survived three semesters before the Marine Corps decided that his grades were too low and rescinded his scholarship.

Charles Whitman occasionally exhibited quirky behavior at UT. With two friends, he had once poached a deer which the three men tried to butcher in the shower of Whitman's dorm. After police arrested them, Whitman was fined $100. On one occasion, while browsing in a university bookstore, he remarked to a friend that someone could stand off an army from atop the University of Texas Tower "before they got him."

The tower Whitman referred to was erected in the 1930's when the old Main Building was razed and a replacement, along with the Tower went up in its place. At 307 feet, the Tower was the tallest and most prominent structure on campus. Originally it was designed as a library repository, but the Tower came to house administrative offices although a three-floor life sciences library remained in place. The building boasted twenty-seven floors, an observation deck on the 28th floor, and a carillon of 56 bells which played once a day.

Whitman's career in the Marines had its ups and downs: At Camp Lejeune, he once freed a Marine by single-handedly lifting his jeep which had gone over an embankment. (That act of comic-book bravado landed him in the hospital for four days.) On the other hand, he was court-martialed for a series of misdemeanors including possession of a firearm on base, and a threat to a fellow Marine over a loan of $30 for which he had demanded 50 percent interest.

After an honorable discharge from the Marines, Whitman returned to UT, this time to study architectural engineering. He complained of debilitating headaches and went so far as to consult a university psychiatrist. The therapist spent two hours with Whitman and wanted him to return for more analysis, but the ex-Marine failed to go back. In a suicide note he wrote on July 31, Whitman referred to this visit:

> I talked with a Doctor once and tried to convey to him my fears that I felt some [sic] overwhelming violent impulses. After one visit, I never saw the Doctor again, and since then have been fighting my mental turmoil alone, and seemingly to no avail.

In the spring of 1966, Whitman's mother left his father and moved to Austin. There she got her own apartment but remained in close contact with Charles. On the evening of July 31, 1966, Whitman and his wife Kathy visited friends just before Kathy reported for work as a telephone operator. Back home, Whitman wrote the suicide note cited above. He meant it to be read the following day. It said, in part:

> I do not quite understand what it is that compels me to type this letter. Perhaps it is to leave some vague reason for the actions I have recently performed. I do not really understand myself these days. I am supposed to be an average reasonable and intelligent young man. However lately (I cannot recall when it started) I have been a victim of many unusual and irrational thoughts. These thoughts constantly recur, and it requires a tremendous mental effort to concentrate on useful and progressive tasks.

Charles Whitman drove to his mother's apartment where he bashed her in the head before stabbing her in the heart. He then carried her body to her bed. There he covered it with a sheet. He left a handwritten note beside her body which read, in part:

> To Whom It May Concern: I have taken my mother's life. I am very upset over having done this. However, I feel that if there is a heaven she is definitely there now. I am truly sorry. Let there be no doubt in your mind that I loved this woman with all my heart.

Whitman then returned to his own home where he stabbed his wife three times in the heart, while she lay in bed asleep. As he had done with his mother, he covered Kathy's body with a sheet. He placed his suicide note beside her body after adding, in pen, the following note:

> I imagine it appears that I brutally killed both of my loved ones. I was only trying to do a quick thorough job. If my life insurance policy is valid please pay off my debts, donate the rest anonymously to a mental health foundation. Maybe research can prevent further tragedies of this type. Give my dog to my in-laws. Tell them Kathy loved `Schocie' very much. If you can find in yourselves to grant my last wish, cremate me

after the autopsy."

On the exterior of an envelope, he scribbled: "I never could quite make it. These thoughts are too much for me."

The evening of his double murder, Whitman wrote a letter to himself in which he confessed:

> It was after much thought I decided to kill my wife, Kathy, tonight after I pick her up from work at the telephone company. I love her dearly. She has been as fine a wife to me as any man could ever hope to have. I cannot rationally [sic] pinpoint any specific reason for doing this. I don't know whether it is selfishness, or if I don't want her to have to face the embarrassment [sic] of my actions would surely cause her. At this time, though, the prominent reason in my mind is that I truly do not consider this world worth living in and am prepared to die, and I do not want to leave her to suffer alone in it. I intend to kill her as painlessly as possible.
>
> Similar reasons provoked me to take my mother's life also....

After killing his wife, Whitman went shopping. At two different stores, he bought 700 rounds of ammunition. He loaded his purchases into a footlocker, which he lugged onto campus on a dolly.

The following day Whitman arrived at the UT Tower just before noon. Dressed in overalls, he identified himself as a research assistant, there to deliver some equipment. The "equipment" he was carrying in a trunk included three rifles, two pistols, and a sawed-off shotgun. The elevator wasn't working, but an employee activated it. Whitman was duly appreciative. "You don't know how happy that makes me," he told the repairman. En route to the observation deck, he bludgeoned to death one receptionist and fatally shot two other people. Once in place on the observation deck, Whitman began picking off pedestrians and passers-by below.

Professors began telephoning the police. "Hello, this is Michael Hall at the history department on the university campus," went a typical call.

"Yes, sir," replied a police operator.

"There's just been a gunshot on the main plaza outside the

main building, and at least one person wounded."

"We'll have an officer come by right away," replied the operator.

Whitman's first victim was a pregnant coed named Claire Wilson, who lay for more than one hour on the pavement in 100-degree heat that Monday morning, beside the body of her boyfriend, Whitman's second victim. The hot concrete under her burned the backs of her thighs.

Neal Speke reported on the shooting live for Austin's KTBC radio and TV station, and he witnessed a remarkable act of heroism: A woman dashed to Claire Wilson's aid while Whitman was still shooting from the Tower. Speke described what happened this way:

> She lay down between Claire and her dead boyfriend, while the shooting is going on and comforts her until they came to rescue her. A red-haired, hippie type girl, and she took her hand and said 'Don't close your eyes, Claire.' Then she came to the hospital a day or two later and brought her a gift of a painting she made to comfort her. And they never saw each other again.

"The bullet went into my side," Claire Wilson said later. "Then it fragmented….so they had to take out five feet of intestine. My ovary, my uterus was just ripped apart, and the baby was hit in the head, and they had to take out the iliac crest. … So if I'm tired I walk with a limp."

She thought that the shooter was targeting her baby in her belly, but Whitman was aiming, it seemed, for his victims' hearts.

Whitman's next target was a newspaper delivery boy, making his rounds on his bicycle. In all, Whitman killed fourteen people that day and wounded thirty-one others. A 15th victim died years later of injuries sustained during the attack.

Another of Whitman's victims was Robert Heard, an Associated Press newsman. Struck in his left shoulder, Heard remarked that Whitman "must be an incredible shot." A UT student was having lunch with two of his buddies at a drug store on Guadalupe Street when they became aware of bullets whizzing past their heads. "A quarter-inch to the right and he could have picked off any one of us." Much later that same student reminisced about his close encounter with death which gifted him with a second chance at life. "Lots of times in my life things don't go my way," he philosophized, "and I say 'Quit complaining, you survived the day.'"

The police, at first outgunned, enlisted the assistance of civilians with rifles. They provided ammunition for the impromptu vigilantes who were told to shoot to kill.

Volunteers telephoned in with offers of assistance. "Y'all need a scope?" asked one caller. "I got a .280 with a scope. I can let y'all have it."

"I'm just gonna say it once," said another caller. "I've got a European model 9mm that will tear him all to hell."

One gun rights advocate said that "the upshot of the Whitman story is that these armed students and citizens kept human carnage to a minimum."

Some professors, however, were leery of armed students on campus. One English prof encountered a student with a rifle in a corridor. He was there, he said, to check his grade.

Two Austin cops eventually made their way up to the terrace where Whitman was holed up. One of them, Houston McCoy, wrote about that day twenty years later:

> I found a student who had a high-powered scoped rifle in his apartment a few blocks away. I drove him to get it, drove to a nearby hardware store and procured some ammunition for the rifle and drove to a building just south of the tower and mall.

Thinking that there was more than one sniper, McCoy told the student he was going to the tower. "He asked what if he should get a bead on one of the snipers," McCoy wrote, "and I told him to shoot the shit out of him."

Keith Maitland, a film maker who directed a movie about the attack, commented that "we live in a world today where you hear a loud sound, like a gunshot, in a public space, and it doesn't take long to kind of assume that there's something happening, that you don't want to be part of…to run and hide. But in 1966, people were surprised, they were confused, and so it made the sniper's job a lot easier to catch people unaware."

Houston McCoy made his way up to the Tower via a maintenance tunnel. Beside McCoy, an Austin cop named Ramiro Martinez eventually inched his way up to and onto the observation deck of the UT Tower. Martinez forced open a door which Whitman had blocked with a dolly, presumably the one which he had rented to carry his recently purchased ammo. Martinez said later that, "Time is passing but you don't feel as if time is passing." Civilians helped by pinning down the assailant with rifle fire. On his way up to the Observation Deck, Martinez had passed a rifle to a university employee, Allen Crum, who followed him up the Tower. Ramiro Martinez was credited with killing Whitman although both he and McCoy fired their weapons at the sniper. Years after the event, McCoy said that Martinez had "jerked the shotgun from my hands and while yelling, ran to [Whitman's] motionless body and fired point blank. "Martinez then forcefully threw my shotgun onto the floor." (McCoy later said), "began jumping up and down and waving his arms, and repeatedly hollered, 'I got him!'"

When he left the Tower, Martinez was still yelling, "I got him!" He confessed later that his knees had "felt like rubber." Forty years after the massacre, the city of Austin designated August 1 as Ramiro Martinez Day. With what sounded like a trickle of a guilty conscience for upstaging McCoy, Ramirez said: "The reason I got the publicity a lot of the time was I was willing to speak to the media; I felt like this was therapy for me, not to keep it bottled up."

Hundreds of people had congregated below the Tower. The assault and the way it ended was not something—in the words of one of them—"you'd expect from our beautiful town." Whitman's rampage had lasted just over one and a half hours. The university recovered quickly, perhaps a little too quickly, from Whitman's massacre. Classes were canceled—in the words of one TV critic—"only long enough to mop up the blood." There were "no vigils, no grief counseling, no closure." There was no mention of the shooting at graduation that year, nor was there any mention of the massacre in the school yearbook. Austin was reluctant to be viewed the way Dallas was after the assassination of JFK three years before.

The filmmaker, Keith Maitland mentioned above, made an unusual and much talked about movie called Tower. It employs rotoscope animation in which live actors are filmed, then replaced by animated cartoon-like images to achieve an effect which TV critic Hank Stuever characterized as "a terrifying sense of urgency and precision." The film garnered top prize at the South by Southwest Film Festival held in Austin in 1966, and it made the shortlist of documentaries considered for a prize at the Oscars. But it didn't get an Oscar nomination. Why? Some critics have faulted Tower for its deliberate omission of any mention of the perpetrator, Charles Whitman, whose name is uttered only once toward the end of the film when commentator Walter Cronkite identifies him as the shooter. In omitting any mention of Whitman, Maitland sought to honor the survivors of the shooting and the policemen who killed the killer. Stuever made the comment that "we don't get anywhere by looking away from things that frighten or disgust us."

So, why did Whitman go off the deep end? Sigmund Freud had a theory—never proved—that people have an unconscious drive which leads to aggressive behavior. The force behind this drive—which Freud identified as Thanatos—builds up until it cannot be controlled. In her article, "The Desire for Revenge," the psychoanalyst Lucy Lafarge wrote that this desire is a "ubiquitous response to narcissistic injury."

Gary Lavergne has written what *the New York Times* has declared to be "the authoritative account of the Whitman case." In 2000, he started working on the ground floor of the Tower in the UT admissions research department. As his name suggests, his family roots lie in Louisiana where his father was a policeman. So Lavergne knew how to sweet-talk the cops, and he got access to everything that Whitman had written before he killed his mother, his wife, and 14 others on the UT campus.

Securing access to Whitman's documents took some doing: Lavergne's book about the massacre was published in 1997, a full thirty years after the event. Having perused what Whitman had written, Lavergne said: "I immediately recognized that it was more an expression of what he wanted me, as a reader, to believe, than what was really going through his mind—he was quite a manipulator."

We could do worse, in elucidating what happened in Austin that hot, sticky day in August 1966, than to seek explanation and examples in literature. From the American lexicon, we glean this from Herman Melville's Moby Dick, a reflection on Captain Ahab's obsession with the leviathan which had robbed him of a leg: "He piled upon the whale's hump the sum of all the general rage and hate…and then, as if his chest had been a mortar, he burst his hot heart's shell upon it."

Or, for our English readers, this from Shakespeare's Richard III: "And therefore, since I cannot prove a lover/To entertain these fair well-spoken days/I am determined to prove a villain/And hate the idle pleasures of these days."

In January 2016, the state of Texas began to allow citizens with a handgun permit to carry their firearms openly. On August 1, 2016, fifty years to the day after Whitman committed mass murder at the University of Texas, the Texas state legislature extended the right to carry handguns openly to public university campuses.

Texas author Lawrence Wright commented at the time that:

> An eccentric feature of Texas' new gun laws is that people entering the state capitol can skip the long lines of tourists waiting to pass through metal detectors if they show guards a license-to-carry permit. In other words, the people most likely to bring weapons into the building aren't scanned at all. Many of the people who breeze through are lawmakers and staffers who tote concealed weapons into offices or onto the floor of the legislature. But some lobbyists and reporters have also obtained gun licenses, just to skirt the lines. I recently got one myself.

Wright went on to write:

> Especially among Texas politicians, there's a locker-room lust for weaponry that belies noble-sounding proclamations about self-protection and Second Amendment rights. In 2010, Governor [Rick] Perry boasted of killing with a single shot a coyote that was menacing his daughter's Labrador. Perry was jogging at the time, but naturally he was packing heat: a .380

Ruger. The gun's manufacturer promptly issued a Coyote Special edition of the gun, which comes in a box labelled 'for sale to Texans only.'

Copycat Murders

A FEW MONTHS AFTER THE SHOOTING at UT, an 18-year-old man from Arizona, Robert Smith, shot to death five people. Smith said that he had been inspired by Charles Whitman. A criminologist and author of the book, *Mass Murder in the United States,* Grant Duwe called it "one of the clearest examples of the copycat or contagious effect."

> The most notorious copycat replay of the UT massacre was committed by Stephen Paddock who killed 58 people in Las Vegas more than one half century later on October 1, 2017. With a variety of firearms, he sprayed bullets down on a crowd of people attending a concert below the Mandalay Bay Resort and Casino where he had a suite on the 32nd floor. A former FBI profiler told a reporter from the *Washington Post* that she "was surprised it took this long to have one so similar." Gary Lavergne had a similar comment to make: "I always wondered how long it would take to see something in a very large gathering of people, not necessarily from a high vantage point, but a concert or football game."

Both Whitman and Paddock had perched on high to take out their victims. Lavergne again:

> Both were interested in the advantages that height gives you, and killing as many people they could, though Paddock's weapons were far more sophisticated and advanced. But the major difference between the two was that Whitman, because of the scope he was using, was able to look at and see the people he was shooting at and dropping down. I think Whitman was determined to show off his marksmanship so when all was said and done, people would talk about how good he was.

David Shepherd, a retired FBI agent concurred on the choice of an eyrie to mow down the shooters' victims: "When you start shooting from an elevated position like that, you're trying to do as much damage as you can, wherever you can."

One difference between the two massacres was the time they lasted: Paddock shot for something like ten minutes. Whitman's rampage went on for ninety minutes. Gary Lavergne points out an important difference between the response times between the two incidents. "Back in 1966, there were no tactical teams, and police officers weren't trained for anything remotely like this."

Why did Stephen Paddock do what he did? Remember that neither Whitman nor Paddock "knew who their victims were and didn't really care" (Lavergne). Paddock's motive—not unlike Whitman's—remains something of a mystery. Paddock's brother speculated that "he had done everything in the world he wanted to do and was bored with everything." That theory seems supported when a reporter for the *Wall Street Journal* viewed video footage of Paddock emotionlessly gambling, eating his meals, and hauling more than twenty pieces of luggage filled with semiautomatic rifles up to his suite on the 32nd floor of his hotel.

Paddock told friends that he always felt tired. Wracked by pain. Ill. He subscribed to conspiracy theories: The FEMA camps set up after Hurricane Katrina in 2005 were, in his opinion, "a dry run for law enforcement and military to start kickin' down doors and confiscating guns."

Instead, was the thirst for infamy what drove Paddock? "Some people kill for notoriety and infamy," said the president of the threat-assessment firm Operational Psychology Services. "And that's what he did."

Paddock's father had been a bank robber and a con man. Stephen was seven years old when the elder Paddock went to jail. He made the FBI's Ten Most Wanted Fugitives list in 1969 when he escaped. In the opinion of one official acquainted with the case, Stephen Paddock "was pissed over getting his butt kicked gambling or he wanted to follow in his father's shoes."

In a way, Paddock really was following in the footsteps of his father's criminal past. His mother somehow managed to support him and his three brothers on a secretary's salary. One of his brothers, Eric, said just after the shooting in Las

Vegas, "I wish I could tell you he was a miserable bastard...but I can't say that; it's not who he was; we need to find out what happened to him."

He gambled heavily and began losing. His bank accounts shrank from $2.1 million to $530,000 in the two years that preceded his rampage. Some people who got to know him described him as arrogant. "He acted like everybody worked for him and that he was above others," said one casino host who saw Paddock frequently from 2012 to 2014. A neighbor in Reno commented that he "always walked across the street and would never pass in front of our house."

An exhaustive investigation by the FBI could determine no motive for Paddock's killing spree. We are left with no more than the speculation of people listed above. Could it be that killing large numbers of people is little more than a sport, like the mass slaughter of bison in nineteenth-century America? Is that how murderers like Stephen Paddock view killing fifty-eight concert goers and wounding nine hundred more? Paddock's killing and maiming nearly one thousand souls was, for him apparently, a blistering-hot thrill, something a Clint Eastwood movie might have conjured up, popping off people like fish in a barrel—rat-ta-ta-ta—just to see how good a score he could achieve.

Paddock's mother, her son's heir by default, transferred her right to his estate in 2018. An administrator appointed by a state court judge estimated that what the gunman left behind—a cache of fifty guns, scopes, a red dot sight, and rifle cases—were worth approximately $62,000. Should this stuff be sold for the benefit of the man's victims and their families or destroyed? "The money that would come from selling the guns...would help to make a difference in people's lives," said the lawyer for the special administration for the estate case. On the other hand, "destroying the guns would send more of a symbolic message to the world that weapons like these should not be sold at any price if death or harm to innocent people cannot be prevented."

The sister of one of Paddock's victims said that she saw no point in destroying his weapons. "Destroying them is not going to change anything and it won't bring back any goodness," she said. "But if some good can come out of selling them, I am for it."

But the son of another of Paddock's victims felt that "the idea of receiving money from equipment that was used by someone who took so many lives is creepy."

The sale of one of Paddock's residences netted the estate $425,000. The buyers, a retired couple from Oregon, were not bothered by Paddock's previous ownership of their new house. "There is room to build a pool," said the wife. "It is a nice clean house that has hardly been lived in, and there are nice neighbors who have been through a lot."

✳✳✳

THE AFOREMENTIONED AUTOPSY WHICH WHITMAN had requested in his suicide note revealed that he had what the neuropathologist who performed the autopsy described as a "pecan-sized" brain tumor, called a glioblastoma, which pressed against the regions of the brain which regulated strong emotions. Had this been the cause of Whitman's headaches? Did it account for his behavior? A commission set up by Governor John Connally of Texas was unable to determine what relationship there was between this tumor and Whitman's actions. The consensus seems to be that the tumor was not the reason Whitman, like a cold-blooded professional killer, snuffed out the lives of his victims.

Lyndon B. Johnson was President at the time of the Tower massacre. He offered his thoughts and prayers to the relatives of the victims. This would not be the last time such a sentiment was uttered. But Johnson went further to urge action in response to the tragedy. "What happened is not without a lesson: that we must press urgently for the legislation now pending in Congress to help prevent the wrong person from obtaining firearms."

Johnson continued: "The bill would not prevent all such tragedies, but it would reduce the unrestricted sale of firearms to those who cannot be trusted in their use and possession... the gun control bill has been under consideration in the Congress for many months. The time has come for action."

There was cautious optimism that some sort of gun control legislation would pass Congress. A drive for "restrictive measures" after President Kennedy's assassination had stalled in the teeth of opposition by the NRA. After the 1968 killings of Martin Luther King and Robert Kennedy, Congress did finally pass a bill which regulated the interstate mail-order sale of rifles, shotguns, and ammunition. Reluctantly LBJ signed the bill which he felt did not go far enough. "The voices that blocked these safeguards were not the voices of an aroused nation," he said. "They were the voices of a powerful gun lobby that has prevailed for the moment in an election year."

Charles Whitman's kill numbers were not topped for sixteen years. During that time, he became what Google later called America's favorite mass murderer.

CHAPTER FIVE:
A Litany of Massacres

A list? Is that the best we can do? That, with a brief commentary for each item. This may be the only way—lame though it be—to chronicle the carnage which the country has witnessed in the past fifty years. We limit ourselves in this chapter to school shootings which have become dismally commonplace. Massacres on campus have become so frequent that the public is numbed by these eruptions of violence against children and young adults. People can absorb only so much before they become callous, accepting as normal what has become a recurring horror.

The Tower Massacre at the University of Texas may have been the first of these. Then there came a hiatus before it began again, what became a kind of epidemic of violence in a school setting. It started in a suburb of Denver called Littleton. The shooting which occurred there on 20 April 1999 took place in a high school named Columbine. The name became synonymous with gun massacres at a juvenile institution.

Like many, most even, high schools in the country, Columbine was one where athletes ruled the social roost. At this school, star jocks could get away with things which other students would be busted for. That riled some students. It stoked a feeling of outrage, murderous outrage in the case of the two boys who perpetrated the massacre at Columbine. Their names were Eric Harris, 18, and Dylan Klebold, 17.

It became clear afterward that Harris was the mastermind behind the attack. He got the lion's share of attention after April 20, 1999. What Harris and Klebold dreamed of was slaughter on the scale of Attila the Hun. They had dumped two duffel bags loaded with propane bombs in the school cafeteria. Fortunately they screwed up the wiring of the bombs which failed to explode. Once they realized that their bombs were not going off, the two conspirators, wearing trench coats—coats which would become infamous in the aftermath of the attack—walked back into the school and began shooting. By the time they finished, twelve students and a teacher lay dead, another twenty wounded. This had been the second phase of their planned attack. A third phase involved more bombs, packed into their cars, designed to kill off those who escaped the school, first responders, and reporters. Shortly after noon, the shooters turned their guns on themselves and committed suicide.

What prompted the two boys to turn mass murderers? Although it appears in hindsight that Harris and Klebold were more often the bullies than the bullied, they were picked on, particularly by athletes: Weeks before the shooting, members of the football team sprayed the two with mustard and ketchup and called them "faggots." There were other incidents, too, in which football players harassed Harris and Klebold. Once, a footballer in a speeding car tossed a glass bottle at the two boys and another friend, Brooke Brown. It shattered at their feet.

"Don't worry, man," Klebold told Brown. "It happens all the time." Later Brown said that the shooting "had to do with the injustice in our society and in the school."

Before the boys opened fire on April 20, 1999, they yelled, "All the jocks stand up." Six of their victims were athletes. None had been among the two boys' principal tormentors.

Ten years after the event, sociologist Ralph Larkin wrote:

> Harris and Klebold committed their rampage shooting as an overtly political act in the name of oppressed students victimized by their peers. Numerous post-Columbine rampage shooters referred directly to Columbine as their inspiration; others attempted to supersede the Columbine shootings in body count. ... The Columbine shootings redefined such acts not merely as revenge but as a means of protest of bullying, intimidation, social isolation, and public rituals of humiliation.

Eric Harris was a psychopath in the opinion of psychiatrists who studied the case. Robert Hare, psychiatrist and author of Without Conscience, said that "Unlike psychotic individuals, psychopaths are rational and aware of what they are doing and why. Their behavior is the result of choice, freely exercised.

Journalist and author, Dave Cullen, who has written what is considered to be the definitive book about Columbine, says that, even overshadowing the boy's obvious hatred was Harris' contempt for just about everything.

"I hate the fucking world," was the sentence which began his private journal. It took authorities seven years to release this book which Cullen secured a copy of.

"You know what I hate!!?" Harris wrote. "Country music."

"Country' was spelt without an `o' but with a string of `u's and `y's."

It was a sentiment which he repeated in videos he and Klebold made together. He also repeated these in his journal.

After country music, Harris listed all sorts of things he hated: people who thought wrestling was real; people who used the same word over and over again; people who mispronounced the words they used; and above all, people who were stupid.

Despite his venomous tirades, Cullen observed that the most common word in Harris' journal was "love." Described as sweet-faced and well-spoken, Harris led a life of unrelenting mendacity. "I lie a lot," he confessed in his journal. He lied "almost constantly, and to everybody, just to keep my own ass out of the water."

Once caught breaking into a van, he apologized to his victim with the words, "Jeez, I understand how you feel." This apology was purely for effect. His entry about the incident in his journal reads quite differently:

> How come...I can't deprive a stupid fucking dumb shit [of] his possessions if he leaves them sitting in the front seat of his fucking van in plain sight and in the middle of fucking nowhere.

Harris derived pleasure out of lying. He seemed to revel in his own hypocrisy. Why then, was he so brutally honest in his journal? Did this compensate for his mendacity? Did it help him keep track of his true feelings?

Cullen believes that the fact that Eric Harris was a psychopath "begins to explain his unbelievably callous behavior: his ability to shoot his classmates, then stop to taunt them while they writhe in pain, then finish them off."

According to one story, the shooters targeted minorities and Christians. One of the boys asked a girl if she believed in God; when she answered "yes," the assailant—either Harris or Klebold—shot and killed her. Or so the fable went. That story, it turned out, was false. But the killing at Columbine was still as horrific as it was sensational.

Once again Robert Hare: "[Some psychopaths] can torture and mutilate their victims with about the same sense of concern that we feel when we carve a turkey for Thanksgiving dinner."

To describe Harris as a psychopath is much more precise than to call him a crazy, even if the term means less to laymen than to psychiatrists and psychologists. It places the American teenager in a pigeonhole which he shares with the poison-spewing villain, Iago, in Shakespeare's tragedy Othello. Is that good enough to get a grip on his character? According to Dave Cullen, Harris "was a brilliant killer without a conscience, searching for the most diabolical scheme imaginable."

The twentieth anniversary of the shooting at Columbine rekindled interest in the massacre. The *Washington Post* ran a review of the revival of a play, Columbinus, written fifteen years before. The play relies on documentary evidence as well as interviews of survivors of the 1999 mass shooting.

Frank DeAngelis, who was principal at Columbine in 1999, came to dread the month of April, the month when Klebold and Harris mowed down a dozen of their fellow students and one teacher—a close friend of DeAngelis. The principal credits his friend with saving his life at the cost of his own. The aftermath of the shooting took its toll on DeAngelis who suffered six car accidents in the years following the attack, all of them in the same fateful spring month. What persuaded DeAngelis that he needed to consult a psychiatrist was the three times—again, always in April—he rammed his own garage door, failing first to open it. Verily April is the cruelest month. DeAngelis has written a book which reads—and here I quote from *The Guardian*—"like a self-help manual for how to cope in the wake of a gun rampage." With his counselor's help, he was able to channel the events of April 20, 1999, in a positive direction, "Instead of mourning their deaths, I began celebrating them," he said. "Now I wasn't seeing the kids dying, I was envisioning them living their lives."

Oddly DeAngelis spends little time in his book covering gun control. It seems, at times, as Dave Cullen has said, that "the US has settled into a state of defeatism" when it comes to school shootings: These can be mitigated but not stopped. "I do worry we are becoming too accepting of these events," said DeAngelis. "We are desensitized and that scares me."

> So why not speak out about the country's lax gun laws? Here I quote DeAngelis' reply, which was "I worry when people state that if we have tougher gun laws, we're never going to have another school shooting... But we need to look at all the pieces of the puzzle." He went on: "If you and I wanted to buy a gun right now and bypass the gun laws, there's somewhere we could do it. It's just America. It's unfortunate but that happens."

After the Columbine massacre, survivors started a group called the Rebels Project, a sort of support network which shares with survivors of other school massacres ways to cope with tragedy. These include therapy, exercise, and hobbies. Robin Gurwitch, a trauma specialist at Duke University Medical Center, says that there is no time limit on when memories of a shooting can come rushing back. Anything can trigger them—anniversaries, a song, or fire alarms. "We don't get over it," says the psychologist. "We don't get over it. We hope we learn to get through it and cope."

✱✱✱

LIKE FILINGS TO A MAGNET DRAWN, hundreds, maybe thousands of depressed and alienated youth in the country, homed in on the Columbine massacre. Even kids not born at the time of the killing. One killer at Santa Fe High School in Texas—an institution to be included in this chapter's list—wore a black trench coat, just like Harris and Klebold, and a T-shirt with the slogan "Born to Kill," an attempted simulacrum of the Columbine shooters and their "Wrath" and "Natural Selection" T-shirts. His weaponry included a sawed-off shotgun. He toted a canister of carbon dioxide gas and Molotov cocktails. Again, like the Columbine kids, the 17-year-old junior had posted a picture on Facebook showing a red-star medallion and a hammer-and-sickle pin on the collar of his trench coat. Another echo of Columbine. A proposal to tear down Columbine was floated to deter copycat killers who sought out the high school as a kind of mass murder mecca. DeAngelis supported the idea.

"If I would have known 20 years ago that we were still going to have tour buses showing up, we were still going to have people infatuated with the two killers," he said, " I would've said maybe we need to look at relocating."

In 2006, an 18-year-old student from North Carolina wrote Frank DeAngelis, who was still principal at Columbine. The principal immediately alerted police but not in time to prevent the young man from shooting to death his own father and wounding two fellow students. The shooter wore a black trench coat, wielded a sawed-off shotgun which he named "Arlene," just as Eric Harris had done. The psychologist, Peter Langman, author of *Why Kids Kill: Inside the Minds of School Shooters*, has said that: "The phenomenon is feeding on itself. It's gaining momentum, and the more there are, the more there will be."

He has done a diagram, a sort of flow chart, linking as many as thirty shooting rampages back to the Columbine killings. Media have played a role in inspiring these attacks. Gunmen admit that they look upon the killings as a competition. Can they kill more than the tallies of previous attacks?

"It seems the more people you kill, the more you're in the limelight." Those were the words of one Oregon killer who racked up nine murders.

Some news services have considered not publishing the names and details of assailants in order to tamp down the competitive urge of school shooters. This suggestion has actually been adopted after some of the later shootings.

***

IT IS THE LEAST SPECTACULAR ACTS of violence which sometimes grab the attention of the nation's press. A 2021 shooting in Arlington, Texas resulted in no fatalities, only four people injured. It was not "somebody attacking our schools," in the words of a police official. Was this meant to be a reassuring comment? Just another aspect of ordinary school life? Authorities said that an 18-year-old student got a gun from his backpack, opened fire, shooting two people, one a 15-year-old boy in critical condition who was left with what are likely to be life-long scars. "Sadly back to school has meant back to school shootings for too many communities across the country," said Shannon Watts, founder of Moms Demand Action, an organization affiliated with Everytown for Gun Safety. The Arlington shooting was not premeditated, like the shootings at Parkland or Sandy Hook, but the result of disputes. Everytown for Gun Safety has assembled a list of recommendations for the Biden administration which include securing firearms so that children can't lay their hands on them.

According to statistics compiled by Everytown for Gun Safety, there were a minimum of 322 unintentional shootings by children in American homes in 2021. They resulted in 132 deaths and 206 injuries. Commenting in *The New York Times*, Gail Collins writes that in the hundreds of school shootings since the Sandy Hook massacre, that "the only real, serious response seems to have been the education of our children in what to do when a classmate starts spraying bullets." She goes on to offer this sarcastic observation: "The US is a world leader in teaching youngsters how to duck and cover behind their desks."

***

WHAT ABOUT THAT LIST? HERE is another item on it:
Virginia Tech. April 16, 2007, almost eight years after Col-

umbine. The shooter thought of Eric Harris and Dylan Klebold as his brothers. Of actual, living friends he had few. Seung Hui Cho had been born in South Korea. He came to the States with his family in 1992. He was a student at Virginia Tech in Blacksburg, Virginia, and on the Ides of April, with two semi-automatic weapons—a 9-mm handgun and a 22-caliber handgun—he took the lives of 27 students and five faculty before turning his weaponry on himself. In two shooting sprees, the second of which lasted a scant ten minutes, Cho ended the lives of 32 people.

Why? That's the question we always ask, isn't it? Cho resented his classmates. He called them "sadistic snobs." Furthermore he went on:

> You have never felt a single ounce of pain your whole life. Did you want to inject as much misery in our lives as you can just because you can? You had everything you wanted. Your Mercedes wasn't enough, you brats. Your golden necklaces weren't enough, you snobs. Your trust fund wasn't enough. All your debaucheries weren't enough. Those weren't enough to fulfil your hedonistic needs. You had everything.

In his last words—videotaped—Cho said: "This is it. This is where it all ends. End of the road. What a life it was. Some life."

Between his two shooting sprees, Cho mailed a package of materials, including a video, to MSNBC. Among these materials was something which came to be known as Cho's Manifesto. It was a profanity-laced compilation, rambling and largely incoherent. It called people—the people to whom the manifesto was addressed—hedonists, Christian Nazis, descendants of Satan. Here is a representative passage: "You had a hundred billion chances and ways to have avoided today, but you decided to spill my blood."

Cho's parents, who lived in Charlottesville, Virginia, spoke little English and avoided the press. Representing the family fell to Cho's older sister, a 2004 graduate from Princeton who was working, at the time of the Virginia Tech massacre, as a contractor for the State Department. "We feel hopeless," she wrote in a publicly-released statement. "We are living in a nightmare. We apologize for the devastation my brother has caused."

It became common after the 2007 slaughter at Virginia Tech for victims who survived other incidents, and for the families of some of the victims, to become activists in the battle to exercise some control on guns. One man named Colin Goddard, who survived being shot four times by Cho, later volunteered for The Brady Campaign to Prevent Gun Violence. When he was interviewed ten years after the shooting by a reporter for *USA Today*, he still had three bullets lodged in his two hips and above his left knee.

Colin was late — as usual — for his 9:05 intermediate French class. That was the Monday morning of the shooting. He knew already that there had been a shooting at a dorm, but a fellow student, Rachel Hill, who arrived later than Goddard, had concluded that things must have calmed down because she had been allowed to go to class. They hadn't. Goddard remembered hearing "weird banging noises" coming, it seemed, from outside the building.

Goddard's French teacher peeked outside the classroom door, then ordered her students to take cover under their desks. Colin spotted someone in khaki pants and a white shirt come through the door into the classroom. The shooter began firing and Goddard felt as if he had been kicked in his leg above his knee. He had been hit.

> I remember smelling the propellant that filled our classroom, which smelled like fireworks (he later wrote about his personal ordeal that day). Then a warm, wet feeling started flowing down my leg — followed by a sharp, burning pain. That's when I realized I had been shot. Everything after that is a blur of bangs, screams and shell casings. All of my senses were overwhelmed, my body was working to keep itself alive, and all I can remember thinking is 'I can't believe this is happening.'

The gunman left but returned to shoot some more. This time he hit Goddard, twice in the hips, once in his shoulder. Both Rachel Hill and Goddard's French teacher were killed.

The mothers of two other victims of the VA Tech shooting also became activists. One of them carried with her to speaking engagements and demonstrations a copy of the front page of The Roanoke Times showing her son being carried to safety by four hefty policemen after he was shot twice by Cho.

There was predictable legislative fallout from the slaughter. Later the same year, George Bush signed the NICS Improvement Amendments Act which tightened the reporting of mental health data. [NICS stands for National Instant Criminal Background Check.] The president of the Brady Campaign to Prevent Gun Violence lauded the move. "As a result of that law, almost every state dramatically improved reporting of that kind of information," he said. "The process is still ongoing today."

There was the backlash, of course. Eric Pratt, the head of an organization called Gun Owners of America, said that shootings like the one at VA Tech could be prevented if more citizens had guns to take down shooters. "We need more lawful people who can protect themselves and stop these mass shootings."

We have heard this argument before and we shall hear it again.

Sandy Hook

SANDY HOOK, DECEMBER 14, 2012. A mentally deranged 20-year-old man shot and killed 20 children aged six to seven, and six adults at a primary school in Newtown, Connecticut. He had first killed his mother as she lay on her bed. The weapons he used in the school shooting belonged to her. At the conclusion of his rampage, he shot and killed himself, just like the juvenile killers at Columbine.

A majority of mass shootings in the country begin as cases of domestic violence. In her book, *No Visible Bruises: What We Don't Know about Domestic Violence Can Kill Us*, Rachel Louise Snyder cites what happened at Sandy Hook as one such example.

The Sandy Hook shootings were particularly horrific in light of the tender ages of the gunman's victims. Police cautioned paramedics arriving at Sandy Hook Elementary School—

where the shooter, a man called Adam Lanza, had killed the kids—that it would be 'the worst day of your life.' In one instance, the bodies of fifteen toddlers lay packed like sardines in a closet where they had sought to escape the madman's onslaught.

Lanza lived with his mother after his parents divorced. Peter, Adam's father, remarried and moved away. Son and mother continued to live in a substantial-looking house in Newtown. There was ample evidence of his abnormality to warrant concern. A former teacher commented once that "Adam's level of violence was disturbing. His creative writing was so graphic that it could not be shared."

The boy had kept a spreadsheet of shootings which went back more than one century. He downloaded on his computer material about Harris and Klebold, the killers at Columbine

Certainly his behavior was bizarre in the three months leading up to the killings at Sandy Hook. His mother Nancy cited a change which occurred when Hurricane Sandy knocked out power in Newtown. Adam blocked the windows of his room with black garbage sacks and communicated with his mother exclusively by email although they lived in the same house. A nurse at a child study center observed that he washed his hands compulsively and would change his socks as often as twenty times a day. His mother refused to give him the anti-depressant and anti-anxiety meds prescribed for him because they made it difficult for him to raise his arm.

Three days before his rampage, Nancy Lanza did something baffling. She left him on his own to go on holiday at Bretton Woods in New Hampshire. She had done this before. She wanted to show that Adam could cope on his own. She confided to a friend that there were difficulties in dealing with her son, but she felt that he could manage.

Emily Miller, an editor at the *Washington Times*, wrote: "We can't blame lax gun-control laws, access to mental health treatment, prescription drugs or video games for Lanza's terrible killing spree. We can point to a mother who should have been more aware of how sick her son had become and forced treatment."

The photo of Adam online makes him look like a drug-addled angel. Six feet tall, he weighed only 112 pounds. He had no friends and spent his days playing violent computer games like *Grand Theft Auto*, *Doom* and *Left 4 Dead*. There was even one called *School Shooter*. Adam sometimes dressed in military-type clothing. He indicated that he wanted to follow in the footsteps of an uncle and join the Marines.

As Adam crossed the threshold of adolescence, his psychological oddities grew more pronounced. He was socially awkward, walked oddly, could not make eye contact with other people. He once asked his father what need was there for friends. In Grade 5, Adam and another boy wrote a story called "The Big Book of Granny." In the story, an old woman with a gun in her cane kills at random. At one point, the old woman and her son express the desire to stuff the body of a boy-victim and to mount it trophy-like over their mantelpiece. From the eighth grade onward, Adam was home-schooled. His mother handled the humanities, his father the sciences twice a week.

With less contact with his peers, Adam Lanza spent hours every day on his computer. Mass murders fascinated him, but he shared his obsession only with online contacts. The Lanzas shepherded their son to a bevy of psychiatrists. A common pronouncement on his troubles was that he was autistic. In 2006, psychiatrists determined that he suffered from what they called (and here I quote) "a profound autism spectrum disorder, with rigidity, isolation, and a lack of comprehension of ordinary social interaction and common emotions."

Somehow Adam showed a sense of humor in the midst of his abnormal behavior. His father shared an anecdote with *The New Yorker*. When he was sixteen, he found a picture of Karl Marx with his bushy beard, a scrawny-bearded Lenin, a mustachioed Stalin, and a clean-shaven Mao. He sent it around with the caption, "Comrades, we must rectify the faltering facial hair standards." His father found it so gut-splittingly funny, he got T-shirts made with images of the four Communists and Adam's words.

Adam was growing increasingly isolated. He refused to see his father, Peter. On the day of the shootings, Peter found his colleagues clustered around a TV set. The news of the shootings at Sandy Hook had broken. An announcer said that two young men, ages 20 and 24, were involved. Twenty and twenty-four were the ages of Adam and his brother Ryan. Unable to work, Peter went home and phoned his wife who heard him say, "It's Peter. I think it's Adam." At first she didn't recognize his voice. But then he said it again: "It's Peter, it's Peter. It's Adam." Still she didn't understand him. He repeated what he had said, "I think it's Adam, it's Adam."

Later Peter confided to a reporter for *The New Yorker* his view that Adam had shot his mother Nancy four times, one time for each member of the family: once for Nancy; once for himself; once for Ryan; once for Peter. One year after the massacre, Peter and his wife sorted letters that they had received. One screwball message suggested that the CIA had drugged Adam, forcing him to kill in order to generate support for gun-control legislation.

Peter Lanza confessed to *The New Yorker* that he had recently had the worst nightmare of his life. As he walked past a door in his dream, someone began shaking it violently. Peter sensed hatred, anger, "the worst possible evil." He saw upraised hands, and he realized it was Adam. "What surprised me is that I was scared as shit," he recounted. "I couldn't understand what was happening to me. And then I realized that I was experiencing it from the perspective of his victims."

A variety of opinion has been offered by experts who have examined what Adam Lanza did. Scientists have even sequenced his DNA to try to shed some light on his actions. But Adam Lanza's slaughter of the children and adults at Sandy Hook remains stubbornly incomprehensible. Sandy Hook Elementary School was razed in 2013, to be replaced by a new building unrelated to Adam Lanza's murderous spree.

※※※

THE NRA'S EXECUTIVE SECRETARY argued at the time that the best defense against such rampages as Adam Lanza's was to install armed police officers at schools like Sandy Hook. When Barack Obama retorted that would be an error, the NRA's PR firm noted in an ad that the President's children benefitted from Secret Service protection. "Are the President's kids more important than yours?" asked a portentous voice-over.

Sandy Hook witnessed the eruption of a vicious phenomenon. Victims of Lanza's slaughter and their families were accused of being "crisis actors." A conspiracy theorist like Alex Jones claimed on his Internet channel *Infowars* that the attack was a fabrication of the federal government and people he called "gun grabbers." He said, in answer to someone who called in to his show on 13 January 2015 that:

> Yeah, when you're trying to decipher cloak and dagger dirty tricks, it's pretty hard to do. It's just that then you learn that they were funded by western funding. Then you learn that it was the same (inaudible) connection, underwear bomber. Then those are big red flags that they were patsy provocateurs. The classic MO has been followed.
>
> And then yeah, it kind of becomes a red herring to say the whole thing was staged because they have staged events before. But then you learn the school had been closed and reopened, and you've got video of the kids going in circles in and out of the building, and they don't call the rescue choppers for two hours, then they tear the building down and seal it, and they get caught using blue screens and a email by Bloomberg comes out in a lawsuit where he's telling his people to get ready in the next 24 hours to capitalize on a shooting.
>
> Yeah, so, Sandy Hook is a synthetic completely fake with actors, in my view, manufactured. I couldn't believe it at first. I knew they had actors there, clearly, but I thought they killed some real kids. And it just shows how bold they are, that they clearly used actors. I mean they even ended up using photos of kids killed in mass shootings here in a fake mass shooting in Turkey—so yeah, or Pakistan. The sky is now the limit.

Jones has claimed that his *Infowars* persona is "performance art." He came to the attention of the nation when he promoted a charge that a Washington D.C. pizzeria named Comet Ping Pong was a front for a pedophilia racket masterminded by prominent Democratic politicians like John Podesta, the Democratic Campaign Chairman in 2016. One of Jones' gullible devotees was so moved by what he heard in Jones' broadcast that he drove all the way from his home in North Carolina to D.C. There he assaulted the pizzeria at gunpoint. That caper earned the perpetrator jail time. Jones finally apologized to the manager of the restaurant for all the trouble that he and fellow conspiracy theorists had caused.

Several parents of children killed at Sandy Hook and FBI officers who took part in the rescue mission at the school sued Jones for defamation of character. The suit wound its way through the courts, and after six years Jones was found guilty. Late in January 2019, a Texas judge ordered Jones and representatives of his company to submit to questioning by lawyers for the mother of one Sandy Hook student. The judge also granted access to Jones' pertinent business records.

In a 3-hour deposition of Jones which appeared on March 29, 2019 on YouTube, lawyers for Sandy Hook parents grilled Jones mercilessly on what he had been saying over the past six years about the massacre.

"Alex Jones has tried to do everything he can to try his case in the media," said Wesley Ball, one of the lawyers representing the Sandy Hook parents. "The best thing we can hope for is to get Alex Jones to trial." In the meantime, the filmed deposition speaks for itself. The shock jock still refuses to acknowledge that what he has done contributed to the grief of those who lost their children in the attack. The lawsuits brought against him, Jones maintains, are retaliation for Hillary Clinton's loss in the 2016 election. Years of corruption in government and institutions has made him deeply skeptical of what he calls "mainstream media" and the "agenda hidden behind things." He goes on to say:

> I myself have almost had like a form of psychosis back in the past when I basically thought everything was staged, even though I'm now learning a lot of times things aren't staged. So I think as a pundit, someone giving an opinion, that—you know—my opinions have been wrong. But they were never wrong consciously to hurt people.

The balding, pot-bellied "pundit" is now ready to admit

that children died at Sandy Hook. But, in his opinion, there was still a cover-up.

> I still have questions about Sandy Hook, but I know people that know some of the Sandy Hook families. They say, 'No, it's real,' people I think are credible. And so over the years, I've—you know, especially as it's become a huge issue, had time to really retrospectively think about it. And as the whole thing matured, I've had a chance to believe that children died, and it's a tragedy. But there are still real anomalies in the attempt to keep it blacked out that generally, when you see that in government, something's being covered up.

Would he admit that he had inflicted harm on the grieving parents and staff of Sandy Hook? "I am not prepared to sign on to whatever you and the mainstream media make up about me," he shot back.

Jones has been banned from several platforms including Facebook, Twitter, Apple and YouTube. This does not seem to have deterred Jones, who played a role in the final days of the Trump presidency. The *Wall Street Journal* reported that he pledged more than $50,000 in seed money for Trump's January 6, 2021 rally—the one that culminated in his supporters storming the Capitol and getting their idol impeached for instigating an insurrection.

According to the Journal, Jones did this in exchange for a "top speaking slot of his choice." The conspiracy theorist helped to arrange for an heiress to Publix Super Markets to commit $300,000 for the event. Jones was photographed, bullhorn in hand, egging on protestors on the Capitol grounds (although he did try to prevent them from entering the Capitol, urging them to be peaceful). In the end, Jones' seed money was used for a rally the day before the Capitol riot. At that rally, Jones said: "I don't know how all this is going to end but if they want to fight, they better believe they've got one."

The stories spread by types like Alex Jones unleashed a flood of vitriol directed at the parents of children killed in the Sandy Hook slaughter. This took the form of email and telephone threats. Jones has invited a retired public school official named Wolfgang Halbig on Infowars. Halbig, a septuagenarian who has obsessed about "this supposed tragedy at Sandy Hook," kept returning to Newtown to demand thousands of pages of public records. These included photos of the scene of the crime and receipts for the cleanup of "bodily fluids, brain matter, skull fragments and gallons of blood." He harried families of the victims and other residents of the small town in Connecticut. Asked by a lawyer for the Sandy Hook families if he thought that Halbig was "a raving lunatic," Jones said only that "he seemed very credible and put together earlier on, but—I can't remember the exact number—he seemed to get agitated about four years ago, three years ago." If he is thwarted in his attempt to get information, Halbig publishes personal items about the people he targets.

"I've said nobody died," the conspiracy theorist said in February 2019. "I've never ever been given the documents to form a true and honest opinion. We want to know the truth so we can teach other school districts to prevent this."

Jones was the principal pest bothering Sandy Hook parents, but he wasn't the only one. Several parents were harassed to the point that they changed their addresses. Two of them, Leonard Pozner and Veronique De La Rosa, wrote a letter to Mark Zuckerberg to complain of the harassment to which they and their family were subjected on Facebook. The letter, reprinted in the British daily, *The Guardian*, read in part:

> Almost immediately after the massacre of 20 little children, all under the age of seven, and six elementary school teachers and staff, the attacks on us began. Conspiracy groups and anti-government provocateurs began making claims on Facebook that the massacre was a hoax, that the murdered were so-called "crisis actors" and that their audience should rise up to "find out the truth" about our families. These claims and calls to action spread across Facebook like wildfire and, despite our pleas, were protected by Facebook.

An example of what the Pozners were complaining about is provided by an anecdote printed in *The New York Times*. Robbie Parker, the father of a Sandy Hook victim was accosted in Seattle in October 2016 by "a middle-aged man dressed in khakis and a sports coat." (This was Parker's description of him.)

The man asked Parker if he had lost a child at Sandy Hook. Parker said that yes, he had lost a daughter. He offered his hand which the man ignored, instead spewing obscenities at Parker. Parker goes on, retelling the incident as follows: "The man trailed me, jabbering in my ear. It was absolute venom. He was absolutely disgusted with the person that he believed that I was."

Robbie Parker was one of the people Alex Jones had ridiculed on his program. He said of an interview Parker gave in Newtown that "he's laughing and then he goes over and starts basically breaking down and crying. This needs to be investigated. They're clearly using this to go after our guns."

Some conspiracy theorists are demonstrably unhinged. One man kept calling a newspaper in Oregon to say that its reporting on Sandy Hook was fallacious. He was imprisoned in 2013 for harassing the families of victims at a mass shooting in a movie house in Aurora, Colorado. When his probation expired, he started harassing the Parker family.

Alex Jones was to find that the accusations he leveled at the parents of Sandy Hook parents came at a price. In December 2019, a Texas judge ordered him to pay $100,000 in legal fees to one of those parents. Worse was to come. The judge said that Jones' failure to cooperate should be treated as contempt of court. "Mr. Jones is learning that he cannot treat the courts with the same contempt he showed my clients," said a lawyer for one of the plaintiffs. "In disobeying court orders, Mr. Jones has shown how desperate he is to ensure nobody finds out how *Infowars* really operates, or the lengths the company went to carry out its five-year campaign of malicious harassment against these parents."

Jones' problems with the law span years. In November 2021, a judge ruled that the showman's refusal to turn over documents meant that he was liable for damages in the lawsuits leveled against him by parents of children killed in the Sandy Hook shootings. The default resulted from Jones' "failure to produce critical material information that the plaintiffs needed to prove their claims," which alleged that Jones had profited from the Sandy Hook massacre and other mass shootings. One of the plaintiffs' lawyers commented that the court ruling made clear that "Alex Jones and the Jones's defendants have engaged in a long, continuous course of misconduct...designed to prevent the plaintiffs from getting evidence about Mr. Jones' business and about his motives for publishing lies about them and their families."

A Connecticut jury found that Jones had to pay close to one billion dollars to the eight families of victims at Sandy Hook and to an FBI agent who responded to the scene of the massacre. One of the attorneys for the plaintiffs described the verdict as "probably one of the largest defamation verdicts in US history." Said Chris Mattei, another of the lawyers for the Sandy Hook families, "We are going to enforce this verdict as long as it takes because that is what justice requires."

For Robbie Parker, the verdict came—and here I quote from the *Washington Post*—as "a moment of vindication and catharsis." Harassment by conspiracy theorists had driven his family to relocate from Connecticut to the Pacific Northwest. The trial had offered Parker "a chance to reclaim these things in my life that were taken from me . . .I got to be who I was again and find my voice."

Parker believed that the best way to deal with bullies was to ignore them. They would go away, like "people taking a break from looking for Big Foot," but this didn't happen.

Jones claimed that he had less than $2 million. "I don't have any money, so this is all a big joke," he said.

Oh?

Bernard Pettingill, Jr., a forensic economist, has ball-parked his net worth to be between $135 million and $270 million. Jones might have been worth more if he had not moved money into companies controlled by himself, friends or family. Over a period of 15 months—from August 2020 to November 2021—Jones' company signed what are essentially IOU's for $55 million to a company owned by Jones and his parents. Attorneys for the Sandy Hook plaintiffs contend that Jones has engaged in this and other transfers to protect his wealth from creditors like the Sandy Hook parents. "*Infowars* had made Jones a wealthy man," observed the *Post*, "to a degree that has become apparent only because of the Sandy Hook litigation. "The bankruptcy court," noted the *Post*, will "ultimately decide which creditors are paid and how much." According to Jay L. Westbrook, a University of Texas bankruptcy law professor, the issue is whether the payments made by Jones were valid payments made in the ordinary course of business.

Jones's reaction to the verdict of the Connecticut jury was captured by the *Post* this way: "After dismissing the judge as a 'tyrant' and the proceedings as a 'kangaroo court,' Jones appeared to laugh as the verdict was read out."

"'This is hilarious,' he said, as the separate awards were listed. He repeatedly pumped his fist in the air before a camera live-streaming his reaction to the *Infowars* site."

Jones lurched from his Sandy Hook (mis)adventure to one fueled by the coronavirus pandemic. The *Infowars* store sold a gamut of products, some of which Jones touted to his virtual audience. "This stuff kills the whole SARS-corona family at point-blank range," he said of one item on March 10, 2020. "It kills every virus." The Food and Drug Administration disagreed. In an open letter, the agency declared, "there currently are no vaccines, pills, potions, lotions, lozenges or other prescription or over-the-counter products available to treat or cure coronavirus disease."

Although the *Infowars* studio is located in Texas, what it broadcasts can be seen wherever viewers have access to the internet. That includes New York which has consumer-protection laws. That state's attorney general, Letitia James, instructed her health-care bureau to issue Jones with a cease-and-desist order. This resulted in the site releasing a disclaimer which stated that "the products sold on this site are not intended for use in the cure, treatment, prevention, or mitigation of any disease, including the novel coronavirus."

"He has added a new disclaimer," said James, "but he hasn't stopped selling the products. We are still in contact with his lawyers, and, at a certain point, if they refuse to comply with our orders,…then we hit them with an array of violations, we issue subpoenas, and we could haul them to court."

She added in a politely menacing tone, "My advice to Mr.

Jones and any other scammers out there would be to heed our warnings because, when we go to court, we have a pretty high success rate."

Jones was a principal speaker at a "You-Can't-Close-America" rally which took place on the steps of the state capital in Austin, Texas in April 2020. Charlie Warzel, commenting in *The New York Times*, said that "the *InfoWars* strategy is simple: Instill a deep distrust in all authority, while promoting a seductive, conspiratorial reality in which Mr. Jones, via his outlandish conspiracies, has all the answers." He observed that the rally in Texas was "to sow division and to reshape public opinion," and he quoted Jane Coaston writing in *Vox* that "[Trump's] message of division [is] designed to pit Republican voting areas of states against their Democratic voting neighbors even rural Republicans against urban Republicans."

In early December 2022, Alex Jones filed for Chapter 11 personal bankruptcy in what one lawyer called "the latest in a long line of tricks by Alex Jones to keep the Sandy Hook families from the justice to which they are entitled."

"The bankruptcy system does not protect anyone who engages in intentional and egregious attacks on others," said Chris Mattei. "The American judicial system will hold Alex Jones accountable."

***

As happened after the massacre at Virginia Tech, many of the families of the Sandy Hook victims became activists. They began to campaign for gun control and related issues. One such issue dealt with photographing the victims of a slaughter like Sandy Hook. The film maker Michael Moore was all in favor of doing just that.

> When the American people see what bullets from an assault rifle fired at close range do to a little child's body [he said], that's the day the jig will be up for the NRA. It will be the day the debate on gun control will come to an end. There will be nothing left to argue over. It will just be over. And every sane American will demand action.

But the state of Connecticut felt otherwise. Its legislature overwhelmingly passed a bill banning the sort of photographs that Moore wanted people to see.

"For the families and the community, we just want to get back to a normal life and that would be a horrendous offense to the families," Dorrie Carolan, co-president of the Newtown Parent Connection support group agreed. "There's no need for any of that… It's going to be a long healing process and to dredge up pictures of the crime scene would not be a good thing. We want to remember the little angels as they were, with their happy expressions and faces and you want to think of the teachers trying to hold them safe and not to see the pictures of their bodies. I think it would be terrible."

Not all the victims' families shared that sentiment. Leonard Pozner and Veronique De La Rosa, the authors of the letter to Mark Zuckerberg which appeared in *The Guardian*, chose an open casket for their son Noah's funeral. A cloth covered the lower half of his face.

"There was no mouth left," Veronique told the *Jewish Daily Forward*. "His jaw was blown away."

Noah had been shot eleven times.

"I owed it to him as his mother—the good, the bad, the ugly," Veronique said. "It is not up to me to say I am only going to look at you and deal with you when you are alive, that I am going to block out the reality of what you look like when you are dead. And as a little boy, you have to go in the ground. If I am going to shut my eyes to that I am not his mother. I had to bear it. I had to do it."

Asked why she requested [Connecticut] Gov. Malloy to view the open casket at the funeral, she said: "I needed it to have a face for him. If there is ever a piece of legislation that comes across his desk, I needed it to be real for him."

Another parent of a child killed at Sandy Hook reported a heart-breaking anecdote of her own:

> After my precious Dylan was killed in the senseless shooting at Sandy Hook Elementary (she writes), my other son Jake asked me not to say Dylan's name aloud. The reminder of how quickly and violently his best friend had been snatched

away was too painful and raw.
In the years after, I sometimes heard Jake talking to Dylan, just chatting to his brother quietly while he played. I had to stop, steel myself, allow myself to feel the anger that Jake could no longer play with his brother, and then remember that this was Jake's way of moving forward, of keeping Dylan's memory alive.

Gun control advocates in general had no problem with legislation banning the public airing of images like those of the Sandy Hook victims.

"The families should have the lead say on this," said Ladd Everitt of the Coalition to Stop Gun Violence. "It's their children or relatives that are involved, that these photographs are of, and if it should be anybody's call it should be their call, and some have stepped forward very vocally and said this [law] would be respectful of their lost loved ones… We can have a hypothetical debate about what effect those pictures would have on the gun debate, but we're not going to stand up and say our word outweighs theirs."

But newspapers objected to the ban which was broadly written. It applied not only to the Sandy Hook massacre but to future homicides as well. Chris Powell, the editor of the *Journal Inquirer* was typical in his criticism of the law:

> Crime scene and autopsy photos and videos probably are not necessary to understanding what happened in Newtown, nor to validation of the official account of most murders (he wrote after the law passed) but crime scene and autopsy photos and videos certainly are necessary to understanding some murders and to guarding against official misconduct and lies. Famous examples from history of the necessity to disclose the image evidence of crime include the assassination of President Kennedy and the mass murder of Polish military officers by the Soviet Union during World War II. But in recent years so many murder convictions in the United States have been disproved by DNA analysis and the recanting of testimony that it is outrageous that any criminal evidence should ever be placed outside public review.

It should be noted that newspapers had previously shown considerable restraint in publishing photos of the victims of mass shootings

On the more ambitious goal of securing background checks for gun buyers, the Sandy Hook activists were less successful. Despite 90 percent public approval, despite massive funding by Michael Bloomberg and intense lobbying by Sandy Hook parents, the bill to expand background checks fell five votes short of passage in the Senate. It was a bitter disappointment for those who had supported it.

"In retrospect Sandy Hook marked the end of the US gun control debate," claimed British journalist, Dan Hodges, in 2018. "Once America decided killing children was bearable, it was over."

However, something seemed to have changed. In the opinion of Senior Editor, Alec McGinnis, of *The New Republic*, "a visible movement for gun regulation [was] emerging." A woman named Shannon Watts, a stay-at-home mother of five, created a Facebook page for an organization which she called One Million Moms for Gun Control. That organization, now called "Moms Demand Action," garnered 100,000 likes. It went on to spawn one hundred chapters in forty states, gaining support from BlastRoots—an Internet application which enables users to organize grassroots advocacy campaigns.

Ladd Everitt of the Coalition to stop Gun Violence commented: "I've been doing this for thirteen years, and I've never seen anything approaching the level we've seen since Newtown."

Newtown made one survivor of the Virginia Tech shooting into an activist. Before April 16, 2007, the day Seung-Hui Cho killed 32 people at Virginia Tech, Colin Goddard was just trying to figure out what to do with his life. The massacre at Virginia Tech gave focus to his life. He began speaking out on the subject of gun violence. "Please ask yourself, 'What was your Newtown moment?'" Goddard challenges the audiences he addresses. "If it hasn't happened yet, please ask, 'What is it going to take?'"

After working three years for the Brady Campaign, Goddard joined Michael Bloomberg's Everytown for Gun Safety. In January, 2020, Goddard released a video in support of

Bloomberg's short-lived candidacy for the presidency. It aired in Virginia which held its primary the following month. Six years before that, Goddard had become the focal point of a film entitled Living for 32 in which he reflected on his own survival the day of the massacre and what he did afterward. Asked what compelled him to change career paths and become an activist, Goddard told the Chronicle of Higher Education:

> I admire my fellow Hokies and classmates who wanted to be engineers and survived the shooting and are now engineers. It didn't knock them off their path. I was one of the college students who didn't really know what the hell to do after graduation. Learning what I did about this issue and continuing to see it happen to more people, and seeing how stuck it was politically, I just saw an opportunity in front of me and a path forward to make some progress on something that I believed in.

Would it have made a difference if Goddard or any of his classmates had been armed?

> I didn't know what the hell was happening until I got shot (he responded). That's what I do know. And I do know that there were many more situations in college where a concealed weapon would have made the situation much more dangerous.

※※※

WAS NRA CLOUT ON THE WANE? "The NRA is just all mythology," said Chris Murphy, the junior Senator from Connecticut. "The NRA does not win elections anymore."

Said Kris Brown, president of the Brady Campaign, "Of all the races that we worked on at the federal level, we won 90 percent of them."

There was some evidence to support President Brown's and Senator Murphy's enthusiasm. After an infamous killing occurred in the state, Florida passed legislation which curtailed gun rights. Said the managing attorney for the Giffords Law Center to Prevent Gun Violence, "To pass a package of bills that included an extreme risk protection order, raised the minimum age to purchase guns, prohibited bump stocks, extended waiting periods, and designated $2 million in funding for urban gun violence reduction programs, I think was tremendous," he said.

Politicians were getting an earful from citizens. A woman whose daughter was killed, not at Sandy Hook, but in another mass shooting, buttonholed a Republican Representative and reduced him to tears:

"When you start a conversation with 'You have a daughter.' I had a daughter. Would you like to see her killed the way mine was killed?' And then you go into a description. [The Congressman] had his head down like he was saying, 'I don't want to hear this,' and I said, 'Imagine it's your daughter pinned down with nowhere to go, and she gets shot six times and the sixth one takes her brain'... I knew he didn't want to be there but he did listen."

One Democrat to cosponsor the background check bill was an erstwhile NRA stalwart: Joe Manchin of West Virginia. What happened to change his attitude? "My God, you had babies slaughtered," he said. Did he have Herod's slaughter of the Innocents in mind? "I've heard people say it's gun control. It's not gun control—it's gun sense."

To get a better sense of what the Senator faced from his constituents, Alec McGinnis of *The New Republic* accompanied Manchin to a couple of town meetings in the coal country of West Virginia. At the more difficult of these get-togethers, McGinnis reported that the vocal opposition was limited to an old woman who sat in the front row and to four men in black NRA T-shirts at the back of the hall.

"How does your bill make these students or any other students safer?" asked the woman in the front row.

"Why pass another gun law when there are already 50,000 gun laws on the books?" shouted one of the men in back.

It wasn't long before the quintet of naysayers was raising hullabaloo about abortion which kills—they professed—fifty thousand babies a day.

Manchin did what he could to stem the flow of invective, but at the end of the day, he stated "If disingenuous criticism could stop someone from taking action, there's no need for me to be here—there's no need to run for public office."

Not surprisingly Manchin discovered in the course of that meeting that many in the audience—perhaps a majority—actually agreed with him. They were intimidated from voicing their support by the raucous minority who kept baiting the Senator.

What happened at Sandy Hook spawned years of litigation. Some of this actually made its way to the Supreme Court. In November 2019, the Court announced that it would not consider an appeal from the manufacturer of the assault weapon which Lanza had used in his attack on the school. This was noteworthy because a federal law, passed in 2005, gave gun makers (and sellers) immunity from most lawsuits. The ruling lets stand a decision by the Connecticut Supreme Court that exploited a loophole in the federal law which permitted plaintiffs to sue gun manufacturers.

Lawyer for the families that brought the suit, Joshua Koskoff said, "The families are grateful that the Supreme Court . . . denied Remington's latest attempt to avoid accountability; we are ready to resume discovery and proceed toward trial in order to shed light on Remington's profit-driven strategy to expand the AR-15 market and court high-risk users at the expense of Americans' safety."

Remington had marketed the weapon under the slogan, "Consider your man card re-issued."

There were financial consequences to the massacre committed at Sandy Hook. Families of some of the victims reported that they had reached a $73 million settlement in their lawsuit against Remington. The families contended that Remington had run afoul of state consumer law by advertising the weapon in a way that appealed to troubled youth. Their achievement was significant because much litigation along these lines had been stymied by a 2005 law entitled the Protection of Lawful Commerce in Arms Act which afforded blanket immunity from prosecution to gun manufacturers. Said Josh Koskoff: "This victory should serve as a wake-up call not only to the gun industry, but also the insurance and banking companies that prop it up."

Parkland

PARKLAND, FEBRUARY 14, 2018. A 19-year-old psychopath named Nikolas Cruz gunned down 17 students and teachers at a high school which he had previously attended. The school, called Marjorie Stoneman Douglas, was about one hour's drive north of Miami. Just weeks after this slaughter, Governor Rick Scott signed the legislation cited above.

Here is a question we shall ask again: Was there a pattern to these recurring mass shootings? For starters, the shooters were all young males seeking notoriety.

Nikolas Cruz wanted to make sure that people understood where he was coming from. He bequeathed researchers a series of three videos on his cellphone.

"When you see me on the news, you'll all know who I am," he boasted in one of them. "You're all going to die."

"All the kids in school will run in fear and hide," he said in one of his videos. "From the wrath of my power, they will know who I am."

Peter Langman, a psychologist who has been quoted before in this chapter, said of the Cruz tapes: "He shows no emotional distress. He doesn't even come across as full of rage or anguish. He just focused on how this is going to enhance his status, how he's going to make his mark on the world."

Cruz had crippling doubts about his self-worth. "I am nothing," he said. "My life is nothing and meaningless." And his defensive riposte to this? "I am going to be the next school shooter of 2018. My goal is at least twenty people."

Here is a bit of background for Cruz. First off, he was an orphan: His adoptive father had died years before the attack on Douglas High School in Parkland. His adoptive mother passed away in November 2017. The boy's problems dated back to Middle School. He scribbled derogatory references to Barack Obama on his homework. The president should be "burned alive and eaten" said Cruz. Infractions in his behavior included insubordination, profanity, and fighting. Every once in a while, "he would just spew something out of his mouth that was inappropriate," said a teacher who had worked with him in sixth grade. He once drew a swastika on a test and what The *Washington Post* described as a Nazi symbol on his book bag. When asked by his mother, Cruz denied knowing what the symbol meant. She made him scrub it off.

Nikolas Cruz had a younger brother—probably half-brother since they look so racially dissimilar. His name was Zach. After the death of their adoptive mother, Zach was Nikolas's only family. The slaughter at Parkland put the murderer's brother in an impossible position. "I always carry it with me. Every day. There is no forgetting," Zach said. "I'm stuck between loving him and hating him because of what he did."

Once Zach had spied on Nik's cell phone, found a message there in which Nikolas was saying, "I'm gonna go to that school; I'm gonna shoot everybody." Zach kept this discovery to himself.

Zach was allowed to visit his brother in jail. A video recording captured their meeting in which Nik is seen to be wearing a hospital gown. Handcuffs restrain his hands behind his back. A chain holds his left foot to the floor.

"What do you think Mom would think right now?" Zach is heard to say.

"She would cry," Nik replies.

"People think you're a monster now," Zach says.

"A monster?"

"You're not acting like yourself," Zach goes on. "This is not who you are. Like, come on, why did you do this?"

"I'm sorry," Nik mumbles.

"This is not even a game," Zach continues, raising his head to the ceiling. "You're not gonna wake up and be out of here."

A memory returns to Zach, who says, "Remember when Mom died? Remember we were walking down the hallway and I told you?"

Nik shakes his head.

"You probably don't because you just did some fucked up shit," Zach admonishes his brother. "I told you when we were walking down the hallway that it's just me and you and I had your back."

Zach leans forward. "I know you, you probably felt like you had nobody but I, I care about you. I know I made it seem like when we were growing up that I hated you...but truth is I just didn't want to look like a—I didn't want to look weak. I love you with all my heart."

Nik starts to shake.

"I know what you did," Zach says. "Other people look at me like I'm crazy for even—and I don't, I don't care what other people think. Like, you're my brother. I love you, I want—I want you to—."

Nik was crying now openly. He emitted a stream of high-pitched sobs. Zach buried his head in his hands. Then he hammered the table beside him with his fist. Then he asked the detective in the room with him and Nik, "Can I hug him?"

Then Zach stood up, walked over to Nik and threw his arms around his sobbing brother.

***

MARJORY STONEMAN DOUGLAS HIGH expelled Nikolas Cruz during his junior year. His expulsion from Douglas High was not the only one in his life. Young Cruz told classmates that he had been expelled previously from two private schools. Besides unruly behavior going back to middle school—bumping into fellow students in the hallway, cussing out staff, even getting up in class and dancing—he passed around pictures of frogs he had killed. One student alleged that the school kicked Cruz out of Douglas High for carrying knives to school. At her wit's end to know how to handle Cruz, his adoptive mother, Lynda Cruz, suborned the police to try to talk sense to her son. To little or no avail.

Cruz developed an infatuation with a girl in the school, to the point where he was said to be stalking her. The girl's mother and Mrs. Cruz agreed that the relationship "was unhealthy for everyone" and should be terminated. At that point, Cruz's behavior began to deteriorate. His rampage at Douglas High occurred on Valentine's Day. In the opinion of those who knew him, that was not a coincidence. On February 14, Nikolas Cruz refused to go to an adult education course which he normally attended. He said that he didn't go to school on Valentine's Day.

Investigators at Florida's Department of Children and Families diagnosed Cruz as autistic—something he had in common with Adam Lanza. He also suffered from attention-deficit hyperactivity disorder (ADHD).

Teachers worked hard to turn Nikolas around, but there were limits to what they could do. The paperwork required to substantiate the boy's needs was daunting. "You have to have just so much information, which we did," one of his teachers said. "We had so much." Still, it did not prevent the Cruz massacre.

The public defender appointed to represent Cruz said:

> What we have gathered so far looks to us like this is a complete multi-system failure, that you had the school system failed...you had the mental health system failed. When he went to purchase a gun, that system failed...the FBI failed. When you look at it, this should never have happened.
>
> This kid exhibited every single known red flag, from killing animals to having a cache of weapons, to disruptive behavior, to saying he wanted to be a school shooter. If this isn't a person who should have gotten someone's attention, I don't know who is.

"There's always more that you could do," said the Broward Schools Superintendent. "But the fact is that there's more that the federal leadership and government could do... They could put resources and make priority investments so that you can properly service these students who are disengaged or have mental health issues." He went on to say in an interview with the press: "We need greater investments in mental health, social emotional services for our kids."

Starting in 2013, Broward County began offering an alternative program for students guilty of rule violations involving things like alcohol and drug use. The program emphasized counseling and the involvement of community social service agencies. Nikolas Cruz began getting into trouble at the time the county initiated the change in policy.

Teachers urged school administrators to have Cruz transferred to Cross Creek, a school which catered to students with emotional and behavioral problems, but the transfer process was cumbersome and slow. "It's very hard to get a kid in there, very hard" said one teacher. "I suspect it comes down to money…so for three fourths of the year [Cruz] went untreated at school."

In February 2014 Cruz was finally transferred to Cross Creek where he stayed two years. After that he moved to Douglas High where he stayed two more years. The beginning of 2017 saw him expelled for what was alleged to be an assault. From Douglas, Cruz went on to an alternative high school.

On the day of the shooting, Nikolas Cruz was totting a duffel bag and a backpack. He set off the fire alarm to lure students out of their classrooms. The weapon he used to mow them down was a semi-automatic AR-15. This he discarded along with a gas mask when he fled the school. Shedding his gear made it possible for him to meld into the mass of students fleeing the scene of the carnage. Police apprehended Cruz an hour after the shooting as he was sauntering down a street in Coral Springs, a city about two miles from Douglas High School.

Politicians' reactions to the killing at Parkland had been predictable, and they fell more or less along party lines. Bill Nelson (D-FL) took to the Senate floor to say:

> At some point, we've got to say enough is enough. Let's talk about that 19-year-old carrying an AR-15. Let's do what needs to be done, and let's get these assault weapons off our streets. Let's accomplish something on background checks.

Speaker of the House, Paul Ryan, shot back that lawmakers "shouldn't just knee-jerk before we even have all the facts and the data; we need to think less about taking sides and fighting each other politically, and just pulling together."

United Church of Christ (UCC) pastor, Peter Luckey, built a Lenten sermon around the rash of shootings in the nation:

> This is a wilderness time in our county. We are living in a wilderness time. I grew up a few miles from Sandy Hook Elementary School in Newtown, Connecticut. I used to run

against the high school kids in Newtown in track. Since 2012, and the killings at Sandy Hook, there have been 239 school shootings in our country. Two hundred thirty-nine. There have been 438 people shot and 138 people killed. We are awash in guns. Three hundred million guns in our country. The Broward County sheriff put it so succinctly the morning after Ash Wednesday. He said, it's catastrophic . . . We're living, friends, in a wilderness time in our country.

The one positive aspect of Cruz's carnage was that the movement to curb gun violence in schools gained incalculable momentum. Appropriately enough, much of this came from Nikolas Cruz's intended victims. While the grown-ups dithered, the kids organized. A group of juniors and seniors at Douglas High School mounted an activist challenge to the gun-lobby status quo. They were responsible for a monster rally in Washington, D.C. The event, called March for Our Lives, attracted hundreds of thousands to the capital in late March 2018. Hundreds of other rallies sprang up across the country, even in foreign lands.

"Welcome to the revolution," said Cameron Kasky, one of the students from Marjorie Stoneman Douglas High School. "Since this movement began, people have asked me, 'Do you think any change is going to come from this?' Look around. We are the change."

Adults were largely barred from the podium at these rallies. The only speakers were teenagers and elementary school children. Another Douglas student, Delaney Tarr told the crowd in Washington: "Today we march. We fight. We roar. We prepare our signs. We raise them high. We know what we want, we know how to get it and we are not waiting any more."

The NRA response? Mostly silence although a commentator on an online video channel, which is NRA-produced, said on the eve of the march, "These kids ought to be marching against their own hypocritical belief structures; the only reason we've ever heard of them is because the guns didn't come soon enough."

Among the Douglas High students, two gained a nation-wide reputation for their work on gun violence control.

One of these was Emma Gonzalez who spoke at the Washington rally. She first read the names of those who had been killed on Valentine's Day, then she stood in silence for six minutes and twenty seconds, the time Nikolas Cruz had torn through the halls of the school shooting students and faculty. She concluded by saying:

> Since the time I came out here, it has been six minutes and twenty seconds. The shooter has ceased shooting and will soon abandon his rifle, blend in with the students as they escape and walk free for an hour before arrest. Fight for your lives before it's someone else's job!

Congressmen missed the March for Our Lives because they had adjourned for their spring break. President Trump spent part of that weekend at the Trump International Golf Club, less than one hour's drive north of Parkland. The president's spokeswoman issued a statement which said, in part, "We applaud the many courageous young Americans exercising their First Amendment rights today."

Gonzalez described herself in a February 2018 essay which appeared in Harper's Bazaar as "18 years old, Cuban and bisexual." An interviewer at Variety described Gonzalez as a "Bright-eyed and jaunty" (teenager) who "voraciously consumes movies and TV shows like 'The Office' on Netflix; she knows all the lyrics to her favorite songs, and her Spotify user name is Gonzalez spelled backward."

Her shaved head reminded me of Ingrid Bergman's portrayal of Joan of Arc at the stake in the Robert Rossellini film of 1948. It made her instantly recognizable to those who followed the Parkland story, and it led to detractors labelling her a dyke. That's wrong, according to Gonzalez. "I like guys and girls." How relevant is that, anyway?

> On her left wrist [the *Variety* interviewer wrote], she wears an array of rubber bracelets memorializing victims who were gunned down at her high school . . . The bands are a stark daily reminder of the painful memories that no young person should ever have seared into her consciousness.

Gonzalez explains how she views herself and those like her:

> We are the people who died in the freshman building on Valentine's Day at Douglas High, and the people who died in every mass shooting in US history. We are everyone who has been shot at, grazed, or pierced by bullets, terrorized by the presence of guns and gun violence in America. We are kids, we are parents, we are students, we are teachers. We are tired of practicing school shooter drills and feeling scared of something we should never have to think about. We're tired of being ignored. So we are speaking up for those who don't have anyone listening to them, for those who can't talk about it just yet, and for those who will never speak again. We are grieving, we are furious, and we are using our words fiercely and desperately because that's the only thing standing between us and this happening again.

Her anger and frustration are apparent when she says: "We are children who are expected to act like adults, while the adults . . . behave like children."

"It should not be easier to purchase a gun than it is to obtain a driver's license [she believes], and military-grade weapons should not be accessible in civilian settings. You don't drive a NASCAR on the street, no matter how fun it might be, just like you don't need an AR-15 to protect yourself when walking home at night."

The second of the Douglas High students to gain nation-wide fame was a friend of Emma Gonzalez. His name was David Hogg. When invited to one of the president's so-called listening sessions, Hogg said: "We don't need to listen to President Trump; President Trump needs to listen to the screams of the children and the screams of this nation."

Temperamental, stubborn as a mule, and dyslexic to boot, David had put up an awful fuss about moving from the West Coast to Florida. His parents had to bribe him with—among other things—a new computer to get him to agree to the move. To a journalist interviewing him, he issued a scathing verdict on US politicians accepting money from gun groups like the NRA:

> The pathetic killers who want to keep killing our children, they could have blood from children spattered all over their faces

and they wouldn't take action because they all still see those dollar signs.

On the Valentine's Day massacre, young Hogg had the presence of mind to turn on his cell phone's video recorder to narrate events as they unfolded. Alone in his car afterward, David Hogg began screaming, "Fuck!" He began smashing his fists on the dashboard. Then he sent his video to a local newspaper where he worked as an intern. His career as a media star was launched.

Biking back to school the day of the shooting, David was interviewed by Laura Ingraham of FOX News. He told her, "I don't want this to be just another mass shooting; I don't want this to be something that people forget."

Six a.m. the following morning he was prepping for an interview with George Stephanopoulos of MSNBC.

The Twitter followings of both David Hogg and Emma Gonzalez soared. As was to be expected, there was a glut of hostility directed particularly against Hogg, who was more acerbic and assertive than Gonzalez. The young man was accused, of course, of being a crisis actor. Death threats poured in. His mother received a note which said, "Fuck with the NRA and you'll be DOA." At the rally in Washington, D.C., Hogg called for a boycott of Laura Ingraham who had accused him of whining because he hadn't been admitted to UCLA. Ingraham later apologized for this slur after a sizeable number of her sponsors—companies like Johnson & Johnson, Nestlé, Jenny Craig and Ruby Tuesday—dropped out. "I'm glad to see corporate America standing with me and the other students of Parkland," Hogg commented. "When we work together, we can accomplish anything." As things worked out, Hogg was admitted to Harvard. UCLA's loss, it turned out, was Harvard's gain. Hogg planned to go to Harvard and study political science there. Emma Gonzalez was accepted at New College, a prestigious liberal arts school in Sarasota, Florida, and she planned to go there and room with her best friend from Douglas High.

March for Our Lives became a fixture in the gun control firmament, long out-living the actual march on Washington which had spawned the movement. Buzzfeed News reported that the incorporation of three young Black students onto its board effectively integrated what had previously been a lily-white group. One of the new board members, Bria Smith, 18, from Milwaukee voiced her objection to the exclusivity of the MFOL leadership this way: "There's a bunch of White kids getting millions of dollars . . .I'm like, what about Black Lives Matter? What about my cousin who was shot and killed and there was no justice for him?"

HuffPost, quoting a PR firm handling press requests for the campaign, reported that a number of celebrities had made hefty contributions. These included Oprah Winfrey, George and Amal Clooney and Gucci, all of whom had ponied up half a million dollars to MFOL. Some of the adults assisting the Parkland students with their finances were well known. These included the chair of the Board of Regents of the University of California and a member of the (Quaker) Friends Committee on National Legislation.

The summer of 2018 Gonzalez and Hogg organized a nation-wide tour to register young voters. It actually registered 50,000. The bus carried between eighteen and twenty-two students as well as one therapist and three security guards. It hit seventy-five cities in two months. One of those cities was Huntington Beach, California. There, David Hogg led a march from the rallying grounds where he shouted out, "Tell me what democracy looks like!

The bus tour opened the students' eyes to a world radically different from their own. David Hogg, for example, lived in a gated community in Parkland, Florida. On the tour, he encountered the father of Michael Brown. Hogg remembered that meeting this way:

> He told us to close our eyes and imagine the person that we love most, that we hold dearest. And then imagine them being shot and left on hot asphalt for four hours. And not knowing where they were, if that was them, and not being able to see them. I imagined my sister. I imagined Emma. I was really just thinking of, like, pretty much everybody on our team, because we're all family now.

The Parkland students were shadowed on part of their tour of the country by a group which called itself the Utah Gun Exchange. That group fancied itself on a "freedom tour." It rode around in a vehicle described by *The New York Times* as "a tank with a machine-gun turret." It is not known whether any body of protestors, like the Utah Gun Exchange, called what the Parkland students were doing a Children's Crusade.

An example of the static which David Hogg provoked on NRATV: It came from that channel's commentator, Colion Noir. Noir—a stage name; his birth name was Collins Iyare Idehen, Jr.—is a gun rights enthusiast. He began raging against Hogg for saying that he was fighting for helpless Black people.

> Who the hell gave @davidhogg111 the authority to put on his White man's burden costume to save me from myself by marching to restrict my right to own a gun that at one point I wasn't considered human enough to own? That is the shit we're cosigning?

There were, of course, positive reactions to the Parkland students' odyssey. Chief among these was a handwritten letter from Barack and Michelle Obama sent only days before the March for Our Lives.

"We wanted to let you know how inspired we have been by the resilience, resolve and solidarity that you have all shown in the wake of unspeakable tragedy," the letter said. "Not only have you supported and comforted each other, you've helped awaken the conscience of the nation."

> Throughout our history, young people like you have led the way in making America better [the letter went on]. There may be setbacks, you may feel like progress is too slow in coming. But we have no doubt that you are going to make an enormous difference in the days and years to come.

In the fall of 2018, days before the midterm elections, an op-ed piece coauthored by Hogg and Gonzalez appeared in the *Washington Post*. They commented on their recent cross-country tour which took them to conservative regions like Bismarck, ND where "the mayor and state representative arrived at our town hall meeting to head a counter-rally right outside." They further wrote:

Other times, people have shown up at our events armed to the teeth shouting our names and accusing us of being 'crisis actors.' We've gone out to meet them. We've explained that we're not the gun-grabbing communists they think we are—that when people advocated for safer roads and cars, they weren't anti-vehicle. We're trying to keep people from dying. Sometimes, the people we talk to end up in tears. Usually we end up finding common ground.

The Parkland students wielded influence world-wide. They inspired among others a young autistic Swedish girl called Greta Thunberg who became an environmental superstar. Her activism gained—and retained—the world's unflagging admiration.

What does the future hold for David Hogg? He has told reporters that, after canvasing for candidates he supported, he would attend college where he planned to read a "shitload of books."

When he turns 25, Hogg plans to run for Congress. How well he would fit in among his future colleagues is anyone's guess. It should come as no surprise that young Hogg was a two-legged lightning rod for the most flamboyant of the gun rights enthusiasts in Congress. Two examples will illustrate the point:

Hogg and a representative from Colorado, Lauren Boebert, once photographed packing a pistol Roy Rogers-style, expressed their distaste for each other in an exchange of tweets. In the wake of the January 6 siege of the Capital by a mob of Trump supporters, Hogg tweeted that "They can put up all the fencing around the capital. The real threat of @mtgreene and @lauren boebert will still be inside until @GOPLeader takes a stand."

Boebert tweeted back: "David, please. We all saw how tough you were when questioned face to face. Give your keyboard a rest, child."

The second target of Hogg's tweet was Georgia representative, Marjorie Taylor Greene (@mtgreene), whose outrageous comments on sundry topics—she contended that several school massacres including those at Sandy Hook and Parkland were staged events and (of course) she refused to accept that

Joe Biden had beaten Donald Trump in 2020—precipitated a resolution to expel her from the House of Representatives. A video captured one cringe-inducing episode which involved Hogg and Greene. In the video, Greene is seen chasing David Hogg down a Washington street, berating him nonstop about his advocacy of gun control which, she claimed, would not work. If one of the enforcement officers assigned to guard Marjory Stoneman Douglas had done his job, she insisted, the massacre would not have happened.

One father of a slain student at Parkland told *The Guardian* that Greene "hasn't said, `I was wrong.' She hasn't said, `I'm sorry to the families I've hurt.' She hasn't said `I accept the truth about Parkland, Sandy Hook and 9/11.' She has let the lie live. That makes her incapable of serving as a representative in Congress."

***

Not only the Parkland students but their parents became political activists. "We've been given this voice through the loss of our loved ones, in my case, my daughter Gina," said one of them, Tony Montalto.

> It's something I feel I need to do [he went on] because as we've watched our country drift further apart, to the far left and far right, I realize there's a voice that's missing and that's from the folks in the middle, the ideological middle of the country.
>
> There's certainly anger at the failures that occurred, there's anger someone would do this to our loved ones, to my little girl. [But] that coming together, that compromise, is what we need to do to start healing things here in America.

Trump's school safety commission's review failed to thrill Montalto and parents like him. "It was a little light on the firearms piece," he commented. "I'm not saying we're disappointed, we're saying we need more." He went on to say:

> We need to take the gains we can get today, take the things we can agree on and enact laws and policies that are going to keep our children and staff members safe at school. Then

we'll come back another day and work on the other things.j

Not all the Parkland parents agreed on the need for gun control. One father, whose daughter was among the victims of Cruz's rampage, said "The easy thing is just to point the finger at guns, that's why I had to get involved." He continued:

When everyone else was focused on gun control the president listened to me, put the commission together, came up with all these recommendations. His policy makers and cabinet members indulged [sic] into school safety and he focused on the facts. And now these recommendations will change education for every child in this country.

National fame has come at a price for the Parkland student activists. Comedian Louis C.K. has made jokes at their expense, apparently in an attempt to make audiences forget his admission that he masturbated in front of female colleagues. He has criticized the students for testifying before Congress.

"What are you doing?" he asked. "You're young. You should be crazy, unhinged. Not in a suit, saying 'I'm here to tell . . .'"

> You're not interesting [Louis C. K. went on] because you went to a high school where kids got shot. Why does that mean I have to listen to you? Why does that make you interesting? You didn't get shot. You pushed some fat kid in the way and then, now I gotta listen to you talking?

One Parkland parent decided to fight fire with fire. Manuel Oliver recorded his own gig. In the recording, he stands on what appears to be a dark stage. Beside him on a stool stands a bottle of water, virtually empty. "Recently I heard this great line from a comedian," he begins. "If you want people to forget that you were jerking off, just make a joke about kids getting shot. And I thought, 'Jokes about kids getting shot.' I can do that."

Oliver talks about his son. He left him off at school on Valentine's Day. "I love you," the son tells his dad before leaving the car. Two hours later he was shot and killed.

"You guys ever heard dead baby jokes? I got a dead baby. His name was Joaquin Oliver. He's going to be 18, but now he's dead."

Oliver pauses. He looks straight at the camera. "And that's not a joke."

In the summer of 2020, March for Our Lives launched a TV ad which aired in nine key states. It was featured at the Democratic National Convention in 2020. Narrated by Emma Gonzalez, the ad calls for the banning of weapons of war. "When we were stuck inside, we wondered, would we face the plague of gun violence again?"

"Will we fear gathering in our schools and our churches again?" she asks. "Will we be shot for the color of our skins again? But a fight for justice forced us out to fill the empty streets."

The group is motivated by issues, not personalities. "We endorse policies, not people," said a spokesman for the March. "The most change we've seen in gun violence prevention happens on the state and local level."

In the summer of 2019, March for Our Lives issued a proposal called "A Peace Plan for a Safer America" which reiterated the group's demands for a federal gun buy-back program, a ban on assault weapons, and the creation of a national gun registry.

Despite their nation-wide recognition, the Parkland gun-control activists suffered a collective body blow on their home turf. In the spring of 2019, the Florida legislature approved legislation permitting teachers to carry guns in their classrooms. The Florida governor was expected to sign the bill into law. From the point of view of the Parkland activists, it was a case of two steps forward, one step backward. Gun control activist, Gay Valimont, who leads the state's chapter of Moms Demand Action for Gun Sense in America, was quick to condemn the bill. "The risks of arming teachers are well documented, as is the research indicating there are much better ways to keep our kids safe in school, "she said.

Passage of the bill was marked by a shouting match among lawmakers. "What happens when [a] teacher [who is overwhelmed] feels threatened?" asked one legislator. "We see accidents happening every day," said one of his Democratic colleagues.

Despite clear opposition to the measure from Florida voters, Republicans who controlled the legislature, pushed through the bill. In so doing, they rejected more than 20 amendments proposed by Democrats. One of these would have required implicit bias training for armed teachers. "I asked for implicit bias training because we're talking about Black boys and girls that are getting murdered by police officers," said the legislator who had proposed the amendment. "There are bad police officers and there are bad teachers."

Said one Republican leader, "When law enforcement can't get there to save others, I hope there's someone in that room who is able."

Fedrick Ingram, president of the Florida Education Association, joined the fray with these comments:

> Parents and educators should ask tough questions. Will teachers wear guns, or how will firearms be stored? Will parents and teachers be told if the teacher in any given classroom is armed? Can parents opt their kids out of a class where the teacher is carrying? . . . If a weapon is accidentally fired or displayed by a teacher, what reporting and disciplinary measures will be in place? There are a lot of questions a district needs to answer if it plans to allow armed teachers.

As happened at Sandy Hook, there were financial consequences to the Parkland shooting. Sixteen of the seventeen students and staff members killed at Marjory Stoneman Douglas High School reached a $127.5 million settlement with the US Department of Justice over the FBI's failure to follow up on a tip it had received five weeks before the Cruz attack. The caller had said that Cruz had bought guns and planned to "slip into a school and start shooting the place up."

✳✳✳

Santa fe high, May 18, 2018. Seventeen-year-old Dimitrios Pagourtzis killed ten students and teachers and wounded thirteen others in a small town thirty miles south of Houston, Texas.

This half hour rampage is the bloody coda of a chapter which contains only a sampling of the school attacks to occur in the past twenty years. There are others—all too many others. School shootings have become so common that people have become anesthetized by them. Their power to shock is dulled by the near-monthly repetition of the massacres. At times they seem to have been woven seamlessly into the fabric of the nation.

Are there any copycat similarities to these butcheries? The shooters at some of these crime scenes sport Nazi symbols on their clothes. Their backpacks. Their book bags. Their weapons include a sawed-off shotgun. Or an AR-15. Or an AK-47. Or a semi-automatic Glock handgun (purchased legally or filched from a parent's gun rack). Or some combination of these. And more often than not, the shooters want to rack up as big a body count as they can, to slaughter at least as many people as the shooters before them.

Pagourtzis, the shooter at Santa Fe High wore a trench coat, again like Harris and Klebold in Columbine. And he wore a T-shirt with "Born to Kill" on it. He shouted something before he opened fire. It sounded like "Surprise!" Then he shot a closet-full of cowering students at the school's art complex. Later he told police that he aimed to spare those students he liked and targeted those he didn't. The shooter was mentally ill. It was crazy watching him shoot and then pump, one Santa Fe student said. The student went on to say, "I remember seeing the shrapnel from the tables, whatever he hit; I remember the shrapnel go past my face."

The Florida Department of Children and Families knew that Nikolas Cruz, the shooter at Douglas High School, had cut his arms and talked of buying a gun. One visit and a handful of questions persuaded the department that he was at low risk of hurting himself or others.

After each shooting, public officials mouth the standard pieties. Consider this pronouncement from a Baptist preacher after the Santa Fe shooting: "We have fallen away from God and put other gods in front of Him. God is not a genie that we can rub from a magic lamp."

Or consider this opinion from President Trump who, after offering prayers and condolences from the victims of the Parkland killings, said: "No child, teacher or anyone else should ever feel unsafe in an American school."

Or this refreshing contrast by Kelly Clarkson, host of Billboard Awards, who said on the night awards were presented:

> Before we start tonight's show, there's something I'd like to . . . this is going to be so hard—there's something I'd like to say about the tragedy, Friday, at Santa Fe High School.

Pausing, she struggled to continue:

> I'm so sorry. I'm a Texas girl and my home state has had so much heartbreak over this past year, and once again we're grieving for more kids who've died for [absolutely] no reason at all. And tonight they wanted me to say that obviously we want to pray for all the victims and pray for their families, but they also wanted me to do a 'moment of silence.'
>
> And **I'm so sick of 'moment of silence.' It's not working,** obviously, so, why don't we **not do** a moment of silence. Why don't we [do a] 'moment of action'? Why don't we do a moment of change? Why don't we change what's happening. (Applause) because it's horrible.
>
> And mamas and daddies should be able to send their kids to school, to church, to movie theaters . . . You should be able to live life without that kind of fear.
>
> So, we need to do better. We need to do better as people. We're failing our children. We're failing our communities, we're failing their families.
>
> I can't imagine—I have four children. I can't imagine getting that phone call or knock at the door. So, instead of a moment of silence, I want to respect them and honor them. Tonight, y'all, in your community, where you live, your friends, everybody . . . **let's have a moment of action—a moment of change.**

Two weeks after the shooting in Santa Fe, Trump visited victims in the hospital. He combined the visit with two big fundraisers in Texas.

The Houston police chief put some teeth in his comment on

Pagourtzis' killings:

> It's a time for asking of God's forgiveness . . . for our inaction, especially the elected officials that ran to the camera today, acted in a solemn manner, called for prayers and will once again do absolutely nothing.

Newspaper photos were virtually interchangeable, from one mass shooting to another. How many times have we seen teenage girls—particularly pretty blonde girls—sobbing in their mothers' arms? Was there a pattern in these mass murders? There seemed to be a pattern in how we perceived them.

But there was a ray of hope that pierced the gloom. Hours after the shooting at Santa Fe, David Hogg and Emma Gonzalez—now media celebrities after March for Our Lives—contacted a student activist in Santa Fe. The student—who recognized that she was in a minority in a gun-besotted suburb of Houston—subsequently participated in a sit-in at the Washington, D.C., office of Texas Senator Ted Cruz.

Changing the way politicians talk about massacres will not be easy. Less than one year after what happened at Parkland, a Republican, Matt Gaetz, who represents Florida's First Congressional district (which spans the state's panhandle), spoke scathingly against murders committed by illegal immigrants. He told the press that better background checks "would not have stopped many of the [massacres], but a wall, a barrier on the southern border may have, and that's what we're fighting for."

Besides the shooting at Parkland, there was a shooting of five people at Fort Lauderdale airport; the killings at the Pulse nightclub in Orlando; and the execution-style slaying of five women who worked at a bank in Sebring. All these occurred less than three years before Gaetz made his remarks. They all occurred in his home state of Florida.

And they were all committed by native-born Americans.

CHAPTER SIX:
Thoughts and Prayers

It was a Thursday, June 28, 2018, when Jarrod W. Ramos, a man with a score to settle, walked into the offices of the *Capitol Gazette* in Annapolis, Maryland, shotgun in hand, and shot to death five people. In a letter to the newspaper's lawyer, Ramos contended that he planned to go to the *Capital Gazette* with "the objective of killing every person present."

Donald Trump made the remark which has become a standard response of politicians, particularly those on the Right, to assaults of this kind: He offered the victims of the attack his thoughts and prayers. To which one reporter, who had spent the slaughter of her colleagues cowering beneath her desk, responded:

> I'm going to need more than a couple days of news coverage and some thoughts and prayers because our whole lives have been shattered. Thanks [Trump] for your prayers but I couldn't give a fuck about them if there's nothing else.

Senator Marco Rubio (R-FL) wasted not one syllable of sympathy for the victims of the shooting itself, but he did take Twitter time to moralize about the journalist's use of profanity: "Sign of our times. The F word is now routinely used in news stories, tweets etc. It's not even F*** anymore. Who made that decision?"

Politicians and public figures have used the phrase "thoughts and prayers" (or some variant thereof) so much that it has become first meaningless, a right-wing cliché, then something to ridicule. The phrase has popped up in responses to every massacre covered in the last chapter, from Columbine to Parkland, to others as well and to natural disasters. President Lyndon Johnson offered thoughts and prayers when Charles Whitman stood on top the tower at UT and killed fifteen people, not including his own mother and wife. Governor Sam Brownback of Kansas fell back on the phrase when he urged people to "send your thoughts and prayers to the people of Hesston" when Cedrick Ford shot up the Excel plant in that town.

One comedian, Anthony Jeselnik, has built a routine on the stock phrase, one which ends with a mocking question. Like the reporter at the Annapolis *Capitol Gazette*, he hears thoughts and prayers, and he asks what that's worth. His answer: "Fucking nothing."

As for the officials who intone that hackneyed phrase, what they're really saying is "Don't forget about me."

The phrase found a place in the first debate between Ted Cruz (R-TX) and his challenger, Beto O'Rourke. Cruz blamed society for removing God from the public square. To which O'Rourke snapped back, "Thoughts and prayers, Senator Cruz, are just not going to cut it anymore."

The survivors of the Parkland shooting used the phrase their own way: They spelled out the words "thoughts and prayers" with body bags on the National Mall in Washington, D.C.—one thousand one hundred—of them. "This is still happening and we need . . . to keep pushing . . . our president and Congress to do something," said one of the cofounders of March for Our Lives.

If Thomas Aquinas were writing this book, he might have composed the following catechismal exchange:

> Q: Why does a politician like Ted Cruz bring up God when he speaks?
>
> A: Because it appeals to his evangelical followers.
>
> Q: What would it mean to restore God to the public square?
>
> A: Probably more talk about religion.

Q: Would that help?

A: That depends. Is there less violence in a theocracy than in a secular society?

The staff at the *Capital Gazette* were included in Time's awards for 2018 Person of the Year whom the magazine called "The Guardians." All those recognized in the award were journalists. They included Jamal Khashoggi and reporters who covered the president of the Philippines, Rodrigo Duterte, and reporters who exposed the murder of Rohingya Muslims in Myanmar (Burma).

"As we looked at the choices," said *Time* editor Edward Felsenthal, "it became clear that manipulation and the abuse of truth is really the common thread in so many of this year's stories, from Russia to Riyadh to Silicon Valley."

It seemed a natural to trot out a phrase involving prayer when public officials commented on shootings which occurred at churches. Here are two examples from the recent past:

FIRST: On June 17, 2015, a 21-year-old white supremacist gunned down nine worshippers at a historic Black church in Charleston, South Carolina.

The church, which was called the Emanuel African Methodist Episcopal Church, dates back to the opening days of the nineteenth century. The oldest Black denomination church in the state of South Carolina, it was cofounded by a man called Denmark Vesey who had purchased his freedom after winning a lottery in 1799. Vesey still associated with and identified with Black slaves. He organized them and freed Blacks to launch a revolt which was scheduled for mid-June 1822. But the plot was discovered. Vesey was arrested and hanged the following month. One of his sons rebuilt the church which Vesey had founded and which had been damaged during the Civil War

One hundred and fifty years later, a young fanatic, Dylann Roof—that was the murderer's name—joined a prayer meeting there. The twelve congregants had met to discuss a passage from the Gospel of St. Mark. Their subject was the parable about the sower: "The sower soweth the word . . . but . . . Satan cometh immediately and taketh away the word that was sown in their hearts."

An hour after arriving, Roof pulled out of his fanny pack a couple of pistols and killed all but three of the participants. This act of race hatred may set him apart from the psychopathic killers listed in the previous chapter, but is this a distinction without a difference? Like Nikolas Cruz, the shooter at Parkland High School, Roof was smitten with insignia associated with the Third Reich in Germany. He loved all things German—everything from one of Goethe's romantic novels to Haydn's Clock Symphony—and prided himself on the Teutonic origin of his last name. White supremacist regimes fascinated him: He had the flags of the (White-run) Rhodesia Republic and apartheid South Africa sewn onto one of his jackets. Roof admitted to police after his arrest that his intent was to spark a race war.

Examination by psychiatrists and psychologists could not dissuade the judge in the case that the young racist was capable of standing trial. He ruled that Roof did "not suffer from any mental disease or defect which renders him unable to understand" his legal situation. One forensic psychologist who examined Roof did produce a laundry list of psychological conditions—including a schizoid personality disorder—from which Roof suffered, but these did not amount to schizophrenia and did not make him psychopathic.

Thoughts and prayers in regard to the church slayings were not long in coming, albeit in a more intelligent way than usual. President Barak Obama said this at a press conference:

> Michelle and I know several members of Emanuel AME Church. We know their pastor, Reverend Clementa Pinckney, who, along with eight others, gathered in prayer and fellowship and was murdered last night. And to say our thoughts and prayers are with them and their families, and their community, doesn't say enough to convey the heartache and the sadness and the anger that we feel.

Nikki Haley, then governor of South Carolina, said:

> While we do not yet know all of the details, we do know that we'll never understand what motivates anyone to enter one of our places of worship and take the life of another. Please

join us in lifting up the victims and their families with our love and prayers.

During Roof's trial, details of the massacre emerged. He had arrived twenty minutes late for Bible study that night. At the conclusion of the meeting, he pulled out a semiautomatic pistol and began shooting.

One woman to attend the Bible study was a 58-year-old hair stylist named Felicia Sanders. She had come with her son Tywanza, a poet and a rapper, and her 11-year-old granddaughter. She testified at Dylann Roof's trial. First she told the jury how she had held her granddaughter to her—"I muzzled her face to my body so tight." Although her son Tywanza had been shot once, he managed to raise himself to his elbows and confront Roof.

"Why are you doing this?" he cried out to Roof.

The generally laconic Roof told him, "I have to do this. I have to do this because [you] sic raping our women and y'all taking over the world."

Tywanza Sanders said, "You don't have to do this. We don't mean you no harm."

Roof then fired five more bullets into Tywanza Sanders' body.

Felicia Sanders told the court that her son, the poet and rapper, crawled across the basement room of Emanuel African Methodist Episcopal Church.

"I watched him take his last breath," Felicia Sanders told the jury. "I watched my son come in this world, and I watched my son leave this world . . . I watched him die."

Dylann Roof's family attended his trial only sporadically. His mother Amy was in attendance during Felicia Sanders' testimony. She started to tremble as the Black hair dresser spoke. She lay down and began to moan. Then she shot up and cried out, "I'm sorry! I'm sorry! I'm sorry!"

Amy Roof collapsed on the floor and was taken from the courtroom on a stretcher. Throughout this drama, Dylann did not so much as turn his head, topped with its pudding-bowl haircut, to look at his mother. Who never came back to his trial. Dylann Roof was found guilty on all counts and sentenced to death.

SECOND: A domestic dispute involving a man and his mother-in-law lay at the root of a church shooting in a small town in Texas, Sutherland Springs, about thirty miles from San Antonio. The killer was an ex-serviceman who had received a bad conduct discharge—which is a level below dishonorable discharge—from the Air Force in 2014. He had worked at Holloman Air Force Base in New Mexico as a logistical readiness airman.

Devin Patrick Kelley was court-martialed in 2012 for assaulting his first wife and a stepchild. He was sentenced to a year in prison and demoted in rank. In the summer of 2014, the year he remarried, Kelley had another run-in with the law. The issue this time was animal abuse. A police report said that Kelley had been beating a brown and white husky. He struck the dog, which was whining and yelping, on the head and chest. Then Kelley picked up the animal and threw it on the ground. The police charged Kelley with animal cruelty. His husky ended up with the Humane Society where it underwent a medical evaluation.

Kelley did not get along with his mother-in-law. Six months before a massacre at the First Baptist Church in Sutherland Springs, he threatened Michelle Shields if she tried to enter the hospital room where his second wife, Danielle, Michelle's daughter, lay after giving birth to the couple's second child.

"I will personally make it my mission to destroy your entire life," he texted her. "I suggest you don't test my resolve."

In another message, he wrote "You think this is a fucking game? It's not."

"I wasn't going to disobey," Kelley's mother-in-law told a reporter from the *San Antonio Express-News*.

It was six months before Michelle saw her new granddaughter. The occasion was a family get-together at a church festival, five days before the massacre. Kelley was on meds for mental illness, and Michelle hoped against hope that her son-in-law was coming round. The shooter's parents had kept him on what a classmate described as "psych" drugs while he was in middle school.

Michelle Shields talked about how Kelley had tried to drive a wedge between her daughter Danielle and her family. When she called, Kelley would turn on the speakerphone so that he could eavesdrop on their conversation. If something which displeased him was said, he would make Danielle hang up.

"He was afraid I was going to try to talk Danielle out of the relationship," Michelle guessed. "I wasn't going to do that. I just wanted her [to be] happy. I just wanted to talk to her."

In an exclusive interview with the *San Antonio Express-News*, she said:

> I want people to never lose contact with their children because you never know what's going on in their relationship. Just stay focused on their lives. You don't have to pry . . . just let them know that you're there and you love them, that a parent's love for their child is unconditional and never-ending and that you'll always be there for them.

Michelle Shields and her husband, Benjamin (Danielle's step-father), were members of the First Baptist Church which Kelley attacked on the morning of November 5, 2017. Kelley was a strident atheist. Religious differences may have been at the heart of his animosity toward Michelle.

Whatever his motive, Kelley donned a face mask emblazoned with a white skull, circled the First Baptist Church in Sunderland Springs on November 5, 2017, a Ruger AR-556 assault-type rifle in hand, and began shooting anyone who got in his path. He then entered the building and methodically began mowing down parishioners, left and right, young and old, ages one and a half years to 77, starting from the front of the church and working his way back. An unidentified man wrenched the gun out of his hands. The day Kelley had chosen for his rampage was one on which his mother-in-law—possibly his intended target—was absent from the church.

As Kelley ran to make his escape, he was confronted by Stephen Willeford, an NRA instructor, who had heard the shots and run barefoot into the road. He confronted Kelly with an AR-15 and shot him before Kelley continued to flee in his SUV. At the same time, a resident named Johnnie Langendorff drove by in his truck. Willeford yanked open the door. "That guy just shot up the Baptist church," he yelled at the driver. "We need to stop him."

Langendorff's two-syllable reply: "Let's go."

Willeford hopped in and off they went.

"I had to make sure he [Kelley] was caught," Langendorff, later told a CNN reporter. When asked what was going through his mind, he replied, "Nothing. Get him."

Why? "Because that's what you do. You chase a bad guy."

The two men chased after Kelley. Both Kelley's Ford SUV and Langendorff's truck careered down the highway at speeds which, at times, exceeded 90 miles an hour. During the chase, Kelley telephoned his father to say that he had been shot and would probably not make it.

Kelley hit a stop sign, lost control of his vehicle and crashed into a ditch. Willeford propped his rifle on the hood of Johnnie Langendorff's truck and yelled at him to get out of his car. Langendorff sprinted into the road to direct traffic. When the police arrived five minutes later, they found that the shooter had ended his life with a bullet to the brain.

A bad conduct discharge from the Air Force meant that Kelley did not have the right to purchase or own firearms like the Ruger handgun and a Glock found in his car just after the shooting. Kelley's first wife told officers of the 49th Security Forces Squadron of her husband's abusive behavior. Late in 2011, Kelley pushed his wife against a wall and choked her. Her offense? She did not want to visit Kelley's family. On another occasion he kicked her in the stomach, dragged her by her hair to the bathroom, and said "I'm going to waterboard you," whereupon he stuck her head under the showerhead.

The Air Force Office of Special Investigations interviewed Kelley on a separate occasion when allegations that he had abused his stepson surfaced. Kelley first denied that he had hurt the child, but he eventually confessed that he had pushed the toddler down and shaken him more than once.

The Air Force neglected to inform Federal officials of Kelley's conviction, and that failure of communication allowed him to purchase weapons which he used in his assault on the church in Sutherland Springs.

Kelley's pursuers were regarded as heroes in Sutherland Springs. Both were members of the NRA and, subsequent to the attack on the Baptist church, Willeford appeared in an NRA ad to recruit new members. His three kids were all expert shots by the time they were eight years old. President Donald Trump invited Willeford to his State of the Union speech in 2018. Both he and Langendorff were recognized at the NRA Foundation Banquet. An NRA publication saw in Willeford a civilian who upheld the organization's slogan that the best way to stop a bad guy with a gun was a good guy with a gun.

The man he did stop, Devin Kelley, perpetrated the worst church massacre in Texas history before Willeford shot him. In fact, it was the worst church massacre in US history. By the time Willeford had pumped a couple of bullets through the interstices of his body armor, Kelley had shot and killed 26 people and wounded another 20. A local sheriff speculated that Kelley might have gone on to attack another church two miles from Sunderland Springs, had it not been for Willeford. But the killer did abandon his rifle at the First Baptist Church.

Johnnie Langendorff is a much younger man than Willeford, lanky and generally laconic. He works at an auto parts store, and he wears a Stetson with a beaded hat band, a feather affixed to it. He also has a steer skull tattooed on his throat, the animal's horns curling up toward his jaws.

Willeford is a grizzled, jowly man, and he is shy of the national press. He posted a hand-written message on a chair on his porch. It read: "Not talking to the media! My time is not free!" He declined several requests to talk to The *Washington Post*. Willeford was willing, however, to be interviewed by the NRA. "We're just concerned that our message is going to change when we do an interview, that it's not going to be exactly what we say or how we feel; it's going to turn into something that it's not."

Thoughts and prayers were not long in gushing from the gullets of politicians, all the way from Donald Trump down through the likes of Speaker of the House, Paul Ryan. This time, however, criticism of the sanctimonious display came from legislators like Elizabeth Warren (D-MA):

> How many kids must die of gun violence on playground & streets every day with no attention at all before we wake up to what's happening? [The Senator from Massachusetts tweeted] Thoughts & prayers are not enough, GOP. We must end this violence. We must stop these tragedies. People are dying while you wait.

Columnist Leonard Pitts of the *Miami Herald* questioned why the American public was so blasé about the mass shootings in the country and he speculated:

> Do you think that if the Texas killer had had an exotic name or began his attack with a cry of 'Allahu Akbar!' our responses would be limited to thoughts and prayers and lawmakers would be content to mouth impotent pieties?

Several months after the attack on the Baptist church in Sutherland Springs, the massacre at Douglas High School in Parkland, Florida unleased a surge of student activism on behalf of gun control. That surge failed to reach Sutherland Springs which remains a bedrock NRA stronghold. There the mantra that "the best way to stop a bad guy with a gun is a good guy with a gun" is accepted as a self-evident truth.

"The illogical rhetoric that came out of Parkland was depressing," said Frank Pomeroy, pastor of First Baptist Church in Sutherland Springs. The tragedy at Parkland was "politicized" in Pomeroy's opinion; it was "overtaken by ideology."

Pomeroy and his wife Sherri missed church that fateful Sunday, thus escaping Kelley's blood lust, but their family did not emerge unscathed from his attack. Their 14-year-old daughter Annabelle was one who died on November 5. Pomeroy said of his wife that she was "still very fragile" after the death of their daughter.

The Houston Chronicle photographed Pomeroy officiating at the pulpit of his church, a Kimber 9mm pistol strapped to his hip. In the foreground of the photo, 34-year-old Kris Workman is strumming on his guitar. Workman is seated in a wheelchair. Kelley had stood over him on November 5 and shot him, severing two vertebrae in his back and partially paralyzing him. Doctors told Workman that he would never walk again, but he has recovered some use of his left leg.

> God is working. God is big, and if he decides that I'm going to walk again, I'll walk again [Workman said]. And if he doesn't, that's OK, too. You know it doesn't matter because whatever I'm intended to do, it's not a surprise to God, and if that includes me being in a wheelchair, that's OK.

Pomeroy has said that, "I keep the memories with me, but I take them with me and move forward, and know that Annabelle is moving forward with me."

Michelle Shields also retained memories. Her son-in-law had killed Michelle's mother at the church on November 5. Michelle could not sleep. She kept imaging what happened in the church that November morning. Months after the event, letters of condolences were still coming from every corner of the globe.

"I've actually gone through reading the notes, and I could just feel the love as they're writing it." She went on to say: "There's a lot of good people in the world that have a lot of kindness and care for each other. You don't see it until something really happens, and then it makes you realize that they are out there, that people do pray, and people do care."

Michelle Shields has given up her bank job which she held for a quarter of a century. She hopes to work for FEMA disaster relief in places like Houston and Puerto Rico.

> I want to go over there and give other people a hand that have different types of pain, or different types of trouble. Just to know there are people out there that care. That's something I feel like I need to do because so many people have done that for us.

The THIRD and last example occurred while this book was being written. On a Sabbath—Saturday, October 27, 2018—a middle-aged gunman tore through the Tree of Life Synagogue in Pittsburgh, PA. He killed eleven, mostly elderly worshippers and wounded six other people, including three police officers. The man accused of the massacre, Robert Bowers, was himself shot and injured and taken to a hospital where, ironically, he was cared for by Jews.

His motive? Bowers had an account on Gab, a social media network, frequented by white nationalists unwelcome on other networks like Twitter or Facebook. On his account, Bowers had a link to a Jewish nonprofit organization, which he had captioned, "You like to bring in hostile invaders to dwell among us?" When he gave himself up to the cops who arrested him, he said that he "wanted all Jews to die and also that they were committing genocide" against his people.

The gunman continued ranting that he wanted "to kill all the Jews" even as he was being treated in the emergency room of Allegheny General Hospital by a team of Jewish doctors and nurses. Head of the hospital, Jeffrey K. Cohen, said of his patient that, "I thought it was important to at least talk to him and meet him. You can't on the one hand say we should talk to each other, and then I don't talk to him. So you lead by example."

Cohen was a congregant at the Tree of Life Synagogue. He views Bowers as the product, not the instigator of bigger problems, what with "all the chaos that's going on." He condemned those who fostered an atmosphere of hatred. "It's time for leaders to lead [he said]. And the words mean things. And the words are leading to people doing things like this, and I find it appalling."

Cohen actually stopped by Bowers' bed to ask him how he was doing. Bowers told him that he was fine. The FBI agent guarding the shooter was impressed by the doctor's humanity. "I don't know that I could have done that," he said.

Bowers had twenty-one guns registered in his name. He carried out his assault on the Pittsburgh synagogue with an AR-15 rifle and three handguns. Neighbors described him as a quiet man who kept to himself. He told one of them that he was a truck driver who used his apartment—described in one newspaper account as a "shabby one-bedroom" place—to store his things. The boyfriend of one of his neighbors told a reporter that, coming home late one night, he saw Bowers sitting in his car "smoking and apparently listening to the radio."

President Trump was not slow to condemn the attack on the synagogue, telling reporters at Andrews Air Force Base, "It's a terrible, terrible thing what's going on with hate in our country."

"The results are very devastating," he went on. If the synagogue "had some kind of protection, it would have been a much different situation."

The president lost no time in deciding to visit the scene of the massacre. His visit, coming three days later, was not universally welcomed. Eleven members of a Pittsburgh affiliate of an organization called Bend the Arc wrote an open letter to Trump to say that he would not be welcome to come to Pittsburgh until he denounced white nationalists.

Bend the Arc is an organization of progressive Jews dedicated to social justice. Thirty-five thousand people signed the letter written on behalf of Bend the Arc which said, in part, that:

> For the past three years your words and your policies have emboldened a growing white nationalist movement. You yourself called the murderer evil, but yesterday's violence is the direct culmination of your influence.
>
> Our Jewish community is not the only group you have targeted. You have also deliberately undermined the safety of people of color, Muslims, LGBTQ people, and people with disabilities. Yesterday's massacre is not the first act of terror you incited against a minority group in our country.

Trump ignored the letter, refusing to comment on it. Despite advice to the contrary, the President flew to Pittsburgh on the Tuesday following the mass shooting. Two days before his visit, there was a vigil in the city that drew more than two thousand people. In his address to the crowd, Rabbi Jeffrey Myers of the Tree of Life Synagogue said that choosing good over evil begins with speech. "It starts with one simple step. Just stop the hate. Don't say it. Zip the lip. It just takes one person to make that difference."

The crowd erupted in an incessant chant: "Vote! Vote! Vote!"

One year after the Las Vegas massacre in 2017, in which Stephen Paddock killed 58 concert-goers, a gunman shot up a bar in the town of Thousand Oaks, CA. The bar was crammed with college kids, some of whom had attended the Route 91 festival in Las Vegas the night Paddock had mowed down attendees. It was a tragic irony that one survivor of the Route 91 slaughter lost his life in the Borderline Bar & Grill in Thousand Oaks. An affiliate of CNN interviewed the victim's mother. "My son was in Las Vegas with a lot of his friends and he came home," she said. "He didn't come home last night." She went on: "I don't want prayers. I don't want thoughts. I want gun control, and I hope to God nobody else sends me any more prayers. I want gun control. No more guns."

"We don't want to be 'Thoughts and Prayers' people," said the Rev. Kathleen Moore, an Episcopal priest in Ohio. The author of a litany to be recited in the wake of mass shootings, she said, "You want to be careful, but also don't throw prayer out—we believe in the power of prayer."

A man who is now an Episcopalian bishop—a man who was shot in the stomach and spent two months in an ICU—explained that:

> The function of this is keeping things in memory. Many people would like to forget it. Memory is one of the most important things, that makes us human. We can look back upon things and learn. It's like 'Say her name: Breonna Taylor!' Repeating it makes the events, the people holy. It sets those people apart with meaning, versus just a senseless act of violence.

Episcopalians are not the only religious group to react to violence. The website of the Jewish Reform movement offers "a Kaddish after Gun Violence, for when humanity fails itself." In 2016, the US Conference of Catholic Bishops issued a "Prayer for Peace in Our Communities" which refers to the violence [which surrounds us] and cries for justice.

CHAPTER SEVEN:
The Amendment

The Second Amendment to the Constitution of the US reads as follows:

> A well regulated Militia, being necessary to the security of a free State, the right of the people to keep and bear Arms, shall not be infringed.

The amendment was authored by James Madison of Virginia who sponsored it to allay the fears of his fellow Virginians—and by extension all Southerners—that a strong federal government would undermine the institution of slavery on which the Southern economy rested.

Chief Justice Warren Burger had this to say about the amendment:

> The gun lobby's interpretation of the Second Amendment is one of the greatest pieces of fraud, I repeat the word fraud, on the American people by special interest groups that I have ever seen in my lifetime. The real purpose of the Second Amendment was to ensure that state armies—the militia—would be maintained for the defense of the state. The very language of the Second Amendment refutes any argument that it was intended to guarantee every citizen an unfettered right to any kind of weapon he or she deserves.

Bret Stephens fell into step with those sentiments in a 2017 op-ed in which *The New York Times* columnist wrote: I have never understood the conservative fetish for the Second Amendment.

> From a law-and-order standpoint, more guns means more murder. "States with higher rates of gun ownership have disproportionately large numbers of deaths from fire-arm-related homicides," noted one exhaustive 2013 study in the American Journal of Public Health. . . . In fact, the more closely one looks at what passes for "common sense" gun laws, the more feckless they appear. Americans who claim to be outraged by gun crimes should want to do something more than tinker at the margins of a legal regime that most of the developed world rightly considers nuts. They should want to change it fundamentally and permanently.

There is only one way to do this: Repeal the Second Amendment.

What did the Founders intend by what became the Second Amendment to the Constitution? The historian Joyce Lee Malcolm wrote that "the right of individuals to be armed had become, as the [English] Bill of Rights claimed it was, an ancient and indubitable right. It was this heritage that Englishmen took with them to the American colonies and this heritage which Americans fought to protect in 1775." Or was it?

In his book, *The Second Amendment*, Michael Waldman, president of the Brennan Center for Justice at NYU School of Law, observes that the Second Amendment is the only one in the Bill of Rights that has an explanatory clause of any kind: A well-regulated Militia, being necessary to the security of a free state. This clause, called in Latin—a language familiar to many if not most of the Founders—an ablative absolute, provides what linguists would contend were "the conditions under which the rest of the sentence is valid."

Waldman asserts that

> We cannot truly know what the Framers intended. But one would have to look far to find evidence that their principal concern was the risk that government would enact gun safety laws, or disarm farmers.

The Second Amendment did not offer any protection to an individual to own a gun. That had been settled before in cases heard before the Supreme Court. Here is a quote from Waldman's book:

In the Reconstruction-era Cruikshank case, it ruled that the amendment did not cover the states. In *Presser [v. Illinois]*, it found that gun rights belonged to militias. In *Miller v. Texas* in 1894, it rejected the criminal defendant's gun right claim. In the 1939 Miller case, it upheld federal gun law, making clear that gun laws could not interfere with actual, current militia service. Lower courts agreed, when they considered the topic at all.

That all changed in 2008, when the Supreme Court issued an opinion in the case of *District of Columbia v. Heller*. The decision, written by Justice Antonin Scalia, reaffirmed the individual's right to bear firearms, independently of membership in a militia. The syllabus (summary) of that finding reads in part:

> The Second Amendment protects an individual right to possess a firearm unconnected with service in a militia, and to use that arm for traditionally lawful purposes, such as self-defense within the home. The Amendment's prefatory clause announces a purpose, but does not limit or expand the scope of the second part, the operative clause. The operative clause's text and history demonstrate that it connotes an individual right to keep and bear arms.

Chief Justice John Roberts entrusted the writing of the majority opinion in Heller to Scalia. Making such an assignment was something which Roberts' predecessor, William Rehnquist, had never done. The Heller decision was the most important piece of writing which Scalia did while serving on the Supreme Court.

In writing for the majority in Heller, Scalia claimed that the Second Amendment meant "the individual" when it said "people." But the decision in *District of Columbia v. Heller* left open the question of government regulation. Here is Scalia again:

> Nothing in our opinion should be taken to cast doubt on longstanding prohibitions on the possession of firearms by felons and the mentally ill, or laws forbidding the carrying of firearms in sensitive places such as schools and government buildings, or laws imposing conditions and qualifications on the commercial sale of arms.

Antonin Scalia is associated with an interpretation of the

Constitution known as originalism. That term means that the way to interpret the Constitution is by trying to understand what the Founding Fathers would have meant by its language. The idea goes back at least as far as the jurist Robert Bork who wrote of "original intent." Only "original understanding... is consonant with the design of the American republic," he wrote two years before President Ronald Regan nominated him—unsuccessfully—to the Court. Justice Brennon dismissed originalism as "arrogance cloaked as humility." How is it possible to plumb the minds of the Founding Fathers who lived in a world where (as Michael Waldman has written) "citizen soldiers bought their own military weapons and stored them at home, and where the idea of a United States Army would be enough to send patriots to grab their musket." More than two centuries have passed since James Madison and Company penned the Constitution. Are courts to disregard all that has happened in that time in rendering their judgments? Had the Framers (as Michael Waldman asks) "wanted us to read their words, their misplaced commas, as if they were Scripture?"

But to return to the specific issue of gun control:

Gary Wills, a theologian and historian, writing in the *Boston Globe*, considered gun control "inconceivable": "Everyone knows that guns are what made this country great, taming the West, keeping up our fighting spirit, shoving sissies aside as we make our tough progress."

> "It is also theologically inconceivable. God gave us guns to show us who we are. Giving up the gun would be surrender to evil, taking us abruptly into eschatological time.
>
> "So this time let us skip all the sighing and promising and moments of silence. Why keep up the pretense that we are going to take any real and practical steps toward sanity?
>
> "Everyone knows we are not going to do a single damn thing. We can't. We are captives of The Gun. The Gun is patriotic. The Gun is America. The Gun is God."

If—as per *District of Columbia v. Heller*—the need to arm men was to support militias, then what were those militias for?

Was it to protect Yankee colonists against British redcoats, like the Minutemen at Lexington and Concord? Not quite. According to prolific author, Roxanne Dunbar-Ortiz, "[they] were intended as a means for White people to eliminate indigenous communities in order to take their land, and for slave patrols to control Black people."

Dunbar-Ortiz buttresses her thesis by citing legal requirements that able-bodied men carry weapons. The colony of Virginia required male travelers to be well-armed. It extracted a fine for those men who went to work or church without an arm. In 1658, every home had to have a weapon. The New England colonies similarly demanded in 1632 that everyone have a firearm, two pounds of gun powder, and ten pounds of bullets. "No man was to appear at a public meeting unarmed," Dunbar-Ortiz writes.

The Second Amendment enshrined the settlers' right to battle indigenous people for their land, their property, their very lives. This is how she describes the conflict:

> Although the US Constitution formally instituted 'militias' as state-controlled bodies that were subsequently deployed to wage wars against Native Americans, the voluntary militias described in the Second Amendment entitled settlers, as individuals and families, to the right to combat Native Americans on their own.

In his paper, "The Hidden History of the Second Amendment," Carl T. Bogus advanced a thesis that:

> James Madison wrote the Second Amendment to assure the Southern states that Congress would not undermine the slave system by disarming the militia, which were then the principal instruments of slave control throughout the South.

A synopsis of the Bogus article to appear in the Violence Policy Center says:

> Virginia was nearly half-Black, and the White population lived in constant fear of slave insurrection. The main instrument of control was the militia. So critical was the militia for slave control that, in the main, the Southern states refused to commit their militia to the war against the British. The

Constitution, however, would transfer the lion's share of the power over the militia to Congress. Slavery was becoming increasingly obnoxious to the North, and Southern delegates to the Philadelphia convention demanded and got an agreement, somewhat cryptically written into the Constitution that deprived the federal government of authority to abolish slavery. [George] Mason and [Patrick] Henry raised the specter of Congress using its authority over the militia to do indirectly what it could not do directly.

Henry spoke at the ratification convention in Virginia, urging delegates to reject the Constitution. It gave Congress too much authority over the states, he argued. "They'll take your niggers from you," Henry said to the laughter of the assembly.

Bogus' account of deliberations in Southern states like Virginia dovetails with what Dunbar-Ortiz writes, to the effect that slave patrols came into existence to control the Black population and to hunt down run-away slaves. Dunbar-Ortiz quotes from an 1860 hornbook (a primer for study), *The Practice of Law in North Carolina,* to illustrate how such patrols were to function:

> The patrol shall visit the negro houses in their respective districts as often as may be necessary, and may inflict a punishment, not exceeding fifteen lashes, on all slaves they may find off their owners' plantations, without a proper permit or pass, designating the place or places, to which the slaves have leave to go. The patrol shall also visit all suspected places, and suppress all unlawful collections of slaves; shall be diligent in apprehending all runaway negroes, in their respective districts; shall be diligent and endeavor to detect all thefts, and bring the perpetrators to justice, and all persons guilty of trading with slaves; and if, upon taking up a slave and chastising him, as herein directed, he shall behave insolently, they may inflict further punishment for his misconduct, not exceeding thirty-nine lashes.

Slaves were a valuable commodity. By the second decade of the nineteenth century, after the soil of Tidewater Virginia had been depleted by mono-production and overproduction, the principal commodity of the plantations was the physical bodies of the slaves. Estates became breeding grounds for slaves. Thomas Jefferson boasted to George Washington that—in Dunbar-Ortiz's wording—"the birth of Black children was increasing Virginia's capital stock by four percent per annum."

Historian and law professor, Sally Hidden, notes that the language of slave patrols persists to this day in expressions used by the police, expressions like "patrol" itself and "beat."

Suggestions of a "cure" for the Second Amendment range all over the ballpark. In an op-ed piece for *The New York Times*, former associate justice John Paul Stevens raised the possibility of radical surgery. "Repeal the Amendment," he wrote. The amendment's concern for a well-regulated militia is "a relic of the eighteenth century." Stevens was one of four justices to dissent in *District of Columbia v. Heller*. Of that case, Stevens writes:

> That decision—which I remain convinced was wrong and certainly debatable—has provided the NRA with a propaganda weapon of immense power. Overturning that decision via a constitutional amendment to get rid of the Second Amendment would be simple and would do more to weaken the NRA's ability to stymie legislative debate and block gun control legislation than any other available option.

Not so fast, cautions Harvard law professor, Laurence Tribe. Stevens' call to abolish the amendment "handed the gun lobby a rhetorical howitzer." A repeal campaign "wouldn't eliminate a single gun or enact a single gun regulation."

Tribe added that:

> There is undoubted emotional appeal in a call to arms organized around an aim as lofty as the elimination of the Second Amendment [Tribe goes on]. Its very unattainability adds to its allure. I can't deny feeling the pull of that appeal myself. But our shared goal is surely not just to make ourselves feel good about our audacious hopes, but also to protect our children from being ripped to shreds by bullets and terrorized by that prospect.
>
> Given that goal, our solemn obligation is to focus on the real obstacle to progress on gun regulation. That obstacle is not the Second Amendment but the addiction of lawmakers to the money of firearms manufacturers and other unimaginably

wealthy funders. That, coupled with the gun lobby's ability to mobilize single-issue gun rights voters, is set against the backdrop of a gun culture and national history that valorizes guns. None of those realities would be eliminated by erasing the Second Amendment's 27 words from the Constitution.

Tribe compared what students like David Hogg and Emma Gonzalez did favorably with what Stevens recommends. Noting that the NRA's strongest rallying cry has been, "They're coming for our beloved Second Amendment," Stevens bolstered the gun lobby by calling for the amendment's repeal. The Parkland students were more astute than that. Wrote Tribe:

> The kids have been savvy enough to know better. They have reminded everyone that the Second Amendment's right to bear arms, even as interpreted by a conservative Supreme Court and the right-leaning lower federal courts is far from absolute. It permits Congress and the states to outlaw what the court in *District of Columbia v. Heller* called 'dangerous and unusual weapons' and those 'not typically possessed by law-abiding citizens for lawful purposes,' and to comprehensively regulate gun sales and places guns can be carried. Over the past decade, the court has let stand bans on semi-automatic assault rifles, limits on the sale of large magazines and restrictions on the number of guns a person can stockpile. It has left no doubt that Congress can require universal gun registration, that states can forbid gun sales to anyone under 21, and that government can red-flag potentially dangerous purchasers, ban concealed carry and enact sweeping safety measures. Relying on that legal reality, the young have reassured Americans fearful of confiscation that they do not seek the repeal of the Second Amendment.

Tribe acknowledges the emotional pull of repealing the Amendment, whose "Very unattainability adds to its appeal."

The National Rifle Association

THE NATIONAL RIFLE ASSOCIATION was established in 1871 by two Union Army veterans, Colonel William C. Church and General George Wingate, in New York. The two officers were appalled by the lack of skill with guns on the part of Union soldiers during the Civil War. One report estimated that it took the Yankee troops one thousand shots to score one hit on a Confederate soldier. The two Union officers aimed to do something about this by "promoting and encouraging rifle shooting on a scientific basis." The state of New York even provided money for the fledgling organization which used it the following year to purchase property in Long Island for a rifle range. Opposition to the goals of the NRA forced the club to move its matches from New York to New Jersey.

Prohibition ushered in an era of armed bank robberies and gangsters like John Dillinger mowing down his competition with machine guns. To counteract this mayhem, Congress enacted legislation to control guns. The most prominent acts which passed Congress included the 1934 National Firearms Act and the Gun Control Act of 1938. One of the men to testify on behalf of the New Deal legislation was Karl T. Frederick, who said: "I have never believed in the general practice of carrying weapons. I do not believe in the general promiscuous totting of guns. I think it should be sharply restricted and only under license."

That comment would have been commonplace among later advocates of gun control, but this stood out because the speaker was Karl T. Frederick. In 1934, Frederick was president of the NRA. Eighty years later, in the wake of the shooting at Sandy Hook Elementary School, the man who was the power behind the throne of the NRA—Wayne LaPierre—said that the problem was not too many guns but too little: More guns were needed to protect children from the likes of Adam Lanza.

Frederick, an Olympic sharpshooter with three gold medals to his credit, was willing to support FDR on the registering and taxing of machine guns and sawed-off shotguns, but not hand guns. One issue was fingerprinting gun owners. Frederick was opposed. "Automobile owners are not fingerprinted and are, as a class, a much more criminal body, from the standpoint of percentage, than pistol licensees," he asserted.

The chair of the House Ways and Means Committee before whom Frederick was testifying was incredulous. "Do you make that statement seriously?" he asked.

"Yes sir," Frederick replied.

The chairman shot back: "That the ordinary man who owns and operates an automobile is more likely to be a criminal than the man who arms himself?"

Frederick again: "I said pistol licensees, those who have gone to the trouble of securing a license to carry weapons, are a most law-abiding body, and the perpetration of a crime by such a licensee is almost unknown."

The president of the NRA went on to enunciate a view which sounds to present-day readers a lot like the argument advanced by gun-rights advocates: "I think we should be careful in considering the actual operation of regulatory measures to make sure that they do not hamstring the law-abiding citizen in his opposition to the crook."

Frederick may have been persuasive in his appearance before Congress: The National Firearms Act of 1934 eliminated the proposed restrictions on handguns but not those on machine guns or sawed-off shotguns.

Cooperation between the National Rifle Association and the federal government on gun control continued through the 1960s, the years when the Kennedy brothers and Martin Luther King were assassinated. The killing of an NRA member in 1971 seems to have been a watershed moment in the evolution of the organization. The man had been hiding what one newspaper called "a large number of illegal weapons."

The reaction inside the NRA prompted the organization to create a lobbying group called the Institute for Legislative Action or ILA. Its first head was a Texan called Harlon Carter, who had previously headed up the Border Patrol. "You don't stop crime by attacking guns," he famously said. "You stop crime by stopping criminals."

Carter was soon at daggers drawn with the leadership of the NRA. The imbroglio exploded in the open at the NRA 1977 convention in Cincinnati. When the dust settled, Carter found himself the executive vice president and the effective head of the organization. One of his first acts was to install a like-minded colleague, Neal Knox, as head of the ILA. Together they oversaw the emergence of the NRA as a fundraising and political campaigning powerhouse. Politicians came to fear the organization's clout and to court its support. It had come a long way from its modest beginnings in 1871. A sign of changing times was captured in the way the Republican Party platform evolved. In 1972, it announced that:

> We pledge a tireless campaign against crime...to restore safety to our streets, and security to law-abiding citizens who have a right to enjoy their homes and communities free from fear. We pledge to. . . intensify efforts to prevent criminal access to all weapons, including special emphasis on cheap, readily-obtainable handguns . . .with such federal law as necessary to enable the states to meet their responsibilities.

Eight years later, the platform declared "We believe the right of citizens to keep and bear arms must be preserved. Accordingly we oppose federal registration of firearms."

Carter's successors as president of the NRA were often less stiff-necked than he was in their opposition to gun control, but one of them, Charlton Heston, was decidedly more flamboyant. The movie star is best remembered for his speech at the NRA 2000 convention when he hoisted a rifle above his head and declaimed, "From my cold dead hands!" That same year, the association set out to defeat the Democratic candidate for the presidency, Al Gore. "I want to say those fighting words for everyone within the sound of my voice to hear and to heed," he intoned, wafting a replica of a revolutionary rifle. "And especially for you, Mr. Gore: From my cold dead hands!" Michael Waldman believes that Heston's speech mimics his famous line from the movie Planet of the Apes: "Take your stinking paws off me, you damn dirty ape!"

Columnist Nicholas Kristof, writing in *The New York Times* in early November 2018, argued a cause for the tenacity with which Americans clutch their weapons:

> Gun carrying has also become an important part of identity and self-esteem for millions of Americans in ways that liberal city-dwellers don't always appreciate. The last few decades have in many ways demoted working class White men—their jobs have become insecure, they may no longer be the family's chief breadwinner, women and people of color have

gained ground—but firing an AR-15 or packing a concealed weapon, offers beleaguered men a chance to reassert their masculinity; to such men, guns provide a sense of purpose, fulfilling a traditional manly role of protecting their families and their communities.

Visitors to NRA headquarters in northern Virginia see, emblazoned on the wall of the building's lobby, a truncated version of the Second Amendment: The right of the people to keep and bear arms shall not be infringed. Note that the ablative absolute—the murky phrase about a well-regulated militia—has been omitted. When the NRA building went up in the 1950s, the slogan to greet visitors read: FIREARM SAFETY EDUCATION, MARKSMANSHIP TRAINING, SHOOTING FOR RECREATION.

Professor of political science, Hahrie Han, of UC Santa Barbara, argues that apart from the financial support that the NRA commands, the organization has grass-roots which gun control groups lack:

> Understanding the choices gun-control advocates have begins with understanding where the outsize power of the National Rifle Association originates . . . Many people assume its power comes from money. The truth is that gun-control advocates have lots of money, too. Billionaires like Michael Bloomberg have pledged fortunes to supporting gun control . . . The NRA's power is not just about its money or number of supporters or a favorable political map. It has also built something that gun-control advocates lack: an organized base of grass-roots power . . . Local gun clubs and gun shops provide a similar structure for the gun-rights movement. There are more gun clubs and gun shops in the United States than there are McDonald's.

The NRA has suffered reverses. The attempt on Ronald Reagan's life led to the so-called Brady Bill in 1993, covered in a previous chapter. Reagan himself, an NRA member, supported the bill. The following year Congress enacted a ban on what were called assault weapons. The NRA, however, did manage to insert in that bill a sunset clause which allowed a Republican-controlled Congress to let the ban expire ten years later.

When a gun-inflicted massacre occurs, the NRA follows what Ron Elving, writing for NPR, has called a "well-established protocol." First the organization observes several days of official silence, offering only sympathy for the victims. At the same time, it expresses the wish that the event "not be politicized." Then a representative of the NRA makes the rounds of TV talk shows to reaffirm his (or her) faith in guns. Then comes the association's view of the Constitution which stresses the following points:

- The Second Amendment guarantees the individual's right to possess firearms;
- Blame for gun violence lies on criminals, Hollywood movies and video games, and a break-down of the nation's mental health program;
- Lastly it is impossible to legislate away the evil which exists in the world.

The liturgical presentation ends with the NRA's slogan:
"The only thing that stops a bad guy with a gun is a good guy with a gun."

Some observers have suggested that the NRA has lost touch with its own members. Substantial majorities of NRA members favor background checks of one sort or another. In fact, nearly three quarters of its membership look with favor on universal background checks, something which the NRA has fiercely opposed. In 2013, explaining his resignation from the organization, Adolphus Busch IV wrote that:

> The NRA appears to have evolved into the lobby for gun and ammunitions manufacturers rather than gun owners. Your current strategic focus places a priority on the needs of gun and ammunition manufacturers while disregarding the opinions of your four million members. One only has to look at the makeup of the 75-member board of directors, dominated by manufacturing interests, to confirm my point.

In apparent agreement with this, J. Adam Skaggs of the Giffords Law Center to Prevent Gun Violence wrote that "the NRA has policy positions and rhetorical positions that are aligned with where the gun industry makes its money." Still it's possible to push this view too far: Commentator Mike Weisser, who writes a blog called *mikethegunguy*, contends that the gun industry and the NRA collaborate to maximize the organization's influence and industry profits.

Is the NRA hurting for money? The organization has raised its membership fees twice in the past two years. This could signify how the NRA is meeting its financial challenges. Its revenue from dues fell from $128 million in 2017, a drop of $35 million from the previous year.

Following the 2017 rampage in Las Vegas in which Steve Paddock killed fifty-eight people attending a music festival, the organization appeared to moderate its opposition to gun control measures. Paddock had used a semiautomatic rifle equipped with a bump stock which allowed his weapon to function more or less as an automatic rifle. The NRA, in line with President Trump and Congressional leaders, said that it was willing to look at banning bump stocks or at least limiting their use. But it soon became clear that the NRA did not favor any change in the law to regulate bump stocks. Executive Vice President Wayne LaPierre took the view that the federal government, acting through the Bureau of Alcohol, Tobacco, Firearms and Explosives (ATF), already had the authority to regulate bump stocks. The ATF simply needed to exercise that authority. Officials at the ATF flatly disagreed with this assessment: Laws would have to be changed for it to ban bump stocks.

In late 2018, however, the Justice Department did ban the use of weapons equipped with bump stocks. At least for anyone other than law enforcement personnel. It did this by reclassifying these weapons as machine guns. "Such devices allow a shooter of a semiautomatic firearm to initiate a continuous firing cycle with a single pull of the trigger," said an official at the Department. Owners of these devices would be given ninety days to destroy them or turn them over to the Bureau of Alcohol, Tobacco, Firearms and Explosives (ATF). Gun-rights groups announced that they would sue the government to halt the new regulation.

A lawyer representing these groups said that "they [the government] are actively attempting to make felons out of people who relied on their legal opinions to lawfully acquire and possess devices the government unilaterally, unconstitutionally, and improperly decided to reclassify as machineguns."

And that was the rub. The ban on bump stocks might be tied up in court for years, warned Senator Dianne Feinstein (D-CA). ATF has consistently warned that bump stocks could not be regulated under the National Firearms Act as it currently stands. The Justice Department's ban rests on what Feinstein called "a dubious analysis claiming that bumping the trigger is not the same as pulling it." The best way to rid the public of the bump stock menace, according to the Director of the ATF, would be to pass a law. That would mean amending the National Firearms Act, something which has not happened since the law was updated in 1986.

In his report for NPR, Ron Elving noted that majority whip, Steve Scalise, suggested that there might be sentiment among House Republicans to introduce legislation that would expand gun rights rather than limit them. This, in the wake of a June 2017 attack on congressional baseball practice which left Scalise wounded and surgery-bound. After months of rehab, Scalise said on NBC's *Meet the Press* that

> Our Founding Fathers believed strongly in gun rights for citizens. Don't try to put new laws in place that don't fix these problems. They only make it harder for law-abiding citizens to own a gun.

When asked if gun rights were unlimited, he agreed.

CHAPTER EIGHT:
What Can Be Done?

WE BEGAN WITH A CHRISTMAS TALE, we end with a Christmas tale. In 2021, Rep. Thomas Massie of Kentucky posted a Christmas photo showing his family lined up in front of a Christmas tree. Each member of the family is holding an assault weapon. "Merry Christmas!" reads the accompanying message. "p.s. Santa, please bring ammo."

Massie posted the message four days after a mass shooting at a school in Oxford, Michigan, in which four students lost their lives.

"That's my kind of Christmas card!" gushed Rep. Lauren Boebert of Colorado in a burst of jingoistic approbation. She posted a photo of her four sons each toting a semi-automatic weapon.

"The AR-15 has become a potent talisman for right-wing politicians," observed the *Washington Post* which went on to decry the obsession with "tactical culture" of a growing number of American civilians. We cite two examples of this, the first from the *Post*, the second from *The New York Times*.

In a campaign ad, a Republican candidate for the Senate in Missouri, Eric Greitens, kicks in the door to a house and bursts in with a group of men carrying assault weapons. They are hunting RINOs [Republican in name only]. "Get a RINO hunting permit," the ad goes on. "There's no bagging limit, and it doesn't expire until we save the country."

Consider that in November 2022, *The New York Times* reported:

Armed protesters appeared outside an elections center in Phoenix, hurling baseless accusations that the election for governor had been stolen from the Republican, Kari Lake. In October, Proud Boys with guns joined a rally in Nashville where conservative lawmakers spoke against transgender medical treatment for minors.

November 2022 was the month in which three mass murders had shaken the country: The murder of three football players at the University of Virginia; the assault on a gay nightclub in Colorado Springs; and the massacre at Walmart in Chesapeake, Virginia. This has not deterred some gun advocates from trying to intimidate those who support restrictions on firearms.

***

THIRTY-EIGHT THOUSAND EIGHT HUNDRED twenty-six. That is the number of gun deaths per year as reported by the CDC, an average calculated over the 5-year span 2015-2019, (this number increased to 45,222 in 2020.) A little less than two thirds were suicides. More than one third were homicides. The suicide rate in the US is ten times greater than those of other high-income countries; the homicide rate is—gasp!—twenty-five times as great as other high-income countries. Women are more than twenty times as likely to be killed with a gun as women in other high-income countries.

Seventy percent of the shooters in one study were found to be suicidal before or during the incidents in which they killed people. This is a significant finding. As Jillian Peterson, a psychologist and co-author of the study said, "We know a lot more about suicide prevention than we do about this issue."

Recently the desire for fame has ballooned in the souls of shooters. Not surprisingly the massacre at Columbine High School has "redefined the school shooting as a media spectacle."

The title of this chapter is a question: **What can be done?**

The way to stop a bad guy with a gun is a good guy with a gun. Donald Trump has adopted this NRA nostrum as his cure-all to curb gun violence. He said so shortly after the attack on the synagogue in Pittsburgh.

This would entail putting armed surveillance in every synagogue, every church, every school, every restaurant and bar, and every music hall in the country.

Be that as it may, people were afraid and craved the security of owning a gun. We cite the following anecdote to illustrate the point: An ex-marine, Ian Long, dressed in a Black trench coat (no less), shot up a bar in Thousand Oaks, California, killing twelve patrons and employees. Long underscored the senselessness of his crime in what he wrote on Instagram: "Fact is I had no reason to do it, and I just thought…fuck, life is boring so why not?"

A couple of neighbors who lived close to the bar later decided to drive the three miles down to VC Defense, the only gun store in the town, to buy handguns. One of them, a single father, had sworn never to have a firearm in the house. Neither was a typical gun owner, but neither felt safe when the specter of a mass shooter or armed intruder loomed in their minds. It was naked fear that drove them to purchase firearms. They were not alone. The day they bought their guns, a banker walked into the store. Two of his son's friends had been killed at the bar which Long attacked. The owner of VC Defense, advised him to buy an ankle holster. With a gun secured in an ankle holster, the banker could grab his gun and fire, even if he was obliged to lie on his back in the middle of a mall. Talk in the store focused on the off-duty unarmed policemen in the bar at the time of the shooting. California law forbids firearms in bars.

"I take this very seriously," said the owner of VC Defense when interviewed by a reporter for *USA Today*. For the interview, he was wearing his workaday outfit of a T-shirt which read, "Don't Tread on me" and cargo shorts. "Some people would love to have all gun shops gone, but without a legal way people will be doing it illegally."

"They're just frightened," he commented of his new clients. "Unfortunately these mass shootings are good for business, and I say that very solemnly." He went on to say: "I get a lot of closet liberals, people who normally would never want anything to do with a firearm, and I train them and they secretly own firearms."

One young veteran who survived the slaughter in Las Vegas was in the Thousand Oaks bar when Long went on a shooting spree. He was one of Long's victims.

> Imagine being called into a room after waiting ten excruciating hours to learn if your child is alive or dead [the father of the young vet told the *Washington Post*]. You find yourself face to face with a somber police officer. The words "I am sorry, your son did not make it" are barely comprehensible as the room swirls around you. You gasp for air as you feel your heart being ripped out of your chest. Your life, along with the lives of your family, friends and community, is changed in that instant. This is the reality of gun violence in America.

Some suggestions of how people might defend themselves against a mass murderer border on the grotesque. In one Pennsylvania school, the superintendent ordered each classroom to be equipped with a pail of river stones.

"They're the right size for hands," he explained to a local TV station. "You can throw them very hard, and they will create or cause pain, which can distract."

As far back as 1970, historian Richard Hofstadter described the country in terms of its gun culture. In fact, an industry has grown up and prospered on the dependence of Americans and their love for firearms.

In a profile written for the *Washington Post* Magazine, Simon van Zuylen-Wood focused on two entrepreneurs spearheading the drive to cash in on the country's gun fetish.

The first of these was Mat Best. Van Zuylen-Wood said of the man—whom he interviewed on his ranch north of Austin, Texas—that "if Abercrombie & Fitch did a photo shoot in Fallujah, it would produce something like this." Best has posted on Instagram a photo of himself, stripped to the waist, a semiautomatic AR-15 hiding part of his tattooed chest, with the caption, "Happiness is a warm gun. Bang bang pew pew. #lifeisepic." Best is not the only man to post things like this on Instagram; there is a slew of such people doing the same thing. Collectively they call themselves the "tactical community." That word "tactical" sells. In 2007, there were a scant ten registered gun sellers with "tactical" in their name. Ten years later, there were 128. Tactical is now used to sell all sorts of merchandise, even baby gear, for parents who tote firearms at the same time they carry their offspring. There are camo-colored back packs and harnesses as well.

Mat Best is their de facto leader. Best has a sense of humor which mocks his macho image. A photo he posted online has him in the background, looking disheveled and growly. A pal in the foreground bares his teeth. A mouthguard with the word "Bears" inscribed on it makes him look like a character in a James Bond film, the one called "Jaws" because his teeth appear to be capped in steel. One of his online ads shows him cradling an AR-15 in one arm while he cuddles a kitten in the other.

An ex-Army Ranger, Best is also co-founder of a company called the Black Rifle Coffee Company which does a land-office business selling to people who glom on his self-image. There is no denying his appeal to a vast audience of gun devotees. "He can write, he can play music, he's a good-looking guy, he's done rap songs, he's sung ballads, he has a beautiful wife on Instagram," says TJ Kirgin, who runs an online retail shop called Tactical Shit. "Who doesn't like Mat? Everybody wants to be like Mat." Kirgin, a retired police officer from Ferguson, MO, started his business in the days after the 2014 riots which broke out after the shooting of Michael Brown.

Guns, van Zuylen-Wood observes, are as much about esthetics as they are about self-defense. "They are, more than anything else, a lifestyle choice."

Amy Robbins grew up in the suburbs of Dallas, TX. Named as one of D Magazine's ten most beautiful women in Dallas, Robbins co-hosted an NRATV show with Colion Noir, the Black guns-right activist who tangled with David Hogg for what he considered the young student's paternalistic pretensions. After her stint with the NRA, Robbins created her own company called Alexo Athletica for women "who want to carry concealed weapons while they exercise." The need for such attire was not at first apparent to Robbins. Then, while training for a marathon, she understood: "I'd be running really early in the morning or at nighttime, and I would have people either follow me, slow down, roll their window down, make comments." There was nothing in athletic apparel suitable for women who wanted to pack heat while they worked out. Robbins seized on the opportunity.

> I knew there were a lot of women that were like me [Robbins says]. All my Highland Park soccer moms have their license to carry. Most of them put their Sigs [Sig Sauer semi-automatic pistols] in their Chanel bags and they run out the door and they're wearing Lululemon. And I'm like, `Ladies, if you had the place to put it on your body, and it still looked as nice as your Lulu, would you wear it?' And they were like, `Absolutely. As long as it makes my butt look good, absolutely.'

A woman van Zuylen-Wood described as a "right-wing provocateur" had this to say about Robbins' wares: "Ladies, chances are your assailant is gonna' be bigger, stronger, and faster and that's why you have @alexoathletica for your gun, your mace or even your phone."

Robbins has a devoted following. "Amy, you would make a great Bond girl," gushed one admirer on Instagram. "Beautiful and classy, [a] perfect combination."

Some efforts to control gun violence are low-key and go unnoticed outside the communities in which they occur. Mayor of Washington, D.C., Muriel Bowser, initiated a program to identify D.C. residents considered to be at risk of committing a violent crime or of falling victim to one. These residents were called "People of Promise." Their names were put on a list. Some of the people on that list were shot dead before they could help or be helped. In another initiative. the city undertook a program of issuing grants of $5000 to people with ideas to help with the city's gun problem. Some of them developed programs to offer job training, gardening lessons, and—in one case—a junket to Wall Street. One group shot a film about gun violence that reduced its audience to tears. A woman whose son had been paralyzed from the waist down by bullets used her grant money to organize a life skills class. "I've had 22 students in the class and one was drunk and one was high and nodding," she said. "I didn't turn them away. I know what they were going through, and why they are pacifying their pain."

The director of DC Gun Violence Prevention acknowledged that they were not the answer to the problem. "We need to support community members who know their communities," she said. "What the answer is in one community is not the same as in another community."

Officials in Washington were not the only ones to explore non-violent responses to gun violence. Motivated by Quaker religious convictions, Friends Committee for National Legislation convened a panel of experts to brief members of Congress on community-based peacebuilding efforts. One speaker, Nicole Warren from Safe Streets of Catholic Charities, spoke of her work to prevent homicide. She knew of three young men who traveled from Baltimore to Philadelphia to kill someone who had robbed them. Warren partially reimbursed the trio and persuaded them of the seriousness of what they were contemplating to do. Once back in Baltimore, the young men began new lives working for Amazon, UPS, and the Post Office.

Warren was assisted in searching for the would-be shooters by "violence interrupters," who operate under the auspices of the Justice Department. These individuals—and here I quote from the DOJ webpage—"because of their past positions in the community or, in some cases, their prior history with a gang, retain the ability to reach and talk to key active gang members."

Baltimore was the hometown of Cory Winfield who witnessed his first shooting when he was ten. The victim was a fourteen-year-old friend. Winfield started selling drugs. He was robbed a few times and at the age of seventeen, he shot and killed a dealer who was trying to rob him. For this offense, Winfield did almost twenty years in prison. Two weeks after he was released from prison, Cory's younger brother was shot and killed. Winfield hunted down his brother's murderer but when he went home he found his aunt sitting alone in the dark. She knew what he planned to do. "Please stop," she pleaded with him, "I don't want to lose another baby." Winfield promised to give up guns. He became a promoter of Violence Interruption in Baltimore, a program based on one in Chicago.

School Safety

A FLURRY OF GOVERNMENT ACTIVITY occurred in the wake of the massacre at Marjory Stoneman Douglas High School. President Trump set up a Commission on School Safety which issued a 177-page report in late 2018. The commission took what it called a "holistic approach" to a problem for which it admitted that no one-size-fits-all solution existed. Critics of the proposed changes objected to the Commission's recommendation that there be a rollback of an Obama-era policy urging schools not to punish minority students at a greater rate than White students. What did school discipline have to do with school shootings? "It is unconscionable to use the very real horror of the shooting at Parkland to advance a preexisting agenda that encourages the criminalization of children and undermines their civil rights," said the president of the Leadership Conference on Civil and Human Rights.

The man slated to become the chair of the US House Committee on Education in 2019 said, "Rather than confronting the role of guns in gun violence, the Trump administration blames school shootings on civil rights enforcement. This guidance has no connection to school shootings."

There was little indication of activity on the part of the Commission between the massacres at Parkland (when it was set up, and the shootings at the Santa Fe High School three months later when Trump urged the Commission "to start the conversation up again." Bobby Scott (D-VA) remarked that "the report makes no recommendations to address the common denominator in school tragedies—easy access to assault-style firearms designed for the battlefield. Rather than confronting the role of guns in gun violence, the Trump administration blames school shootings on civil rights enforcement."

Worse yet, when Sen. Pat Leahy (D-VT) asked Secretary of Education, Betsy DeVos, whether the commission would look at the role of firearms in the problem of school gun violence, the Secretary replied: "that was not part of the commission's charge, per se."

The Commission did, in fact, not recommend that the minimum age to purchase a gun be raised. It did recommend that schools "consider arming and training teachers… to respond to threats of violence."

✳✳✳

After David Hogg and Emma Gonzalez, the two Parkland students, wrote their op-ed article for the *Washington Post* in early November 2018, they believed that a lasting change could take place on election day. That could occur if young people like themselves went out and voted. A Harvard National Youth poll found that more than forty percent of youth, aged between 18 and 29, said that they would definitely vote during the midterms.

> How many more shootings must there be [Hogg and Gonzalez asked] before our leaders listen to us?
>
> We have a simple answer: Young people must vote—all sixty-two million of us.

Were Hogg and Gonzalez satisfied with voter turnout for the 2018 midterms? Probably. One exit poll indicated that 31 percent of the age group 18-to-29 years old turned out to vote. That represented a fifty percent increase over the previous midterm election of 2014.

"Young people approached the 2018 midterms with a resolve to change the American political landscape through peer-to-peer action, and yesterday they demonstrated their power," said the director of the firm that had done the exit poll. He went on to say:

> These data estimates represent a huge increase in youth participation and are a testament to the efforts that a diverse group of youth organizers built and sustained in communities and on campuses across the country. This year we also saw new stakeholders, including more universities, the private sector, and even celebrities, strengthen and deepen their approach to youth outreach and non-partisan voter engagement efforts.

Young people favored Democrats overwhelmingly, helping to win back for the party more than three hundred state legislature seats. Activists for March for Our Lives—this was the organization that the Parkland students had started—wore shirts with codes which, when scanned, gave information on voter registration. In Wisconsin, a surge in youth participation in the midterm election contributed to the defeat of Republican governor, Scott Walker.

In an op-ed piece for *The New York Times*, former Supreme Court justice, John Paul Stevens, hoisted once again a not-so-modest trial balloon: Repeal the Second Amendment. Stevens argues that the concern that a national standing army would threaten the security of the states was a relic of the eighteenth century. For two centuries it was understood that the Second Amendment placed no limit on the power of the federal and state governments to control guns. Stevens went on to cite Chief Justice Burger's condemnation of the NRA's claim that regulating firearms violated the Second Amendment.

Stevens was one of four justices on the Supreme Court to dissent from the court's decision in *District of Columbia v. Heller*. He argued that the decision disrespected "the well-settled views of all of our predecessors on the court, and for the rule of law itself." Two years later Stevens dissented from another court decision regarding gun rights, writing:

> The reasons that motivated the framers to protect the ability of militiamen to keep muskets, or that motivated the Reconstruction Congress to extend full citizenship to freedmen in the wake of the Civil War, have only a limited bearing on the question that confronts the homeowner in a crime-infested metropolis today.

Laurence H. Tribe of Harvard joined the legal fray which Stevens had initiated by producing his own op-ed piece for *The New York Times* which has been cited in a previous chapter.

Columnist Leonard Pitts Jr. of the *Miami Herald* has written that

> As Canada proves daily, it's entirely possible to balance gun rights with common-sense restrictions that save lives. Comprehensive background checks and a ban on private ownership of high-capacity magazines and semi-automatic weapons

would be a good place to start. What we lack is not a way to stop tragedies but a will.

Other countries have taken drastic action to limit gun violence. We have already cited the example of Australia, which acted in 1996 to buy back military-type weapons from civilians after a massacre in that country. New Zealand did something similar after a gunman mowed down 50 Muslims at two mosques in 2019 in Christchurch. mosques in 2019. Jacinda Ardern, the prime minister of New Zealand, announced a ban on semi-automatic weapons and all high-capacity ammunition magazines.

"What we're banning today are the things used in last Friday's attack," she said. "It's in the national interest and it's about safety."

"The guns used in these terrorist attacks had important distinguishing features," said the P.M. who emphasized that the government would buy back the weapons now being banned. "First big capacity, and also their delivery. They had the power to shoot continuously, but they also had large capacity magazines."

Praise rained down on the prime minister for her decisive action. "A very bold move," said Philip Alpers of the University of Sydney. The president of New Zealand's police association al+so praised the move. "It's exactly what we wanted," he said.

There remain some differences in the approaches adopted by New Zealand and Australia. "In Australia, it was a very simple definition, all semiautomatic rifles and shotguns, full stop," said Alpers, who heads up GunPolicy.org at the University of Sydney. "Here I can see a few grey areas."

"Glad I took my AR-15 for a walk up the range today," said one New Zealander. "We had a blast [and] it could be the last time."

The challenge for New Zealand would come in getting guns and ammunition out of circulation. The country registers only four percent of its weapons. Police reckon that a quarter million people own more than one million firearms. "New Zealand is at a considerable disadvantage to countries that have had registries," said Alpers. "There's no way of tracing the firearms because they don't know who's got them."

Jacinda Ardern has been critical of the world's social media for their role in spreading hate messages which encourage violent acts. "There are some things we need to confront collectively as leaders internationally," she said at Christchurch, scene of the mosque massacres. "We cannot, for instance, allow some of the challenges we face with social media to be dealt with on a case-by-case basis."

Might the US follow the example of these two South Pacific nations? Probably not although the countries have much in common, including a lack of universal gun registration rules. Then there is the power of the gun lobby which, in the words of Philip Alpers, dictates policy to the government. "They are listened to far more acutely by the government, and they have managed to water down every single attempt at improving the gun laws. The gun lobby is directly responsible for having defeated the amendments that could have prevented [the mosque massacres]."

If New Zealand could rein in its gun violence, why can't the US follow suit and do likewise? For one thing, rural voters have more clout than their counterparts in New Zealand, and they are the fiercest advocates of gun rights. The way congressional districts are drawn in the US favors rural (and Republican) voters. "Our form of government," claimed Daniel Webster. the director of the Johns Hopkins Center for Gun Policy and Research, "with a Senate that gives extraordinary power to rural states over urban states and is deferential to states' rights, makes it difficult to advance relatively modest gun-control measures, much less more sweeping measures."

Finally there is the Second Amendment and the way the Supreme Court has interpreted it to give people the right to own guns. Again Daniel Webster: "The gun lobby has been very influential in convincing people the [Second Amendment prohibits any] form of gun control, which affects the politics over even modest measures."

Be that as it may, one state after another has adopted measures to curb gun atrocities. Red flag laws allow law enforcement officials and immediate family members to petition courts to deprive people who appear to be prone to violent behavior from owning guns, at least temporarily. Not surprisingly, given the popular support such measures enjoyed, the NRA reversed course in its opposition to these laws. The organization had opposed them in three states—New Jersey, Minnesota, and Missouri—before coming round to support them elsewhere. "This can help prevent violent behavior before it becomes a tragedy," said the NRA's chief lobbyist.

A Catalogue of Actions/Inactions

Despite the attention paid to mass murder in the media and—let's be honest—in this book as well, the vast majority of gun violence victims are casualties of non-mass-murder incidents. Of the thirty thousand Americans killed every year by firearms, two thirds are suicides, five hundred are accidents, and almost all the rest are run-of-the-mill homicides. This equates to nearly 23,000 people commit suicide every year by shooting themselves. In 2020, the economic recession and the coronavirus epidemic proved to be "a toxic combination" according to Sarah Burd-Sharps, director of research at the Everytown Support Fund. Noticeably hard hit were regions in the south and west, with Native American and Alaska native communities particularly susceptible. About 90 percent of suicide attempts using guns prove lethal. "One of the most effective things you can do to help people in crisis," said Burd-Sharps, "is to keep a gun out of their hand."

Just before Thanksgiving, 2018, the *Washington Post* ran a photo essay on gun violence in the country. It depicted scenes of gun violence over a 24-hour period. What the *Post* picked up was the following:

> 12 pm EST: Police discovered in the basement of a row house in southwest Philadelphia the bodies of four adults, two men who were cousins and two women. All four had been shot once in the head, execution-style.

3 pm EST: A man killed his ex-fiancée in the parking lot of the Chicago hospital where she worked as an emergency room physician. He then entered the hospital and shot dead a police officer and a pharmacy resident. Mayor Rahm Emanuel commented on the slaying: "The city of Chicago has lost a doctor, pharmaceutical assistant and a police officer, all going about their day, all doing what they loved. This just tears at the soul of our city. It is the face and a consequence of evil." Doctors at Mercy Hospital who spoke out against the NRA were advised by that organization to "stay in their line." The doctors had called for more medical research into gun violence.

3:19 pm CST: A man walked into a Catholic supply store in a St. Louis strip mall and sexually assaulted a 53-year-old woman. He then shot her. She died several hours later.

4 pm MST: A man fired on a group of apparently homeless people a few blocks from the Denver baseball stadium. One of his victims later died, four others were wounded and hospitalized.

6:20 EST: A 5-year-old girl was shot in the groin outside her West Baltimore house. She is expected to live. Her brother, 7-year-old Taylor Hayes, was not so lucky: He was killed last summer as he sat in the back seat of a car. Said Acting Baltimore Police Commissioner, Gary Tuggle: "We've got to do more. Not just as a police department but we have to do more as a community. We have become so desensitized to the level of violence in this city that it is just totally, totally inacceptable."

Just after the *Post* published its list of gun-related injuries/fatalities, *The New York Times* ran a story about a 13-year-old girl who was killed by a stray bullet as she watched TV in her Milwaukee home. The girl, Sandra Parks, had written an award-winning essay about gun violence when she was in the sixth grade.

"She was everything this world is not," her mother told a local newspaper. "She was my angel from the time she was in my womb to the time she came out."

Sandra had chosen the subject of her essay because "all you

hear about is somebody dying or somebody getting shot and people do not just think about whose father or son or granddaughter or grandson who it was that was just killed."

Sandra's homicide was the seventh in the Milwaukee public schools for the year. Mayor Tom Barrett told the press that "It's part of the insanity we see in Milwaukee. I look at where we are now as a city and it breaks my heart to stand here. As a dad, it breaks my heart."

Sandra Parks had hoped to attend college and become a writer.

How has the federal government responded to the threat of gun violence in the country? Here is a catalogue of actions/inactions taken since 2000 by government officials, starting from the top (the president) on down to Congress.

George W. Bush had implemented a program of voluntary trigger locks when he was governor of Texas. These were installed through police stations and fire departments. He also pushed for limited background checks. Bush's election to the presidency in 2000 pleased the NRA. The gun rights group claimed that its close alliance with the President-Elect gave the gun rights group ready access to the White House. It came as something of a shock, therefore, when Bush indicated that he would support a renewal of the Assault Weapons Ban initiated by his predecessor, Bill Clinton, if it reached his desk. This position represented a significant break between Bush and the NRA. An organization spokesman said that "it's just unbelievable to gun owners that he would really sign the ban." It would put the president at odds with his own political base, said Michael Franc of the conservative Heritage Foundation.

A spokesman for the gun-control advocacy group Americans for Gun Safety Now, commented that "I think Bush realizes that, number one, this is the right thing to do, number two, he promised to do this in the 2000 campaign, and number three, he knows that it's good politics and this is an extremely popular measure."

The NRA focused its energy on seeing that legislation to renew or extend the ban would never reach Bush's desk.

"We hope the president will not just say he supports the

ban but will work to get it passed," said Democratic Senator Charles Schumer of New York. "This will be a good measure of the compassion in his compassionate conservatism."

Gun rights groups like the NRA contended that the ban had had at best a minuscule effect in fighting crime "and the Democrats know that," in the view of Grover G. Norquist of the NRA. Republicans in Congress saw to it that no action on renewing the ban was taken, and so no legislation to renew the ban ever crossed Bush's desk.

Barack Obama's first term as president saw little action on gun control. Then came the massacre at Sandy Hook elementary school in Newtown, Connecticut. That attack, which took the lives of twenty children and six adults, clearly shook Obama. In a tearful press conference in December 2012, the president said, "Every time I think about those kids, it gets me mad. We're going to have to come together" (he went on) "and take meaningful action to prevent more tragedies like this, regardless of the politics.".

.."Sandy Hook was only one of the massacres which took place during Obama's eight years as president. There were as well:

- The attack on the church in Charleston;
- An armed forces' recruiting center in Chattanooga;
- A community college in Roseburg, Oregon;
- A community center in San Bernardino, CA;
- A movie theatre in Aurora, CO;
- A Sikh temple in Oak Creek, WI;
- Two separate incidents at Fort Hood, TX;
- The Washington Navy Yard;
- The Pulse nightclub in Orlando, FL (where the gunman killed 49 and wounded 53).

During his re-election campaign earlier that year, Obama had indicated that he supported a re-introduction of the Assault Weapons Ban. "Weapons that were designed for soldiers in war theatres don't belong on our streets," he said. A lack of interest in Congress doomed that prospect from the get-go. Instead Obama concentrated on what he could do through executive actions which did not require Congressional approval.

These included an emphasis on mental health, limiting magazine size, strengthening background checks, and relaunching gun violence research.

"There is little more that Obama could have done on gun control," commented Adam Winkler, an expert on constitutional law. "The president's power is limited, and the NRA wrote the laws to restrict what the executive can do." He added ominously: "Obama's executive actions on guns are likely to be reversed quickly; the NRA has close ties to (Donald) Trump and the organization is eager to reverse Obama's reforms."

As president, Donald Trump did reverse many of Obama's executive orders. One that concerns the subject of this book was a restriction on the purchase of guns by mentally ill people, implemented after the Sandy Hook Elementary School massacre. The repeal of this measure counted organizations other than the NRA as supporters. Disability rights groups opposed the rule as did the American Civil Liberties Union which argued that:

> ... it advances and reinforces the harmful stereotype that people with mental disabilities, a vast and diverse group of citizens, are violent. There is no data (sic) to support a connection between the need for a representative payee to manage one's Social Security disability benefits and a propensity toward gun violence.

Sensing perhaps that his move would not be viewed with favor by the public, Trump signed the bill repealing the Obama executive order without a photo-op and with little hoopla. Only an announcement squirreled away at the bottom of an email detailing other legislative matters mentioned his action.

Still the NRA praised the move. John Feinblatt of Everytown for Gun Safety termed the President's decision "just the first item on the gun lobby's wish list."

In an email statement, Senator Chris Murphy (D-Conn) commented:

> Republicans always say we don't need new gun laws, we just need to enforce the laws already on the books. But the bill signed into law today undermines enforcement of existing laws that Congress passed to make sure the background

check system had complete information.

The massacre at Parkland occurred on Donald Trump's watch. A week later the president presided over a meeting (which was televised) with students from the high school. The White House had invited to the meeting parents of children killed at Columbine High School and Sandy hook elementary school.

"I don't understand how I can still go in a store and buy a weapon of war," said Sam Zeif, a Stoneman Douglas High student. The shooter at Parkland had shot his victims with an AR-15 rifle. Zeif continued:

> I was reading today a person 20 years old walked into a store and bought an AR-15 in five minutes with an expired ID. How is it that easy to buy this type of weapon? How have we not stopped this after Columbine, after Sandy Hook? I'm sitting next to a mother who lost her son [at Sandy Hook]. It's still happening.

One father's son texted him from a closet at Marjorie Stoneman Douglas as the shooter, Nikolas Cruz, rampaged through the school. "I love you," the son wrote.

> And then his phone died [the father later said]. I didn't know what happened for another hour or so. Seventeen lives are gone. I was lucky enough to get my son home. It's not left or right. It's not political. People are dying. And we have to stop this. If [Cruz was] not old enough to buy a drink, to buy a beer, he should not be able to buy a gun at 18 years old. That's just common sense. We have to do common sense.

Sam Zeif talked of the case of Australia after that country had experienced a school shooting at the end of the twentieth century.

> Can anyone here guess [he asked] how many shootings there have been in the schools since then? Zero. We need to do something. That's why we're here. So let's be strong for the fallen who don't have a voice to speak anymore. And let's never let this happen again. Please. Please.

Trump took advantage of the forum to unearth one of his

old chestnuts: The need for schools to arm some members of staff, a long-standing piece of NRA advice. He ignored the fact that Stoneman Douglas, like other schools, had armed security guards. The president lauded an assistant football coach whom Cruz had killed in his attack on the school.

> This coach was very brave [Trump said]. Saved a lot of lives, I suspect. But if he had a firearm, he wouldn't have had to run. He would've shot and that would've been the end of it.

Of his solution to the problem of gun violence on campus, Trump went on to elaborate:

> This would only be, obviously, for people who are very adept at handling a gun. It's called conceal-carry. A teacher would have a concealed gun on them. They would go through special training. They would be there and you would no longer have a gun-free zone. A gun-free zone, to a maniac—because they're all cowards. A gun-free zone is 'Let's go in. Let's attack because we know bullets won't be coming back at us.'

Trump's remarks went over like a lead balloon with the Parkland activists who were agitating for gun control.

"I'm glad to see that he did take action, and he did seem to take steps in the right direction," David Hogg told CNN. But the young student from Parkland went on to criticize the president:

> But then once he met with the NRA, he showed that he's no better than all the other politicians because he's owned by them, too. And it just shows the inaction because of this lobbying organization that's continued to terrorize our children and hurt our futures.

Hogg also tore into Secretary of Education, Betsy DeVos, whom the administration chose to head a commission to identify ways to keep schools safe from gun violence. "She doesn't really have any experience in this area," he said. "And she paid over $200 million just to get this title."

Inaction, rather than action, has characterized legislative responses to gun violence this century. After the killing in the Sutherland Springs church, Chris Murphy (D-Conn), a vocal leader in the anti-gun violence campaign, issued a statement condemning the lack of political will of the nation's legislators. So insightful and pulling-no-punches was Murphy's communiqué that the Washington Post ran it in toto, all four paragraphs:

> The paralysis you feel right now — the impotent helplessness that washes over you as news of another mass slaughter scrolls across the television screen — isn't real. It's a fiction created and methodically cultivated by the gun lobby, designed to assure that no laws are passed to make America safer, because those laws would cut into their profits. My heart sunk to the pit of my stomach, once again, when I heard of today's shooting in Texas. My heart dropped further when I thought about the growing macabre club of families in Las Vegas and Orlando and Charleston and Newtown, who have to relive their own day of horror every time another mass killing occurs.
>
> None of this is inevitable. I know this because no other country endures this pace of mass carnage like America. It is uniquely and tragically American. As long as our nation chooses to flood the county with dangerous weapons and consciously let those weapons fall into the hands of dangerous people, these killings will not abate.
>
> As my colleagues go to sleep tonight, they need to think about whether the political support of the gun industry is worth the blood that flows endlessly onto the floors of American churches, elementary schools, movie theaters, and city streets. Ask yourself: How can you claim that you respect human life while choosing fealty to weapons-makers over support for measures favored by the vast majority of your constituents.
>
> My heart breaks for Sutherland Springs. Just like it still does for Las Vegas. And Orlando. And Charleston. And Aurora. And Blacksburg. And Newtown. Just like it does every night for Chicago. And New Orleans. And Baltimore. And Bridgeport. The terrifying fact is that no one is safe so long as Congress chooses to do absolutely nothing in the face of this epidemic. The time is now for Congress to shed its cowardly cover and do something.

Murphy offered an illustration of the frustration and anger

that he felt in his gun-violence campaign when Ailsa Chang interviewed him on NPR:

> CHANG: Since you've been elected to the Senate, you've seen Sandy Hook, Orlando, Las Vegas, Parkland and many more shootings in between. There's been virtually no movement on gun control legislation in that time. What keeps you going?
>
> MURPHY: The worst day of my political career was the day that the background checks bill failed in the Senate.
>
> CHANG: April 2013.
>
> MURPHY: The Sandy Hook parents started out that debate thinking that they were going to get a ban on assault weapons. They didn't think they were going to have to settle for a debate on background checks. And to walk out of that Senate chamber and see those parents and tell them that we had failed, it was just awful. And one of the parents grabbed me, and I said, 'we'll keep going.' And he said, 'listen; I didn't become an advocate for four months. I'm an advocate for 40 years.' And it's those parents who inspire me to keep going.
>
> Great social change movements, the ones that change this country, are the ones that persevere even when they get handed defeat over and over and over again. We've had a lot of defeat. I would argue we've had some victories, too. We've seen progress out there in the states. We haven't seen as much progress in Washington. But I'm not going anywhere. Those families in Sandy Hook aren't. So as long as they're in it, I'm in it.

Why does government lack the will power to counter the gun lobby? Are politicians afraid of losing NRA endorsements? Or the drying up of their war chest funds? Do their convictions on the Second Amendment override common sense measures to contain the carnage? Senator Murphy's comments cited above offer a clue to these politicians' motives.

***

To return — one last time — to the title of this chapter: *What can be done?*

Advocates noted that financial institutions could see, if they so chose, how a potential killer behaved. *The New York Times* examined thirteen mass shootings in this century and discovered that, in at least eight of them, killers financed their slaughter with credit cards. Without those cards, the killers might otherwise not have afforded the weapons and ammunition that they bought.

Example A: The man who shot up the Pulse nightclub in Orlando, FL, killing 49 people and wounding 53 others, used six credit cards to buy two guns and thousands of rounds of ammunition.

Example B: The killer who attacked a movie house in Aurora, Colorado shelled out $11,000 on his credit card to buy a .40 Glock handgun, a 12-gauge shotgun, a 223-caliber AR-15, a bulletproof vest, five thousand rounds of ammunition and a gas mask. "This was a civilian making these orders, not the police and not the military," said the mother of a girl who died in the attack on the movie house. "Someone should have noticed."

Example C: Stephen Paddock, a man of means, stockpiled a veritable arsenal of weaponry in his suite at the Mandalay Bay Resort in Las Vegas, Nevada. Records show that he spent close to $95,000 on firearms and weapon-related paraphernalia. Paddock made some of these purchases online. Police found four credit cards in his hotel rooms.

A former New York Police fraud investigator commented, "Banks will complain [that tracking killers' spending] is the government's job and it's not our job, but you know what? They are the only ones with the ability to do this."

Echoing this perceived response from the purveyors of credit cards, a spokeswoman for Visa told *The Times* that: "We do not believe Visa should be in the position of setting restrictions on the sale of lawful goods or services." She stated further:

> Our role in commerce is to efficiently process, protect and settle all legal payments [she went on]. Asking Visa or other payment networks to arbitrate what legal goods can be purchased sets a dangerous precedent.

Nonetheless, under provisions of the Patriot Act, enacted

after the September 11 attack on the Twin Towers in Manhattan, banks are required to submit what are known as Suspicious Activity Reports for transactions in excess of $5,000 if they have reason to suspect that they involve a violation of or an attempt to evade any federal law.

A thicket of rules prevents banks from knowing exactly what customers using their credit cards are actually buying. Still, as the president of the Anti-Money Laundering Training Academy observed, "They can fine-tune their own systems because in these cases the suspicious purchasing patterns could have been picked up on and quite frankly should have been picked up on."

"They have all the infrastructure in place," said a former federal counterterrorism prosecutor and a staff member of the FBI's 9/11 Review Commission. "It would just be tweaking it to consider firearm-related information."

Some bankers are reluctant to speak of ways the industry might get more involved in helping to stop mass gun killings for fear of antagonizing the Second Amendment claque. But both Citibank and Bank of America decided to discontinue financing gun manufacturers. PayPal has instituted rules that prevent the sale of guns and gun-related items. Still, banks had reason to be cautious. Senator Kennedy (R-LA) introduced legislation which "prohibits the federal government from giving contracts to banks that discriminate against lawful businesses based solely on social policy considerations."

In a mocking defense of his bill (called the No Red and Blue Banks Act), Kennedy tweeted that "our friends at Citigroup and Bank of America apparently aren't busy enough with their banking business; they have decided that they are going to set policy for the Second Amendment."

The ACLU also had concerns that attempts to stem the epidemic of mass shootings in the country might infringe on individual rights. "The implication of expecting the government to detect and prevent every mass shooting is believing the government should play an enormously intrusive role in American life," wrote a senior policy analyst at the ACLU in July 2018.

Is there a happy medium between external security and individual rights?

A chief counsel for the Giffords Law Center to Prevent Gun Violence believes there is:

> There are a lot of steps that credit card companies can take that could prevent some of the tragic gun violence in the country. For companies to say they can't solve the entire problem and therefore shouldn't take any steps is just blindly ignoring what they can contribute to the solution.

Following the mass shooting at Pulse, the Orlando nightclub, JPMorgan Chase donated more than $300,000 to the victims of that attack and their families. The father of one of the victims, Christopher Sanfeliz, learned that his son, a personal banker at Chase, had been employed by the same company which had unwittingly functioned as a cash cow for other shootings. "Something needs to be done to prevent more attacks," he said. "I live with this torment every day of my life."

Gun Control Groups

SEVERAL MAJOR GUN CONTROL ADVOCACY groups arose in the aftermath of gun massacres on American soil. These included:

The Brady Coalition to Prevent Gun Violence. As recorded in the chapter on political assassinations this group, named after Jim Brady who was injured and permanently paralyzed in John Hinkley's attempt on the president's life, came into existence in 1974. It provided the impetus behind the passage of the so-called Brady Bill which required background checks to ferret out domestic abusers, felons, and fugitives and stop them from acquiring guns. In 2018, the organization celebrated the twenty-fifth anniversary of the passage of that bill.

The Giffords Law Center/Americans for Responsible Solutions (ARS) Gabby Giffords and Mark Kelly began the ARS in 2013. In 2016, ARS merged with the Law Center to Prevent Gun Violence to become the Giffords Law Center. The organization has an address in the financial district of San Francisco. If you go to the address listed in its web page, you find yourself in a UPS office. A mistake? No. The Law Center is concerned about security. Who knows if some gun nut might try to shoot up the office?

Everytown for Gun Safety. This group began under a different name—Mayors Against Illegal Guns. It was founded by Michael Bloomberg and other mayors of major US cities in 2006. In 2014, the group Moms Demand Action joined, and the new organization adopted the name, Everytown for Gun Safety.

The organization issued a report in early February 2019 which examined the effects of gun violence on victims. It recounts the story of one Indianapolis teenager, DeAndre Knox. The boy attended a friend's birthday party. An argument broke out, shots were fired—about twenty of them—and DeAndre was struck on the left side of his head. The bullet left him paralyzed, a quadriplegic. He lost the ability to speak. His mother DeAndra Dycus, was appointed his legal guardian for the rest of his life.

"All his friends are going off to college," she said. "You can't help but think of the what-ifs. My son was a basketball player like his friends were. He wanted to go to Indiana University."

The survey by Everytown for Gun Safety found that 58 percent of American adults have suffered from trauma at some time in their lifetimes. That's trauma related to gun violence. "Gun violence in any form leaves an indelible mark on the lives of those who are affected," says Christopher Kocher, director of the Everytown Survivor Network. Caring for a survivor of gun violence does not come cheap. The average cost for a hospital admission ranges from $19,175 for a handgun injury to $32,237 for an assault weapon injury. The stats cited at the beginning of this chapter come from a study done by Everytown.

Everytown has an extensive network of followers. The organization claims three million of them. This army can be mobilized to lobby for legislation that Everytown endorses. A day after the carnage at the Pulse nightclub in Orlando, postcards went out to friends and family of the victims to offer condolences. Everytown exists as a resource for such people. "The gun lobby has had its way in state legislatures for decades," said Everytown's Executive Director, John Feinblatt, a former aide to Bloomberg. "They wanted to convince the American public of their invincibility, to convince the American public that what America stood for was guns anywhere, held by anyone, at any time. There has been no friction in many ways."

The number of employees at Everytown has exploded from about a dozen in 2014 to 130 five years later. Bloomberg has pledged $50 million to support Everytown. That sum is dwarfed by what the NRA has spent: $345 million in 2014. Not surprisingly the NRA is critical of Everytown:

"They use tragedy and exploit victims to push their policy agenda because they can't win the argument based on facts," said the director of public affairs for the NRA's lobbying division. "The tragedies Michael Bloomberg's gun-control group exploit to push their agenda would not have been prevented by the gun-control policies they want to enact."

"They have a lot of financial resources," the director of Everytown explained. "That's why their voice is being heard."

Everytown counters that many of their one-hundred-odd-thousand donors cough up donations in increments of ten-to-twenty-five dollars.

Colin Goddard—the man who was shot multiple times at Virginia Tech in 2007—is a senior policy advocate in the organization's Washington office. "The work is difficult," he says. "You feel like you make a lot of progress, but then you hear of a shooting and feel like you're back at square one . . . I don't want to do this forever."

Following a suggestion made by the father of a shooting victim, Everytown created an online postcard which people could send their elected representatives. Ultimately volunteers sent 1.2 million cards to the White House, Congress, and governors' offices.

Everytown has scored some legislative successes. It has pushed for stricter gun laws in five states since 2013. It has also enlisted the aid of celebrities like Stephen Curry and Chris Paul of the NBA to create TV commercials for gun control.

Said Executive Director John Feinblatt:

> In so many respects, the gun lobby was just given the turf for

> decades and that was the only voice you heard. I think it's very important that people have multiple ways of raising their voice and saying 'We want to live in a different world. We want to live in a world that's safe.

Most of the time these groups act independently. But one example of coordination was a forum on gun safety sponsored by March for Our Lives and Giffords/ARC in Las Vegas, held one day after the second anniversary of the Route 91 Harvest music festival massacre. The event attracted a number of Democrats vying for their party's presidential nomination. The candidates agreed on stricter gun control measures although there was a clash between Beto O'Rourke and Pete Buttigieg on the mandatory vs. voluntary buyback of assault weapons. O'Rourke argued that the program should be mandatory whereas Buttigieg advocated a voluntary approach. Buttigieg was "afraid of doing the right thing," claimed O'Rourke; Buttigieg ridiculed mandatory buyback as a "shiny object." Did he mean by shiny object the Holy Grail? An American politician, particularly one who was a Rhodes Scholar, had to be careful not to appear too highfalutin by making a reference to the Holy Grail. Mayor Pete said, "Calling for mandatory buyback derailed a serious attempt to institute background checks, red flag laws, and the sale of assault weapons.

The 2018 midterm elections saw a change from previous elections. NRA-backed candidates faced new challenges which some of them could not overcome. The ARS notched up six wins for the candidates that the group supported for Congress. These victories came, of course, at a stiff price: ARS spent more than one million dollars apiece to retire five Republicans running for seats in the House of Representatives; and one Republican, Dean Heller, running to retain his seat in the US Senate. All these defeated candidates were pro-gun politicians.

Probably the most encouraging news for gun control advocates came from the cordial reception accorded the Parkland High School activists whose efforts received wide recognition. Several of them flew to Cape Town, South Africa to be awarded the International Children's Peace Prize. In making the presentation, Archbishop Desmond Tutu said:

> The peaceful campaign to demand safe schools and communities, and the eradication of gun violence, is reminiscent of other great peace movements in history. I am in awe of these children whose powerful message is amplified by their youthful energy, and an unshakeable belief that children can—no, must—improve their own futures.

March For Our Lives issued a statement about this accomplishment. "We are truly humbled and grateful for this award," the statement read, "but know that our work will not stop until we end the appalling and preventable epidemic of gun violence in the United States."

The father of one of the Parkland victims, Joaquin Oliver, spoke at Cape Town. Manuel Oliver would later castigate the comedian, C.K. Louis, for ridiculing the Parkland student activists (as recounted in a previous chapter). Now he stood beside a life-size statue of his son and said:

> Joaquin has a voice through art, he is an activist and not a victim. We work along with Joaquin, we work supported by Joaquin's legacy and his presence through art, through his cultures. Joaquin's always there and that helps us [since] we don't have our son any more. Physically we don't, but emotionally he's right there stronger than ever.
>
> By practicing the idea that Joaquin is an activist, by bringing him to the places that we are, people understand that as something that is really happening. It's not someone who's alive and speaking out, this is a more powerful force coming from this kid that is still here and he's able to fight back. I live that feeling.

The group was achieving results. More than twenty-five states passed legislation consistent with its mission. One Parkland High student gloated over the defeat of one particularly prominent NRA protegée. David Hogg tweeted, "Bye@BarbaraComstock."

When Hogg and some of his friends walked past the Congresswoman's office in D.C., her staffers had alre ady slammed their door shut. Hogg's sister Lauren tweeted, "Sending my thoughts and prayers to every NRA-backed politician tonight" (November 6, 2018).

Not everything went the way that the Parkland activists wanted: Pro-gun candidates won the contests for the two highest offices up for election in Florida in 2018, the governorship and a seat in the US Senate. "I'm shaking with anger right now," said one of the students. "We're not going to stop fighting," she continued. "I can tell you, I'm doing this for the rest of my life."

`It just proves we have a lot further to go," said David Hogg. "This is going to be a long uphill battle."

Students expressed concern that the governor-elect, Ron DeSantis, might try to roll back the modest package of gun control compromises that the Florida legislature had passed after the shooting at Marjory Stoneman Douglas High School. DeSantis lost no time, upon becoming governor of Florida, in suspending Broward County Sheriff Scott Israel, a Democratic appointee whose handling of the Parkland school massacre had been sharply criticized. The sheriff, DeSantis' office asserted, had "repeatedly failed and [had] demonstrated a pattern of poor leadership."

A Florida panel, charged with investigating the rampage at Parkland, dealt another blow to the student activists. It issued a unanimous report urging the state legislature to approve a measure to permit teachers "properly selected, thoroughly screened and extensively trained to carry concealed firearms on campus for self-protection, and the protection of other staff and students in response to an active assailant incident." This recommendation flew in the face of the views of the state teachers' union. Former New York City Police Commissioner Bill Bratton said that arming teachers was "the height of lunacy."

"People love their guns here," said the father of one of the Parkland students killed in the shooting on February 14, 2018. "I just don't know what it is with them. They just don't get it. They just don't feel it."

"It's hard emotionally," said an English teacher at Marjory Stoneman Douglas. After the results of the 2018 midterms came in, she said that she would urge her students "to keep using their voices."

The New York Times reported in mid-December 2018 that

state legislatures had passed sixty-nine gun control measures since the Parkland massacre. Michael Bloomberg's group, Everytown for Gun Safety, said that around ninety percent of NRA-supported bills went down to defeat in state legislatures in 2018. "Michael Bloomberg-funded gun control groups have invested unprecedented resources in their state lobbying and public relations effort shifting the gun control battleground to the state level," stated the NRA.

"A lot of policies that we have been working on as a movement for years were pushed across the finish line because of Parkland," said an attorney for the Giffords Law Center. As one might expect, Democratic state legislatures passed more than twice as many gun restrictions as Republican legislatures in 2018. More than half of these came in March and April of that year, in the wake of the Parkland attack.

"There was this structure we had built that could take in all of that anger and heartbreak and make it into action and put it into passing laws," said a spokesperson for Everytown.

"Another factor was strategic," wrote *The New York Times*.

> Many people who wanted stricter gun laws despaired when Congress didn't pass any after Sandy Hook. But it was precisely that inaction in Congress that prompted advocates to start focusing on state legislatures instead.

There is almost unanimous support among the public for universal background checks. Red flag laws, which permit judges to confiscate guns from people whom family or police suspect of posing an imminent threat, especially command widespread support. Such laws, it has been pointed out, might have prevented the Parkland massacre.

Desmond Tutu's praise for the Parkland student activists was by no means the only recognition that they received. The students took pride their place on Time's list of one hundred most influential people in 2018. The five students who started #NeverAgain donned formal apparel and appeared at Time's gala in New York City on April 24, 2018.

Their profile was written by former president, Barack Obama. It reads:

America's response to mass shootings has long followed a predictable pattern. We mourn. Offer thoughts and prayers. Speculate about the motives. And then—even as no developed country endures a homicide rate like ours, a difference explained largely by pervasive accessibility to guns; even as the majority of gun owners support commonsense reforms—the political debate spirals into acrimony and paralysis.
This time, something different is happening. This time, our children are calling us to account.

The Parkland, FL students don't have the kind of lobbyists or big budgets for attack ads that their opponents do. Most of them can't even vote yet.

But they have the power so often inherent in youth: to see the world anew; to reject the old constraints, outdated conventions and cowardice too often dressed up as wisdom. The power to insist that America can be better.

Seared by memories of seeing their friends murdered at a place they believed to be safe, these young leaders don't intimidate easily. They see the NRA and its allies—whether mealy-mouthed politicians or mendacious commentators peddling conspiracy theories—as mere shills for those who make money selling weapons of war to whoever can pay. They're as comfortable speaking truth to power as they are dismissive of platitudes and punditry. And they live to mobilize their peers.

Already, they've had some success persuading statehouses and some of the biggest gun retailers to change. Now it gets harder. A Republican Congress remains unmoved. NRA scare tactics still sway much of the country. Progress will be slow and frustrating.

But by bearing witness to carnage, by asking tough questions and demanding real answers, the Parkland students are shaking us out of our complacency. The NRA's favored candidates are starting to fear they might lose. Law-abiding gun owners are starting to speak out. As these young leaders make common cause with African- Americans and Latinos—the disproportionate victims of gun violence—and reach voting age, the possibilities of meaningful change will steadily grow.

Our history is defined by the youthful push to make America more just, more compassionate, more equal under the law. This generation—of Parkland, of Dreamers, of Black Lives Matter—embraces that duty. If they make their elders uncomfortable, that's how it should be. Our kids now show us what we've told them America is all about, even if we haven't always believed it ourselves: that our future isn't written for us, but by us.

David Hogg responded to this encomium. How else? In a tweet, of course, in which he wrote: "Thanks, Obama."

The NRA Hemorrages

THE NRA WAS GOING THROUGH a rough patch, and one commentator—E. J. Dionne of the *Washington Post*—went so far as to headline one of his opinion pieces 'It's the beginning of the end for the gun lobby's power.'

The 2018 election was a watershed: Voters for whom gun policy was the paramount issue in the campaign opted for the Democrats, seventy percent to twenty-nine percent. 2018 was also the year that saw gun control groups outspend gun rights groups significantly: close to $55 million as opposed to $3 million for the gun rights groups. (These figures come from the Center for Responsive Politics.) Dionne credits the shift in public opinion to the Marjory Stoneman Douglas High School student activists and the gun control groups that sprang up after the massacres, some of which are described in this book.

According to a lengthy article to appear in *The New Yorker* (17 April 2019). The NRA was hemorrhaging money, sometimes to the tune of $40 million a year. Memos written by someone identified in the article as a senior NRA employee alleged that "management has subordinated its judgment to the vendors." As far back as December 1996, the NRA finance committee acknowledged that the organization had been "technically insolvent for several years."

One indication of the gun-rights group's problems was its public rift with its long-time public relations firm, Oklahoma-based Ackerman McQueen. The PR firm is a family business which employs more than 200 people in offices in cities like Dallas and Colorado Springs. Some NRA staff members felt that Ackerman was too expensive. One man, Aaron Davis, who worked for the organization's fund-raising, told *The New Yorker* that Ackerman was "just using the NRA to make a massive profit." For its part, the NRA did not stint on its own promotional events. Davis confessed that he was doing "fund-raising dinners with other NRA executives where "wine was pouring freely . . . at dinners where the bill would be a thousand dollars—just to go out to dinner!"

Davis had to admit that Ackerman was good at what it did. "They were topnotch; they did beautiful graphic design, great writing, and we started to lean on them."

There was resentment at how the NRA was spending its money. Davis recalls taking a board member to lunch to ask for a donation. His guest on this venture told Davis, "I like you, but I hate your department."

"Why?" asked Davis.

"Because NRA is not fancy Italian shoes with thousand-dollar suits; NRA is the backbone of this country, wearing blue jeans and boots, and your division is taking us to a whole 'nother place.'" Certainly some senior officials at the NRA were handsomely paid. For example, its executive director of general operations copped nearly $800,000 in 2017.

In 2017, the NRA began to promote a scheme called Carry Guard which offered training by Special Forces members, and liability insurance to protect policyholders who shot people in self-defense. The program was intended to safeguard the organization's financial security. After splurging $50 million on the 2016 election—mostly to ensure Donald Trump's election—the NRA needed a cash injection.

Critics of Carry Guard labeled the program "murder insurance." In May 2018, the New York Department of Financial Services ruled that Carry Guard could no longer be sold in the state. The NRA countered by suing the department, claiming that New York's action had led to "tens of millions of dollars in damages." Ackerman McQueen received $6 million for its work on the program when it was introduced in 2017.

As Davis stated earlier, a sizeable chunk of the NRA's money problems was due to what the organization was paying Ackerman McQueen. The NRA's 2017 tax filings indicated that more than forty million dollars was paid to the PR firm and its affiliates. Payment through a variety of entities made it difficult to track where exactly the money was going. This is not illegal, but as a former IRS manager told *The New Yorker*, "multiple names for the same entity suggest an effort to disguise the extent of contact."

The NRA ultimately sued Ackerman McQueen (with which it had been associated for more than thirty years) for denying the organization access to its business records. The lawsuit against Ackerman McQueen alleged that the PR firm had overbilled the NRA. Ackerman McQueen said of the suit that it was "frivolous, inaccurate and intended to cause harm to the reputation of our company."

It would be hard to exaggerate the intimate relationship between these two entities. Ackerman produced the NRA magazine America's 1st Freedom. It also produced a series called "Freedom's Safest Place" in which a country music star warned "the ayatollahs of Iran" that they might know the country's 45th "fresh-faced flower-child president," but they didn't know "the people who will defend this nation with their bloody, calloused bare hands." This sounds like a rehash of Charlton Heston's famous one-liner in Planet of the Apes.

"I've been working on gun safety for fifteen years," said John Feinblatt of Everytown for Gun Safety, "and I've never seen the NRA this weak." This is something the NRA would deny, of course, but it could not but concede that the opposition was now well-funded. Democratic candidates running for the presidency in 2020 hopped on the gun-control bandwagon to a degree that Feinblatt described as a "seismic shift." There has been a surge in gun-control measures being considered in Congress. It is a fact that laws backed by gun-control groups passed in twenty-odd states. These groups point to the defeat of a "Stand-your-Ground" bill in Arkansas as evidence of their increased clout and a corresponding weakening of the NRA.

In the past, the organization had been flush with funds.

It now seemed strapped for cash. Losses of $64 million for 2016 and 2017 are credited with the NRA's raising of its fees in 2018 for a second year in a row. "We're facing an attack that's unprecedented not just in the history of the NRA but in the entire history of our country," wrote Wayne LaPierre in a fund-raising effort. The chair of the accounting department at Ohio State University's Fisher College of Business analyzed eleven years of the NRA's financial statements, 2007-2017, and concluded that in seven of those years the organization "owed more money to others than it had at its discretion to spend." A 2017 audit showed that it had just about exhausted a $25 million line of credit.

Ackerman-McQueen created and operated the online channel NRATV. Most of the firm's efforts seem to involve what one former employee described as "servicing the NRA." The firm's services came with a hefty price tag, $40 million a year according to The New York Times. Inevitably, as collaboration between Ackerman-McQueen and the NRA intensified, resentment on the part of rank-and-file NRA employees could not be disguised. An anecdote which ran in *The New Yorker* illustrated the point: The juxtaposition of Ackerman-McQueen Lexus vehicles in the parking lot of the NRA headquarters in northern Virginia and the far more modest cars which NRA employees drove spoke volumes about the disparity between the two organizations. "They had a lot going on for them," noted one former NRA fund-raiser, "but they weren't your folks who were interested in Second Amendment politics." Said Adam Winkler, a professor at the UCLA School of Law and a gun rights expert: "The battle in the NRA board that must have occurred with this breakup of a decades-long relationship must have been something."

The NRA charged in its lawsuit that some NRA members have questioned NRATV's ventures into subjects remote from the Second Amendment. The controversy ultimately pitted the NRA's president, Oliver L. North—he of Iran-contra infamy—against Wayne LaPierre, the organization's long-time executive secretary who rose to that level of prominence in the NRA from his first position as a lobbyist. Described by associates as a meek man, LaPierre has hurled verbal thunderbolts at the elites he professes to despise. He issues jeremiads like this one: "We're standing at the edge of fear, staring into the abyss of the demise of our country and its freedom we care about most."

North asked LaPierre to resign, but LaPierre turned the tables on North. "Yesterday evening, I was forced to confront one of those defining choices—styled in the parlance of extortionists—as an offer I couldn't refuse," the executive secretary wrote. "I refused it."

"All of this is painful for me," LaPierre retorted in connection with his spat with North. "I will not judge Col. North but must report what many of you already know: He has contractual and financial loyalties to [Ackerman McQueen]." LaPierre claimed that he had been threatened with "accusations of wardrobe expenses and excessive staff travel expenses" if he did not resign. In a letter to the NRA board's executive committee, North alleged that LaPierre had charged more than $200,000 of wardrobe expenses to a vendor.

(What happened was this: LaPierre was running up astronomical tabs at what must have been one of his favorite stores, the Italian men's clothier Ermenegildo Zegna in Beverly Hills. On one particular occasion, he spent almost $40,000 using a credit card billed through Ackerman-McQueen and reimbursed by the NRA. After the rupture between the NRA and its PR firm blew up in public, Ackerman made the catty observation that "Wayne continues to blame others for his own actions. No one forced Mr. LaPierre to walk into a Beverly Hills Zegna store and buy a quarter million dollars of clothing he personally did not pay for." Was there anything illegal about any of these purchases? A former chief of the charities bureau of the New York Attorney General's office offered this opinion: "If the expenses incurred by Mr. LaPierre were not legitimate business expenses of the NRA and if he conspired with others within or outside the NRA to incur those expenses in a way that would conceal them, then criminal charges could not only be brought against Mr. LaPierre but also the others who were involved in the scheme.")

A lawyer for the NRA has said that "there is no suggestion

that any of Mr. LaPierre's expenses were improper in any way," but as E.J.Dionne crowed, "it must be nice to have your life style financed by the people you spend your time scaring to death." In fact, senior NRA executives get handsome salaries: *The Times* found that eight of them make more than the head of the American Red Cross which has ten times the revenue of the NRA. On 26 November 2019, the *Washington Post* ran a story stating that compensation for the NRA's top officials had climbed by 41 percent the previous year while spending on its education and training budget, hunter services, and field services plummeted, in some cases by more than half.

In an ironic twist of fate, it was Oliver North, not Wayne LaPierre, who was forced to withdraw as the president of the NRA. "Please know I hoped to be with you today as NRA president, endorsed for reelection" North wrote in a resignation letter which was read aloud at the NRA 2019 convention in Indianapolis. "I'm now informed that will not happen." That ended North's one-year stint as the head of the organization, a position which was largely ceremonial. The turmoil in the high command was felt by attendees at the convention in Indianapolis where it burst into the open. "I'm hoping that this isn't our last NRA convention," said one man at the organization's massive display of weapons called the "Wall of guns."

North's role in the matter was complicated by what Ackerman McQueen paid him, a sum which LaPierre claimed amounted to millions of dollars every year. The press had published allegations of financial impropriety and North said that he was setting up a special committee to investigate. "I did this," he said, "because I am deeply concerned that these allegations of financial improprieties threaten our nonprofit status."

In fact, the New York attorney general, Letitia James, had initiated an investigation into the NRA's tax-exempt status. James has described the NRA not as a charitable organization but as a terrorist organization. How seriously James' investigation could impact the NRA, which is chartered in the state of New York, became clear in early August 2020 when she sought to dissolve the organization in a suit which alleged fraud. The organization, she claimed, had diverted millions of dollars from the NRA's charitable mission to pay for its leaders' lavish life style. Corruption was so bad that the NRA's leadership had "basically destroyed all the assets of the NRA." The lawsuit alleged that the NRA and its high command had violated state and federal laws by enriching themselves. A personal travel consultant for LaPierre had earned $13.5 million, and LaPierre had taken numerous trips to the Bahamas, staying sometimes on a 108-foot yacht owned by an NRA contractor. James asked that LaPierre and three of his colleagues in the NRA high command be barred from serving in a leadership position for a New York charity.

The NRA had been involved previously in clashes with the state, notably New York's Department of Financial Services (DFS), which prohibited the sale of the organization's insurance policy. The NRA subsequently sued the DFS and New York governor Andrew Cuomo, claiming that the department's decision had resulted in "tens of millions of dollars in damages." The organization has its own insurance policy, which protects NRA directors and officers against charges of mismanagement of NRA assets. Insurance costs skyrocketed 341 percent from 2018 to 2019. "To say this is a major increase would be an understatement," the deputy director of the Insurance Law Center at the University of Connecticut, told *The New Yorker*. "This seems to be pretty direct evidence that the NRA's problems are not due to New York but rather to how the organization conducts itself."

"The NRA will fully cooperate with any inquiry into its finances," said the organization's outside counsel. "The NRA is prepared for this, and has full confidence in its accounting practices and commitment to good governance."

The suit against New York, Wayne LaPierre told an audience at the Conservative Political Action Conference (CPAC) in 2019, "will decide whether or not government can be weaponized against you if your opinion differs from theirs." In fact, the NRA set up a web page specifically to solicit funds to pursue its lawsuit. "Please give as generously as you can," pleads the page, "and help with this life-or-death legal battle for the survival of the NRA and freedom."

In January 2021, the NRA declared bankruptcy and sought to move its HQ from New York to Texas in a move that was interpreted as a tactic to avoid accountability. In the opinion of one man who had been a special counsel in James' office, "This is a long-shot effort to avoid liability in New York and it has a very slim chance of succeeding." Kris Brown of the Brady Group said, "The NRA can run, but they can't hide. No organization is above the law." A major contributor to the NRA lodged a complaint to prevent the NRA from sidestepping more than $60 million of debt on the grounds that it had been improperly incurred. "The NRA is still an old boys' club," he told The Guardian. "[It] is unaccountable to the 5.2 million members who pay for everything."

If the NRA had sought to evade accountability in the state of New York by declaring bankruptcy and transferring its HQ to Texas, the ploy did not work. A federal judge in Texas ruled that the group had filed in bad faith in an attempt to ward off the lawsuit by James. "The Court finds, based on the totality of the circumstance that the NRA's bankruptcy petition was not filed in good faith but instead was filed as an effort to gain an unfair litigation advantage...``to avoid a regulatory scheme," ruled the presiding judge, Harlin Hale.

Letitia James was exultant. "The NRA does not get to dictate when and where it will be held accountable," she told reporters. "This decision sends a loud and clear message that no one is above the law—not even one of the most powerful lobbying organizations in the country."

Ackerman McQueen had joined with the AG of New York to try to dismiss the bankruptcy case. "This decision underscores the incompetence and failure of the NRA leadership and its legal team," claimed an Ackerman executive who had been a former NRA spokesman. Gun control groups were equally quick to pounce. "Today's disastrous decision for the NRA shows that they can't even file for bankruptcy correctly," said John Feinblatt of Everytown for Gun Safety. Another member of the same group, who had previously worked for James, said, "This bankruptcy was a Hail Mary attempt by the NRA to avoid accountability but the court saw right through it."

"The NRA was forced to hang its dirty laundry out for the world to see, and has nothing to show for it but another stack of legal bills." Karen Brown of the Brady Campaign, who had previously mocked the NRA as a propaganda machine ("They deserve a nonprofit status like a Superfund [site] deserves organic certification.") now expressed the opinion that "the NRA cannot escape justice."

The New York Times reported that the NRA Foundation—a charity affiliated with the NRA—had transferred more than $100 million since 2012 to the NRA. This is important because contributions to the Foundation are tax-deductible whereas those to the NRA itself are not. "It tells me that the NRA itself is in very poor financial health and they're being subsidized in large part by their foundation," said a former partner at a firm which specialized in tax-exempt groups. "They're kind of running the organization into the ground."

A former head of the IRS division that oversees tax-exempt enterprises reviewed documents obtained by a reporter for *The New Yorker*. He said:

> The litany of red flags is just extraordinary. The materials reflect one of the broadest arrays of likely transgressions that I've ever seen. There is a tremendous range of what appears to be the misuse of assets for the benefit of certain venders and people in control ... These facts, if confirmed, could lead to the revocation of the NRA's tax-exempt status.

Former members of the NRA have criticized the way the organization is run. One of them, Steve Hoback, wrote in an open letter that the NRA has "become the swamp that many have lashed out against in our Federal government." Another former member, Andrew Lander, has written that "the things that are taking place within the organization, I feel are things that corrupt Congressmen would be doing." In the previously cited article in the Post, a lifetime NRA member, Rob Pincus, is quoted as complaining that "money flowing away from programs and into executives' pockets is causing many longtime members to join the ranks of American gun owners who have lost faith in the NRA, especially its leadership." An example of the extension of NRA largesse to its higher-ups is provided by the salary increase granted its chief strategist, Chris Cox. He pocketed, in 2018, annual compensation of $1.4 million, a 17-percent bump-up over the previous year. For several years, the organization has held its World Shooting Championship at a center owned by the NRA's director of competitive shooting. The center received $70,000 in 2018 for hosting the event although federal rules restrict transactions that benefit economically high-ranking employees of tax-exempt organizations.

The brouhaha at the NRA caught the attention of Donald Trump, a past beneficiary of the organization's largesse. Trump tweeted a directive that the gun-rights group "stop the internal fighting & get back to GREATNESS—FAST!" Despite the turmoil roiling the organization, it maintained its ties—and its influence—in the Trump administration. Wayne LaPierre conferred with the president in September 2019 and told him "to stop the games" on gun control legislation in return for NRA support.

John Feinblatt summed up the situation this way:

> Every day there's a new drip, drip, drip. The NRA is not a gun advocacy organization but a business that has been engaged in self-dealing, awarding contracts with little accountability to their friends, and it seems like a business run amok. It's questionable whether they can play in 2020 the way they have in the past.

The infighting at the NRA was clearly taking a toll on Wayne LaPierre. Speaking of himself in the third person, he confided to an investigative reporter for The New York Times, that "all these horrible tragedies—after every one, Wayne would be the guy going out there in the media. From Columbine to—you name it—to the Navy Yard to Aurora to Sandy Hook. Every one of them, I was the guy—Parkland—I was the guy out there in the media."

Wayne LaPierre was not cut from the same cloth as Charlton Heston. Described as mild-mannered—even meek—he executive director of the NRA was said (by Ackerman McQueen) "to know little about guns or how to actually use them."

The coronavirus epidemic of 2020 hit all US companies hard, and the NRA was no exception. In the spring of 2020, the organization announced that it was cutting salaries by 20 percent and canceling its April meeting. It was also canceling all its Friends of the NRA banquets and its gun shows. Wayne LaPierre saw his salary slashed by more than 20 percent. (Mind you, his salary had been increased in 2018 by 40 percent; that year he received $2.2 million from the NRA and related entities.)

If its financial situation were not enough to give the NRA elite sleepless nights, the organization also faced scrutiny over its involvement in a cloak-and-dagger caper which starred a confessed Russian operative named Maria Butina. The 30-year-old Butina was a twenty-first century version of Mata Hari who spent years trying to infiltrate the gun activist group. Her goal—according to Butina herself—was to "establish unofficial lines of communication with Americans having power and influence over US politics."

"The public record is clear that the NRA bent over backwards to help a Russian agent insinuate herself into conservative political circles," commented Sen. Ron Wyden of Oregon. "The public has a right to know who at the NRA knew Butina's [and her Russian handler's] agenda and why they were so eager to help these Russian agents."

The Russian government was eager to cultivate good relations with the NRA. In late 2015, a group of NRA big shots visited Moscow where Butina and her Russian handler hosted them to caviar and vodka dinners. The NRA delegation met high officials in the Russian government while they were in Moscow. Wayne LaPierre had disparaged the junket. "Are you crazy?" he rhetorically asked the NRA members who went.

Ultimately the Russian agent, who was credited with building a network that penetrated Donald Trump's inner circle, was sentenced to 18 months in prison. A US District Judge granted a request to deport Butina after she served her sentence. "Though it was not my intention to harm the American people," she said at the time of her sentencing, "I did that by not notifying the Attorney General of my actions. Please accept my apology and allow me to begin again." Her once-upon-a-time business partner was a former president of the NRA.

Butina was interviewed only once by the team working under Special Investigator Robert Mueller III and her case is not mentioned in the 448-page report which Mueller later issued. Russian president, Vladimir Putin, denounced Butina's sentence as an outrage, an attempt by the US government to save face. "It's not clear what she was convicted of or what crime she committed," he said.

What did the Russians hope to accomplish by cozying up to the NRA? The NRA spent close to $30 million to elect Donald Trump to the presidency in 2016. Was any of this money Russian? No evidence has been found to support the allegation that Russians channeled a ton of rubles through the NRA to help elect Trump. All that the NRA will admit is that the organization received about $2,500 from Russian sources for "non-electoral purposes "in the 2016 cycle.

"It's smart to follow the money," said one NRA ally. "[The Russians] were trying to open US markets. They were interested in export business, not just for arms but ammunition as well."

A parting note: A lobbyist for the NRA offered this blunt assessment of the advantages conferred on members who pay their dues:

> to protect them from anti-gun legislation and anti-gun policies, and quite frankly, we gave them a president who appointed two good Supreme Court justices and over 100 lower court judges to protect them for a generation or two. And we did that because that's what our members expect us to do.

There is no denying the continued if diminished strength of the gun lobby in the US. During the coronavirus epidemic which swept the country in the spring of 2020, some local ordinances declared gun stores as essential for the safety of citizens and allowed them to stay open while non-essential stores were ordered to close. This happened in Illinois and Pennsylvania. And in Connecticut, the state represented in the US Senate by Richard Blumenthal who said, "Plain and simple, there is no reason why gun stores should be given the exemption [to stay open]." That opinion was echoed by San Jose mayor Sam Liccardo, who told the *Wall Street Journal* that "since we don't live in the wild west, where people are dependent on guns for food, and we do have a well-functioning police department, it would be hard to articulate a basis for arguing that a gun shop would be an essential service."

On A Positive Note

THE SUBJECT OF THIS BOOK CAN depress readers. I am aware of this and have chosen to wrap things up on a positive note. Two unrelated items: On April 11, 2020, President Joe Biden announced that the Bureau of Alcohol, Tobacco, Firearms and Explosives (ATP) would henceforth regulate ghost guns like other guns. (Ghost guns are firearms which can be ordered piecemeal online and assembled like Legos. Customers can do this in about half an hour.) Ghost guns are proliferating—the Department of Justice said that more than 20,000 were collected in law enforcement agencies in 2019, a tenfold increase in three years. No background checks have been required of people who purchase ghost gun kits. The change in regulations is expected to close a significant loophole in the country's gun laws.

Here's a second dollop of feel-good news: In 2019, The Guardian ran a year-long series on the decline of gun-related homicides in the Bay Area. Despite an alarming increase in homelessness, the region registered a thirty percent fall in gun homicides from 2010 to 2019. The cities of Oakland and Richmond in the East Bay pumped millions of dollars in a public health approach to preventing gun violence. It seems, at first blush, paradoxical that the population in state prisons decreased twenty-five percent since 2006. This occurred after California voters approved a reduction in criminal penalties for non-violent crimes. Robyn Thomas of the Giffords Law Center told The Guardian that the state had enacted thirty gun-control laws in the decade ending in 2019. Investment in local prevention strategies, she said, was "the key change."

Contrary to insinuations that immigrants account for more

than their share of criminal activity in the country, The Guardian pointed out that well over half a million residents of the Bay Area were born in Mexico. Why then the decline in gun violence? Dollars and data, claimed The Guardian reporters who wrote the story, and community leadership, some of it provided by previous inmates of state prisons.

Early in March 2020, there occurred a celebratory parade in Oakland to highlight the city's success in reducing gun violence. The coach of the Golden State Warriors, Steve Kerr, and two of his most well-known players, Steph Curry and Klay Thompson, took part in the short march. "I get some pushback but I really don't care because it's too important and too many people are affected," said Kerr in a post-march press conference. During the march there were chants of "I believe that we will win" and "Black Lives Matter." Kerr's own father was shot and killed in Beirut in the 1980s. He alluded to his loss in a town hall meeting later that day. "As someone who's been directly impacted by gun violence," he said, "it's great to see the collaboration of people, like victims and perpetrators of violence, police and the mayor, who in the past wouldn't have collaborated." Support for actions like counseling and job training have been credited for Oakland's success. Gabby Giffords joined the march, walking beside Klay Thompson. The former Congresswoman's eponymous group praised the reduction in Oakland's gun homicide rate.

Captains of industry were beginning to weigh in on the issue of gun control. In September 2019 the CEOs of 145 companies sent a letter to the US Senate urging expanded background checks and permitting courts to take away guns from people they deem dangerous under the red flag law. This was less a breakthrough than it might first appear: Some companies declined to sign the letter and some of those that did wouldn't talk about it. Still, signing the letter was a sign of the times, and some signatories were passionate in their support for gun control. CEO for Levi Strauss, Chip Bergh, had organized the letter campaign along with Everytown for Gun Safety. "Doing nothing about America's gun violence crisis is simply unacceptable," the letter declared. "And it is time to stand with the

American public on gun safety."

* * *

READERS WILL ASK, I REALIZE, what are my own opinions about what can be done. Given the complexities of the problem—and with the experience of writing this book behind me—I tread with circumspection. This will read much like a pamphlet written by March for Your Lives. Be that as it may, here are a couple of thoughts/convictions with the objections that will be raised to them.

1) **Restore the ban on assault weapons.**

"I feel very strongly we should not have people 18 to 21 with guns," Jonathan Metzl, a psychiatrist at Vanderbilt University, has said. "There's a lot of research about how [young adults'] brains are not fully developed in terms of regulation," Metzl said. According to him, the prefontal cortex, which is crucial to understanding the consequences of one's actions and controlling impulses, does not fully develop until about age 25. Thus a shooting "certainly feels like another kind of performance of young masculinity."

Kami Chavis, director of the criminal justice program at Wake Forest University School of Law, has said that "We need to pay attention to the scientific evidence that suggests these young minds may not be capable of having the serious responsibility of owning an assault rifle."

I would go further: Assault weapons should not be in the hands of civilians, regardless of their age, as Barack Obama has said. A previous attempt to ban them during the Carter administration was allowed to lapse by a Republican congress. It was claimed at the time that the ban had a negligible effect on the kinds of massacres detailed in this book. The recent interpretation of Second Amendment rights after *District of Columbus v. Heller* may be cited as the reason such a ban is now unconstitutional, although that would be an issue for the courts to resolve. In stating the majority position in the finding, Scalia wrote that bans on "unusual and dangerous weapons" were still permissible. A spokeswoman for the Brady Campaign also found that the court finding did not negate such gun laws as background checks.

Be that as it may, there is still opposition to a prohibition on civilian ownership of assault weapons. For starters, there is the matter of definition. What is an assault weapon? What are military-type firearms? Much of these objections are an exercise in quibbling. What is clearly meant is that a gun like an AR-15 should not be in the hands of a civilian. Historian and criminologist James Alan Fox has observed that "semiautomatic handguns are far more prevalent in mass shootings." He suggests that limiting the size of ammo clips "would at least force a gunman to pause to reload or switch weapons." My view: Ban semiautomatic weaponry as well as guns like the AR-15.

It has been pointed out that a miniscule percentage of deaths by firearms can be attributed to the sort of weaponry that would fall under a proposed ban on what we call here assault weapons. The ban imposed during the Carter Administration did not affect significantly the homicide rate. Elsewhere banning assault weapons has not been successful. In Australia, for example, ten years after that country enacted strict gun control laws, authorities estimated that there were a quarter million guns illegally in the possession of citizens. What happened in New Zealand was similarly discouraging: A buy-back of weapons netted only 700 out of an estimated 1.5 million guns. People just don't comply with laws that restrict their ownership and use of banned weapons. Photographed in the national media, a prominent sign at the January 2020 guns-right rally in Richmond, VA proclaimed, "WE WILL NOT COMPLY," all in capital letters. It might help to slap a stiff fine on recidivist gun-owners who refuse to relinquish outlawed weapons. My view: Failure in other countries to enforce gun laws should not deter authorities in this country from enacting and enforcing gun control measures. Any attempt to control guns, as advocated here, is bound to end up in the Supreme Court. So be it; DC vs. Heller is overdue for a second look.

Daunting as it may be, grabbing guns like the AR-15 from

civilian hands will not affect the homicide rate due to firearms, but it will diminish, if not outright curtail, the sickening phenomenon of gun massacres committed by psychopaths with access to such weapons. Killings like those at the Pulse Nightclub in Orlando or the Route 91 Harvest music festival at Las Vegas were perpetrated by men in possession of military-caliber firepower.

Other writers share my view. Writing in the *Post* in 2018 (and updated four years later), Assistant Editor Robert Gebelhoff advocated banning weapons of war. He acknowledges that the previous ban which expired in 2004 was insignificant, but the ban was full of loopholes. Nonetheless, "semiautomatic weapons and weapons with high-capacity magazines are more dangerous than other weapons."

2) Adopt a stricter attitude toward mental health.

James Alan Fox has observed that mass murderers resist attempts that encourage them to seek help. I still feel that efforts like Valerie Johnson's, detailed in the opening chapter of this book, to nip in-the-bud homicidal tendencies on the part of her son Shawn, should be encouraged. Even in this brief survey, there are at least two examples of shooters hearing voices in their heads: Valerie's son thought the Angel Gabriel was talking to him; Nikolas Cruz claimed to be hearing voices which urged him to kill, to burn, to destroy. Can the disclosure to the appropriate authorities of auditory hallucinations like these be made mandatory for family members who know of them? Should the families of potential mass murderers be required to turn their crazy kin in for psychotic evaluation/treatment? Red flag laws adopted by many states give these families the power to report their concerns about potentially violent relatives. All states should have such laws. Gebelhoff included in his list of potential solutions to gun violence, strengthening red flag laws and background checks.

To explore these questions, I turned to a personal friend, Michael Seely, who is a psychiatrist. I've consulted him before about the motives of mass killers. The principal problem, Seely points out, is that there is no obvious "mechanism of action." If a parent of a mentally unstable child complains to the police, their response is likely to be a shrug. What can we do? To commit someone involuntarily to a mental institution is not easy. It requires evidence that the person to be committed poses an imminent danger to himself/herself or to others. The threshold of proof is high.

There is a misconception in this country, Seely believes, about safeguards to protect the public against mentally suspect behavior. He suggests that companies which insure gun owners might have a role to play in controlling violent behavior by flagging signs of antisocial tendencies.

3) Institute universal background checks for the purchase of firearms.

Enforce the prohibition to buy firearms for those people deemed to be violence-prone. That is the thrust of the red flag laws now being adopted by a number of states. In an article for *The New York Times* which he wrote in the wake of the mass shooting at Sutherland Springs, TX, Nicholas Kristof advocated background checks and protection orders targeted at men prone to domestic violence. Kristof's approach is a public health consideration, modeled after automobile regulations. The liberal approach, he notes, has failed and he cites as evidence how little the ten year ban on assault weapons accomplished. Yet he goes on to observe that the ban was ineffective because "definitions were about cosmetic features like bayonet mounts."

Kristof is certainly not opposed to regulation. "In many places," he says, "there is more rigorous screening of people who want to adopt dogs than of people who want to purchase firearms." He compares the situation in two states—Connecticut, which tightened its gun laws in 1995, and Missouri which eased its laws in 2007. Connecticut saw a 40 percent drop in firearm homicides while Missouri suffered a 25 percent increase. *The Times* re-ran Kristof's op-ed piece in 2019, after the mass shooting at Virginia Beach.

James Alan Fox again: "Mass killers will always find an alternative way of securing the needed weaponry." My view: We need to eliminate those alternative ways.

Fox is dismissive of other proposed panaceas: Increase security in schools ("a minor inconvenience" for those bent on mayhem); expand right-to-carry laws (this will "potentially catch countless innocent victims in the crossfire"); enforce existing gun laws including capital punishment for perpetrators of massacres ("mass killers typically expect to die").

Fox has a measured view. He argues that:

> Sensible gun laws, affordable mental-health care, and reasonable security measures are all worthwhile, and would enhance the well-being of millions of Americans. They may do much to impact the level of violent crime that plagues our nation daily. We shouldn't, however, expect such efforts to take a big bite out of crime in its most extreme form. Of course, a nibble or two from the prevalence of mass murder would be reason enough. And efforts to promote real change in our social policies would be a fitting legacy to the tragedy of Newtown.

Acknowledgments

As explained in the first chapter, the genesis of this book lies in the senseless attack on Alex Melchert. I am grateful for the cooperation of the entire Melchert family in the writing of this book and hereby dedicate it to Alex, in particular, and to all victims of gun violence in this country.

I need to acknowledge the assistance and insight which Valerie Johnson, Shawn Johnson's mother, offered in compiling material for the first chapter of this book.

Let me express my gratitude to two clinical psychiatrists, Paul Linde and Michael Seely, who offered their professional help with the actions of some of the characters who appear in these pages. Paul's experience in this country and in Africa were especially illuminating.

I thank Edward Brunt for his careful and insightful reading of the chapter on Kansas. A 30-year veteran of the Lawrence police force, he offered helpful criticism of that chapter.

I am indebted to Dan Close of the *Wichita Eagle* for helpful advice about making contact with potentially recalcitrant interviewees.

Without my journalistic sources, principally *The New York Times*, the *Washington Post*, and the British daily *The Guardian*, this book would never have seen the light of day.

References

(n.d.). Retrieved from Parents Against Gun Violence: http://www.parentsagainstgunviolence.com/

Ali Rowhani-Rahbar MD, P. M. (2017). "Loaded Handgun Carrying Among US Adults", 2015. *American Journal of Public Health*.

Anderson, P. (2017, October 17). Man arrested Tuesday after eight-hour standoff in East Lawrence. Retrieved from *The Topeka Capital-Journal*: https://www.cjonline.com/story/news/crime/2017/10/17/man-arrested-tuesday-after-eight-hour-standoff-east-lawrence/16524302007/

Asmelash, L. (2020, July 26). How Black Lives Matter went from a hashtag to a global rallying cry. CNN.

Assesment, F. B. (2006). White Supremacist Infiltration of Law Enforcement. FBI Counterterrorism Devision.

Barajas, J. (2018, August 7). Kansas man sentenced to life in prison for 2017 shooting that targeted Indian men. Retrieved from PBS New Hour: https://www.pbs.org/newshour/nation/kansas-man-sentenced-to-life-in-prison-for-2017-shooting-that-targeted-indian-men

Beauchamp, Z. (2020, July 7). "What the police really believe." Vox.

Cox, J. W. (2021). "Children Under Fire: An American Crisis. "*Ecco*.

Dodge City, Kansas – A Wicked Little Town. (n.d.). Retrieved from Legends of America: https://www.legendsofamerica.com/ks-dodgecity/

Editors, H. (2013). Florida teen Trayvon Martin is shot and killed. HISTORY.

Editors, H. (2021, February 22). Ahmaud Arbery is shot dead while out jogging. HISTORY.

Eversley, M. (2016, February 25). Three dead plus gunman in Kansas shootings; 14 injured. Retrieved from *USA Today*: https://www.usatoday.com/story/news/2016/02/25/reports-2-dead-hesston-kansas-workplace-shooting/80954886/

Fieldstadt, E., Chribas, K., & Saliba, E. (2020, May 26). 'I can't breathe': Man dies after pleading with officer during Minneapolis detainment. NBC News.

German, M. (2020, August 28). "The FBI warned for years that police are cozy with the far right. Is no one listening?" *The Guardian*.

Held, K. S. (2022, November 3). "Richard Emery formally sentenced for St. Charles quadruple murder." Fox 2 News.

Howard, J. (2018, May 21). "NRA's incoming president ties Ritalin to school shootings, but here's what the science says." Retrieved from CNN: https://www.cnn.com/2018/05/21/health/ritalin-school-shootings-oliver-north-bn/index.html

Indian engineer killed in Kansas: "5 things we know about gunman Adam

Purinton." (2017, February 28). Retrieved from *Hindustan Times:* https://www.hindustantimes.com/india-news/indian-engineer-killed-in-kansas-5-things-we-know-about-gunman-adam-purinton/story-hIQSHZlnJ50Aje9Kn4n3dI.html

Jones, R. (2021, October 28). "Facing Up to the Racist Legacy of America's Immigration Laws". Retrieved from *The New York Times:* https://www.nytimes.com/2021/10/28/opinion/race-immigration-racism.html

Kansas gun law may prompt congressional backlash. (2016, September 19). Retrieved from Lawrence Journal-World: https://www2.ljworld.com/news/2016/sep/19/kansas-gun-law-may-prompt-congressional-backlash/

Kansas Personal And Family Protection Act. (2013, July 1). Kansas, United States.

Lawhorn, C. (2017, October 1). 5 people shot in downtown Lawrence; 3 dead. Retrieved from Lawrence Journal-World: https://www2.ljworld.com/news/2017/oct/01/three-people-reported-shot-downtown-lawrence/

MacGillis, Alec, *Stopping the Violence,* **The New Yorker,** Feb 6, 2023

Multiple Weapons Found in Las Vegas Gunman's Hotel Room. (2017, October 2). *The New York Times.*

No charges to be filed in officer-involved shooting of Joseph Weber. (2016, September 29). Retrieved from KSNT: https://www.ksnt.com/news/no-charges-to-be-filed-in-officer-involved-shooting-of-joseph-weber/

Our dreams turned short because of one person: Full statement by Srinivas Kuchibhotla's wife in US court. (2018, May 5). Retrieved from *Hindustan Times:* https://www.hindustantimes.com/india-news/our-dreams-turned-short-because-of-one-person-full-statement-by-srinivas-kuchibhotla-s-wife-in-us-court/story-eSymB4USa2q7QqCX66E2OO.html

Parker, K., Horowitz, J. M., Igielnik, R., Oliphant, J. B., & Brown, A. (2017). *America's Complex Relationship with Guns.* Pew Research Center.

Safran, E. (2016, October 5). Ohio gunman 'needed help,' mother says. *Post Crescent.*

Staff, K., & Auld, A. (2021, February 25). Hesston community remembers Excel shooting 5 years later. Retrieved from KWCH: https://www.kwch.com/2021/02/25/hesston-community-remembers-excel-shooting-5-years-later/

State v. Roberts, 503 P.3d 227 (Supreme Court of Kansas February 4, 2022).

Sullivan, J., Anthony, Z., Tate, J., & Jenkins, J. (2018). Nationwide, police shot and killed nearly 1,000 people in 2017. *Washington Post.*

Tapper, J., Diaz, D., & Raju, M. (2021, January 12). Metal detectors installed outside House floor as Democrats express safety concerns about their colleagues. CNN.

Timeline of events in shooting of Michael Brown in Ferguson. (2019, August 8). *Associated Press News*.

Valentine, H., & Balsamo, M. (2021). Padres-Nats game suspended after shooting outside DC stadium. *Associated Press News*.

Washington Post Police Shooting Database 2015-2023. (2023, January 11). Retrieved from *The Washington Post*: https://www.washingtonpost.com/graphics/investigations/police-shootings-database/

About The Author

Bob grew up in Los Alamos, New Mexico, where his father helped make the atomic bomb and where Bob worked in the Los Alamos National Laboratory during summer vacations while at at Pomona College. Bob then moved to Canada. After graduating with his PhD at the University of British Columbia (1963-65), he moved to the Middle East, where he lived the next twenty years. He taught at the American University in Cairo where he learned a smattering of Arabic. In the summer of 1966, at the height of the Cold War, he drove across Russia to present a paper at the International Conference of Mathematicians in Moscow.

The next ten years he taught mathematics at the American University of Beirut, then the leading university in the region.

When the Arab-Israeli war broke out June 5, 1967, Bob and his wife Jean were evacuated from Beirut to Greece. On their return to Lebanon, Bob edited the newsletter *Arabs for Justice* in the Middle East. In 1976, he was again evacuated from Beirut, this time by the U.S. Marines.

In Dhahran, Saudi Arabia, he taught mathematics at the University of Petroleum and Minerals. An occasional freelancer for Arab News, he interviewed the boxer Muhammad Ali when he came to do the pilgrimage to Mecca.

In 1986, Bob returned to the U.S. to teach mathematics at Ripon College, a liberal arts school and then at Louisiana State University where in his free time, he sang in a Black choir. He moved to Lawrence, Kansas, in 1997, to chair the mathematics department at Baker University. His professional writing includes *Calculus for a New Century,* and *War Stories from Applied*

Math.

In retirement, Bob wrote *The Greening of Oz* (2012), about the town of Greensburg in western Kansas, that "came back green" after a tornado almost wiped it out, and in 2020, *The Road through San Judas* (2020), about the struggle between landless farmers and the wealthy Mexican family who wanted them gone.

Bob lives in Lawrence, Kansas, and spends his summers in a 15th century home in rural France.

Index

A

Ahmaud Arbery 20, 21, 23, 26, 27, 203

B

Best, Mat 153, 154
Black Lives Matter 6, 10, 11, 20, 111, 181, 194, 203
Bogus, Carl T. 139
Bowers, Robert 139
Brady, James 83, 84, 98, 99, 146, 173, 188, 189, 196
Brown, Michael 12, 14, 15, 16, 17, 18, 19, 20, 23, 34, 111, 154, 205
Butina, Maria 191, 192

C

Chauvin, Derek 8, 154, 203
Cho, Seung Hui 82
Clarkson, Kelly 119
Columbine High School 151, 167
Cory Winfield 156
Cox, John Woodrow 3
Crump, Ben 8, 17, 18, 20, 25
Cruz, Nikolas 102, 103, 104, 105, 106, 107, 108, 118, 124, 167, 197
Cullen, Dave 77, 78, 79

D

DeAngelis, Frank 78, 80
De La Rosa, Veronique 91, 96
District of Columbia v. Heller 137, 138, 141, 142, 159
Dodge City 32, 203

E

Emanuel African Methodist Episcopal Church 123, 125
Everytown for Gun Safety 81, 98, 166, 174, 179, 183, 188, 194

F

Ferguson 12, 13, 14, 15, 16, 17, 18, 19, 22, 154, 205
Frederick, Karl T. 143
Friends Committee for National Legislation 156

G

Garfield, James A. 48
Garza, Alicia 9, 10, 11
Giffords, Gabrielle 99, 147, 173, 176, 179, 193, 194
Gonzalez, Emma 108, 109, 110, 116, 120, 142, 158
Greene, Marjorie Taylor 2, 27, 113
Guiteau, Charles 49

H

Harris, Eric 75, 77, 78, 80, 82
Hesston 41, 43, 122, 204
Heston, Charlton 145, 183, 190
Hogg, David 109, 110, 111, 112, 113, 114, 120, 142, 154, 158, 168, 177, 178, 181

J

Johnson, Lyndon B. 59, 73
Johnson, Shawn ix, xiii, xiv, xv, 201
Johnson, Valerie ix, xiii, xiv, xvi, xvii, 197, 201
Jones, Alex 88, 89, 90, 92, 93, 95

K

Kelley, Devin Patrick 126
Kennedy, Bob 59
Kennedy, John F. 54
King, Martin Luther (MLK) 28, 61, 74, 144
Klebold, Dylan 75, 82

L

Langendorff, Johnnie 127, 128, 129
Lanza, Adam 85, 86, 87, 105, 143
LaPierre, Wayne 143, 148, 184, 185, 186, 187, 190, 191
Lincoln, Abraham 47, 49
Linde, Paul ix, xiv, 201

M

Maitland, Keith 66, 68
March for Our Lives 107, 108, 110, 112, 116, 120, 122, 159, 176
Marjorie Stoneman Douglas High School 107
Martin, Trayvon 6, 7, 8, 9, 10, 12, 20, 23, 34, 203
McCarthy, Mike 12, 16

McCoy, Houston 66, 67
McKinley, William 51, 52
McQueen, Ackerman 181, 182, 183, 185, 186, 188, 190
McSpadden, Lezley 16, 17, 18
Melchert, Alex ix, xi, xiii, xvii, 201
Murphy, Chris 99, 166, 168

N

National Rifle Association (NRA) 56
North, Oliver L. 184

O

Obama, Barack 43, 87, 102, 165, 179, 195

P

Paddock, Stephen 2, 70, 71, 72, 133, 171
Pagourtzis, Dimitrios 117
Parker, Robbie 91, 92, 93
Pitts, Leonard 5, 24, 130, 159
Pomeroy, Frank 130
Pozner, Leonard 91, 96
Purinton, Adam 37, 40, 203
Pythia xv

R

Rittenhouse, Kyle 26
Robbins, Amy 154
Roberts, Anthony L. 35
Roof, Dylann 123, 125
Roosevelt, Franklin 54

S

Sandy Hook Elementary School 84, 87, 106, 143, 166
Santa Fe High School 79, 119, 157
Scalia, Antonin 137
Schroeder, Doug 42
Second Amendment 44, 69, 135, 136, 137, 139, 141, 142, 146, 147, 159, 161, 170, 172, 184, 195
Sharpton, Al 25, 28

T

Tometi, Opal 10
Tribe, Laurence 141
Trump, Donald 39, 114, 121, 129, 151, 166, 167, 182, 190, 191, 192

V

Virginia Tech 81, 82, 83, 95, 98, 175

W

Waldman, Michael 136, 138, 145
Warren Commission 57
Whitman, Charles 61, 62, 63, 68, 70, 74, 122
Willeford, Stephen 127
Wilson, Darren 12, 16, 18
Winfield, Corey 156
Wright, Lawrence 69

Z

Zimmerman, George 7, 10

Other Books To Enjoy From Anamcara Press Llc

ISBN: 9781941237-76-2
$18.99

ISBN: 9781941237-73-1
$21.99

ISBN: 9781941237-32-8
$19.95

ISBN: 9781941237-13-7
$18.95

ISBN: 9781941237-18-2
$21.95

ISBN: 9781941237-08-3
$24.95

Available wherever books are sold and at:
https://anamcara-press.com/
Easy to Order

Thank you for being a reader! Anamcara Press publishes select works and brings writers & artists together in collaborations in order to serve community and the planet.
Your comments are always welcome!

Printed in the USA
CPSIA information can be obtained
at www.ICGtesting.com
JSHW080538280823
47302JS00003B/106